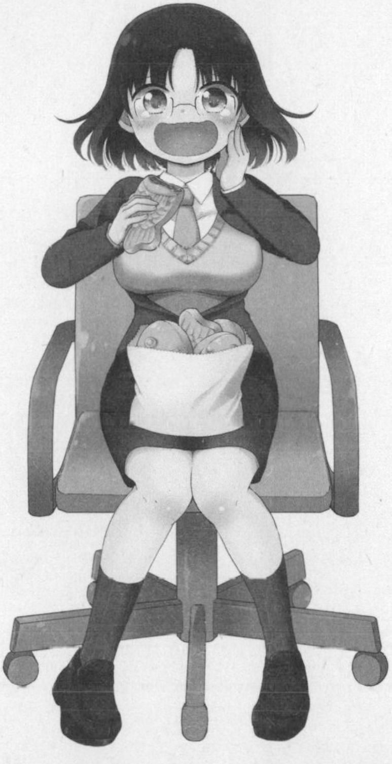

Miss Kobayashi's
Dragon maid
Elma's Office Lady Diary

2

story & art by
Ayami Kazama

original story by
coolkyousinnjya

Miss Kobayashi's Dragon Maid
Elma's Office Lady Diary

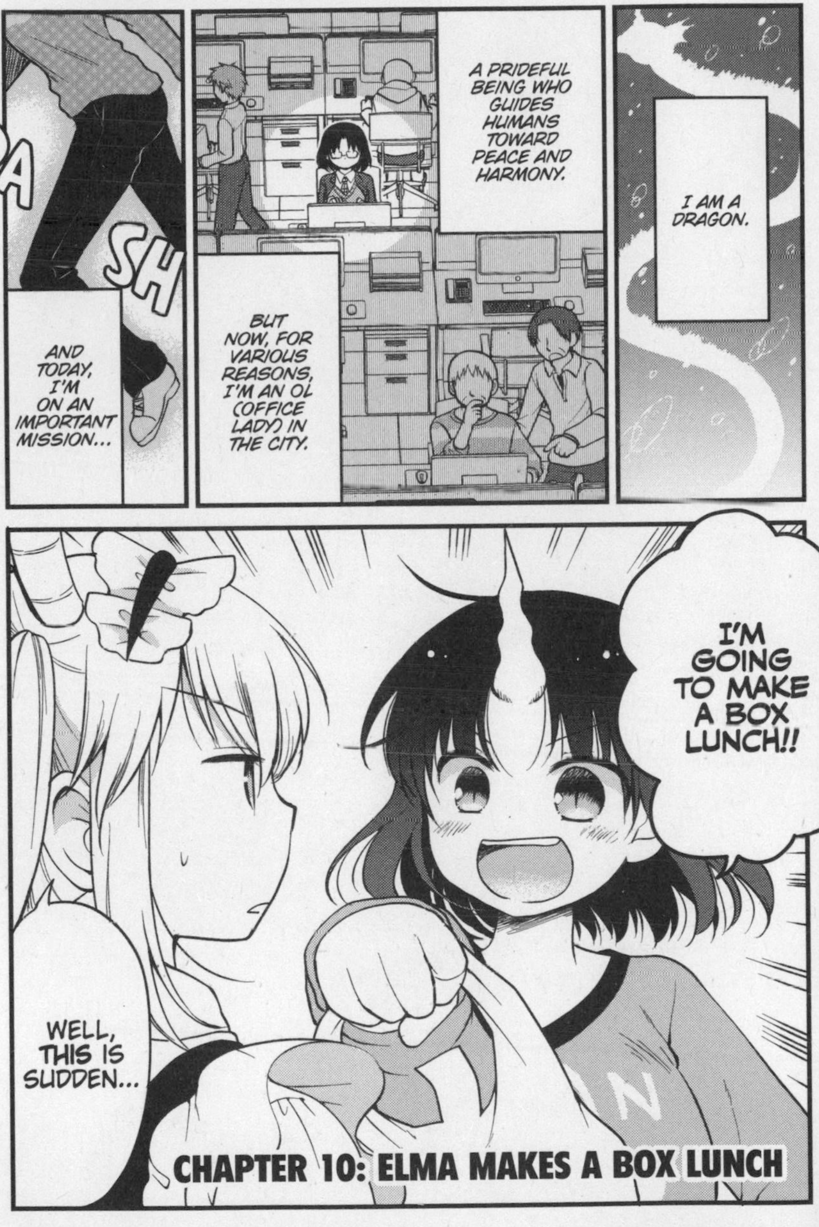
I AM A DRAGON.
A PRIDEFUL BEING WHO GUIDES HUMANS TOWARD PEACE AND HARMONY.
BUT NOW, FOR VARIOUS REASONS, I'M AN OL (OFFICE LADY) IN THE CITY.
DASH
AND TODAY, I'M ON AN IMPORTANT MISSION...
I'M GOING TO MAKE A BOX LUNCH!!
WELL, THIS IS SUDDEN...

CHAPTER 10: ELMA MAKES A BOX LUNCH

HERE'S THE CULPRIT

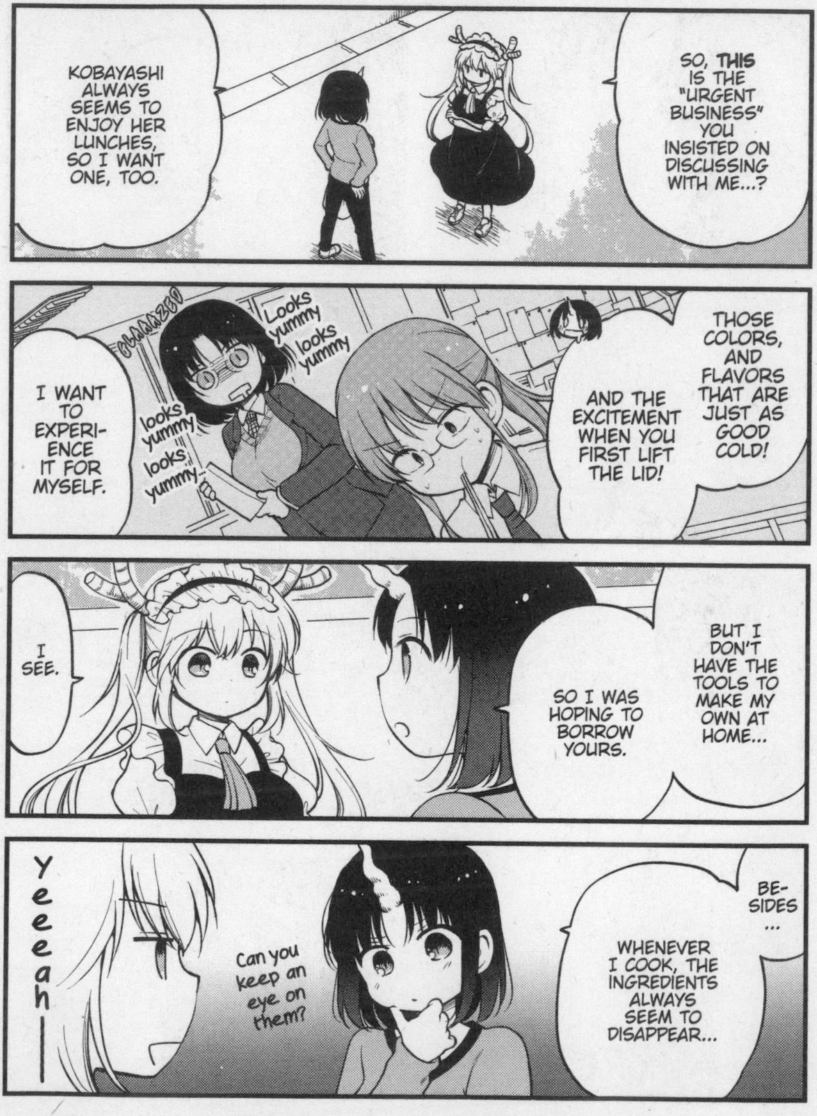
SO, THIS IS THE "URGENT BUSINESS" YOU INSISTED ON DISCUSSING WITH ME...?
KOBAYASHI ALWAYS SEEMS TO ENJOY HER LUNCHES, SO I WANT ONE, TOO.
THOSE COLORS, AND FLAVORS THAT ARE JUST AS GOOD COLD!
AND THE EXCITEMENT WHEN YOU FIRST LIFT THE LID!
Looks yummy looks yummy
looks yummy looks yummy
I WANT TO EXPERIENCE IT FOR MYSELF.
BUT I DON'T HAVE THE TOOLS TO MAKE MY OWN AT HOME...
SO I WAS HOPING TO BORROW YOURS.
I SEE.
BESIDES...
WHENEVER I COOK, THE INGREDIENTS ALWAYS SEEM TO DISAPPEAR...
Can you keep an eye on them?
Yeeeah—

WITH OUR POWERS COMBINED!!

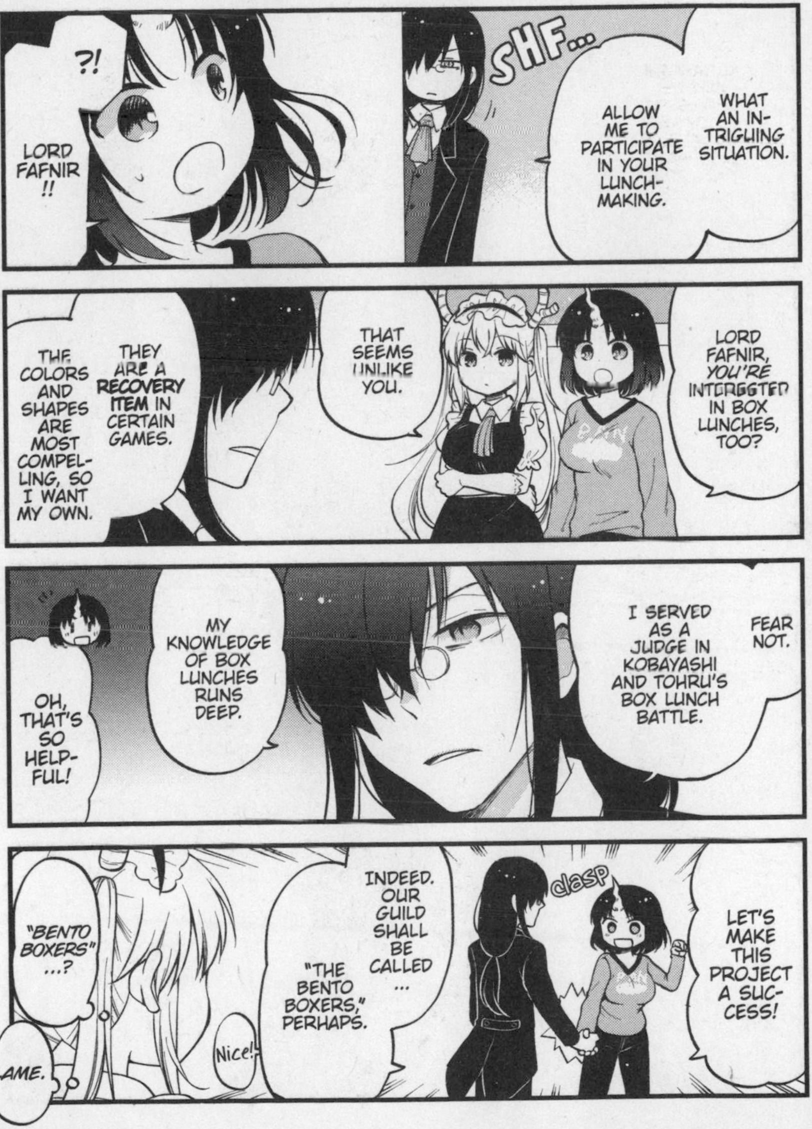
SHF...
WHAT AN INTRIGUING SITUATION.
ALLOW ME TO PARTICIPATE IN YOUR LUNCH-MAKING.
?!
LORD FAFNIR!!
LORD FAFNIR, YOU'RE INTERESTED IN BOX LUNCHES, TOO?
THAT SEEMS UNLIKE YOU.
THEY ARE A RECOVERY ITEM IN CERTAIN GAMES.
THE COLORS AND SHAPES ARE MOST COMPELLING, SO I WANT MY OWN.
FEAR NOT.
I SERVED AS A JUDGE IN KOBAYASHI AND TOHRU'S BOX LUNCH BATTLE.
MY KNOWLEDGE OF BOX LUNCHES RUNS DEEP.
OH, THAT'S SO HELPFUL!
LET'S MAKE THIS PROJECT A SUCCESS!
clasp
INDEED. OUR GUILD SHALL BE CALLED ...
"THE BENTO BOXERS," PERHAPS.
Nice!
"BENTO BOXERS" ...?
LAME.

ONE HIT WONDER

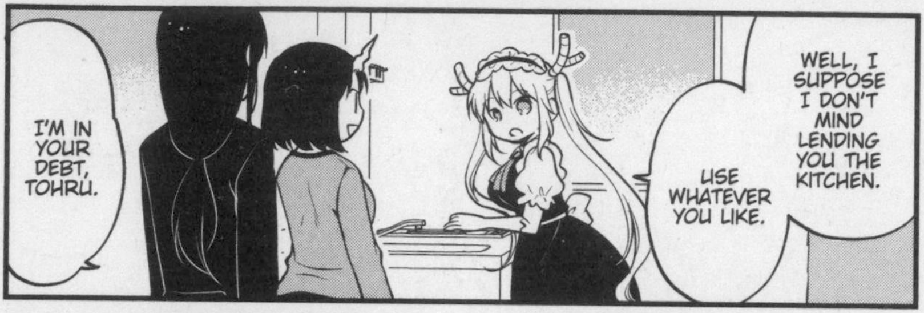
WELL, I SUPPOSE I DON'T MIND LENDING YOU THE KITCHEN.
USE WHATEVER YOU LIKE.
I'M IN YOUR DEBT, TOHRU.

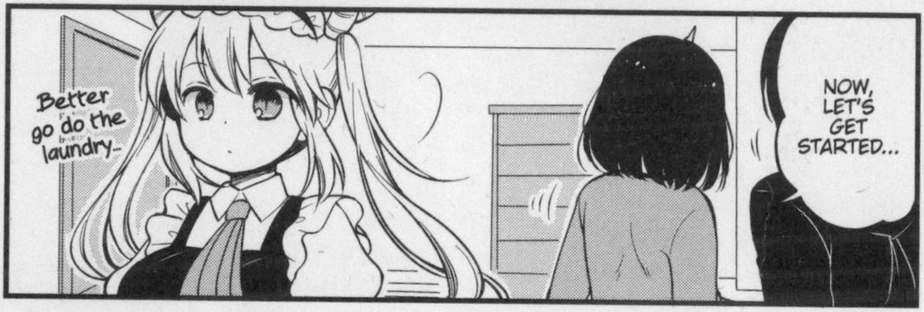
NOW, LET'S GET STARTED...
Better go do the laundry...

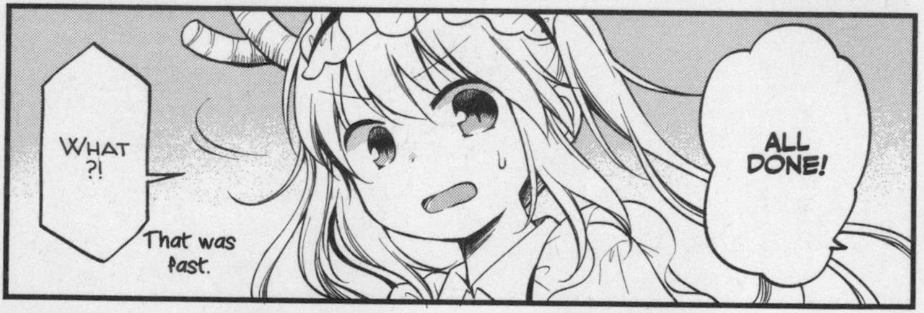
ALL DONE!
WHAT?!
That was fast.

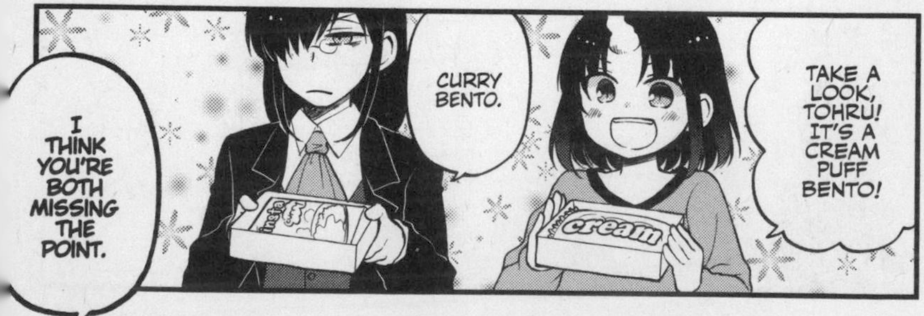
TAKE A LOOK, TOHRU! IT'S A CREAM PUFF BENTO!
cream
CURRY BENTO.
I THINK YOU'RE BOTH MISSING THE POINT.

FAFNIR STYLE

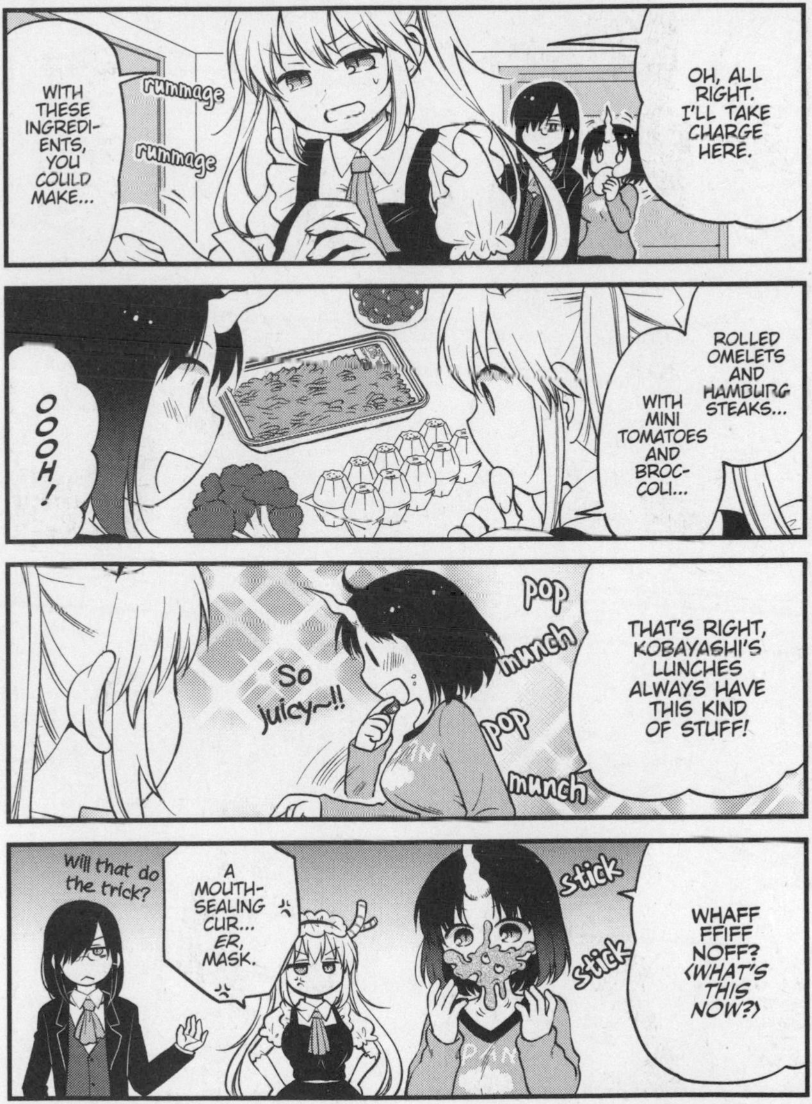
OH, ALL RIGHT. I'LL TAKE CHARGE HERE.
rummage
rummage
WITH THESE INGREDIENTS, YOU COULD MAKE...
ROLLED OMELETS AND HAMBURG STEAKS...
WITH MINI TOMATOES AND BROCCOLI...
OOOH!
THAT'S RIGHT, KOBAYASHI'S LUNCHES ALWAYS HAVE THIS KIND OF STUFF!
pop
munch
pop
munch
So juicy~!!
WHAFF FFIFF NOFF? ‹WHAT'S THIS NOW?›
stick
stick
A MOUTH-SEALING CUR... ER, MASK.
Will that do the trick?

CURSE OF THE ROLLED OMELETS

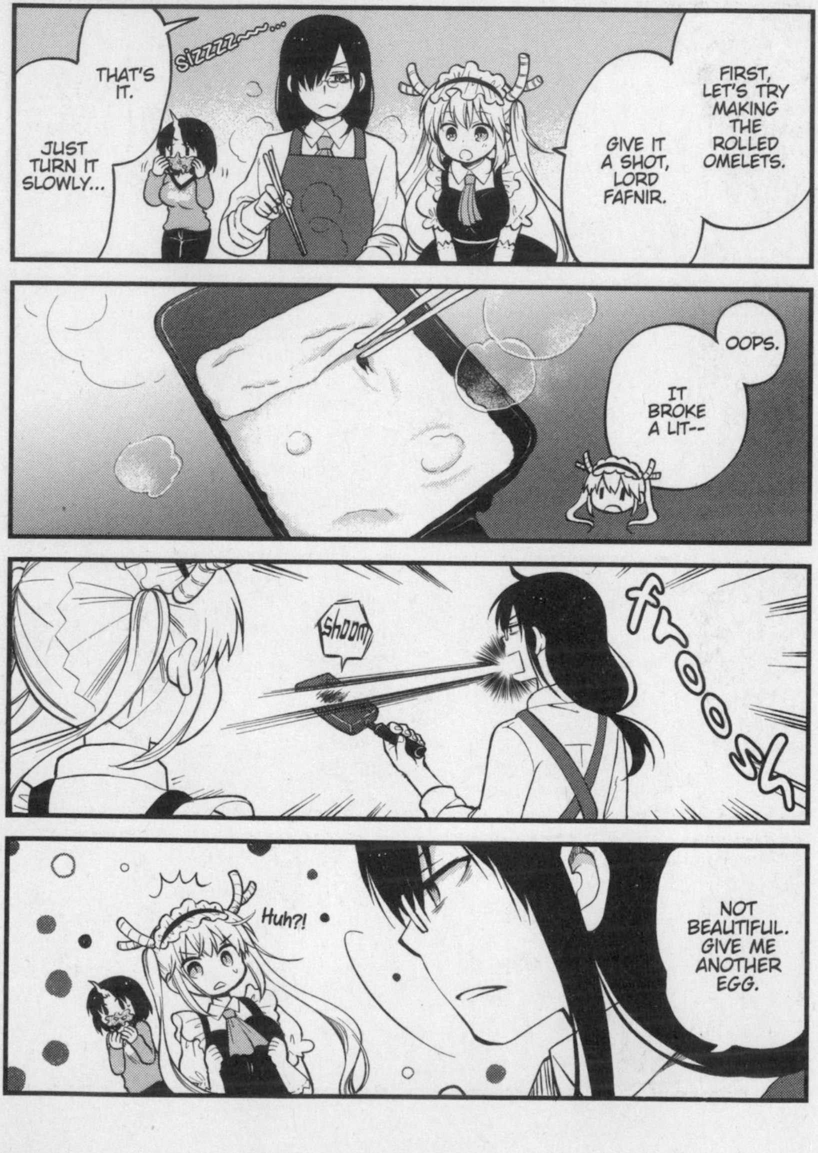
FIRST, LET'S TRY MAKING THE ROLLED OMELETS.
GIVE IT A SHOT, LORD FAFNIR.
THAT'S IT.
JUST TURN IT SLOWLY...
OOPS.
IT BROKE A LIT--
froosh
shoom
NOT BEAUTIFUL. GIVE ME ANOTHER EGG.
Huh?!

EGGSPENSIVE

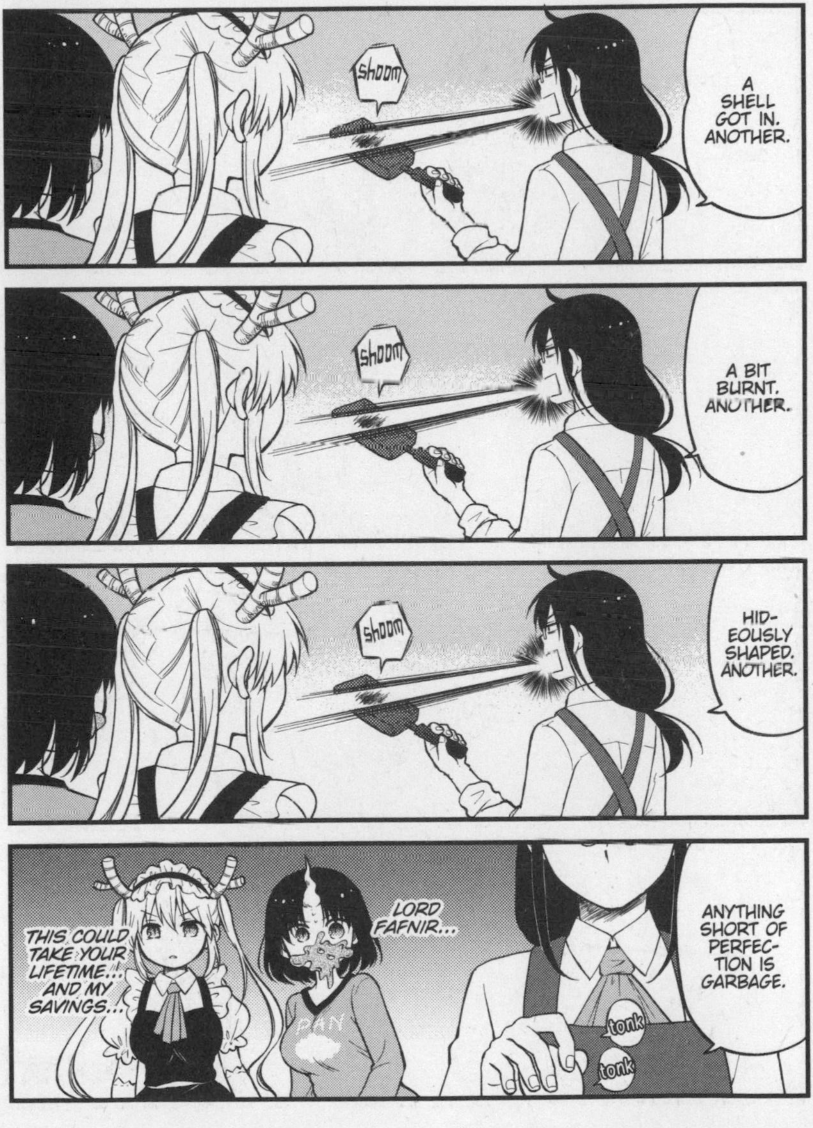
A SHELL GOT IN. ANOTHER.
shoom
A BIT BURNT. ANOTHER.
shoom
HID-EOUSLY SHAPED. ANOTHER.
shoom
ANYTHING SHORT OF PERFEC-TION IS GARBAGE.
tonk
tonk
LORD FAFNIR...
THIS COULD TAKE YOUR LIFETIME... AND MY SAVINGS...

THE HAMBURG TRAGEDY

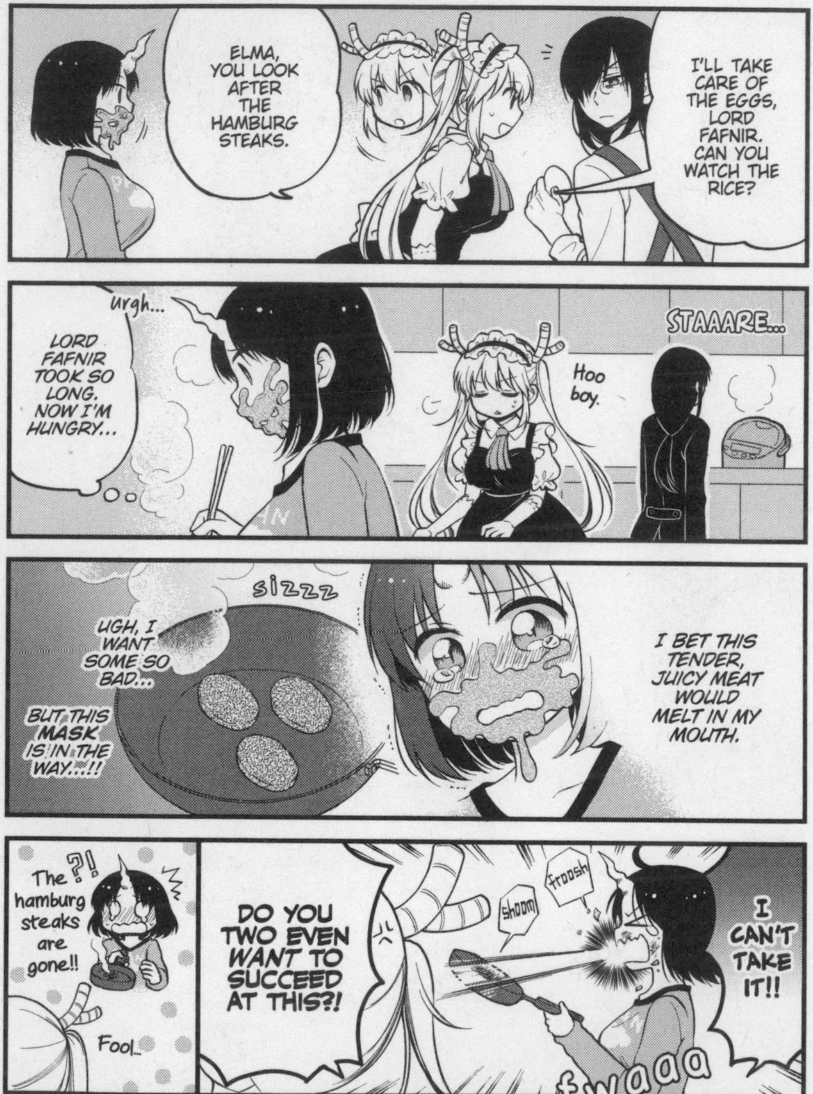
I'LL TAKE CARE OF THE EGGS, LORD FAFNIR. CAN YOU WATCH THE RICE?
ELMA, YOU LOOK AFTER THE HAMBURG STEAKS.
STAAARE...
Hoo boy.
urgh...
LORD FAFNIR TOOK SO LONG. NOW I'M HUNGRY...
I BET THIS TENDER, JUICY MEAT WOULD MELT IN MY MOUTH.
sizzz
UGH, I WANT SOME SO BAD...
BUT THIS MASK IS IN THE WAY...!!
I CAN'T TAKE IT!!
froosh
shoom
DO YOU TWO EVEN WANT TO SUCCEED AT THIS?!
fwaaa
?!
The hamburg steaks are gone!!
Fool..

THE FRUITS OF OUR LABOR

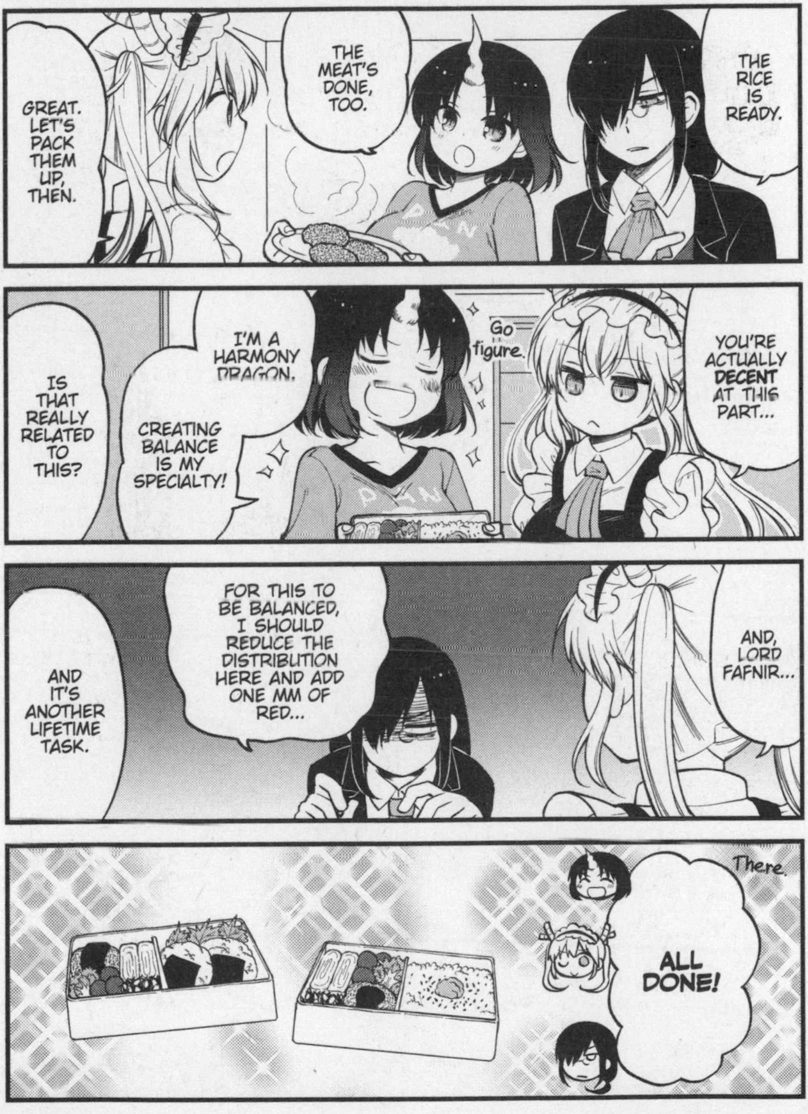
THE RICE IS READY.
THE MEAT'S DONE, TOO.
GREAT. LET'S PACK THEM UP, THEN.
YOU'RE ACTUALLY DECENT AT THIS PART...
Go figure.
I'M A HARMONY DRAGON.
CREATING BALANCE IS MY SPECIALTY!
IS THAT REALLY RELATED TO THIS?
AND, LORD FAFNIR...
FOR THIS TO BE BALANCED, I SHOULD REDUCE THE DISTRIBUTION HERE AND ADD ONE MM OF RED...
AND IT'S ANOTHER LIFETIME TASK.
There.
ALL DONE!

DO WHAT NOW?

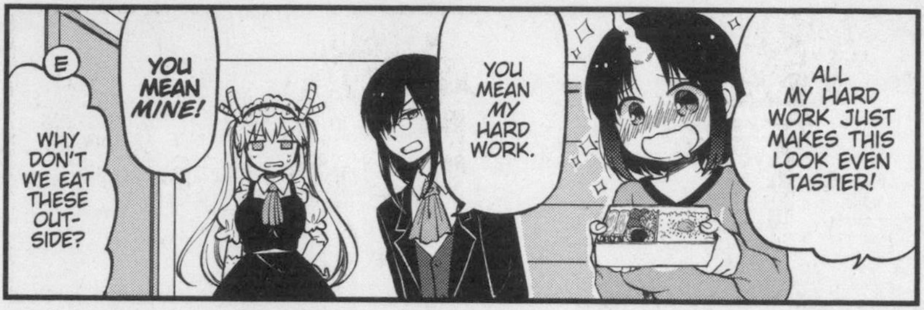
ALL MY HARD WORK JUST MAKES THIS LOOK EVEN TASTIER!
YOU MEAN MY HARD WORK.
YOU MEAN MINE!
E
WHY DON'T WE EAT THESE OUT-SIDE?

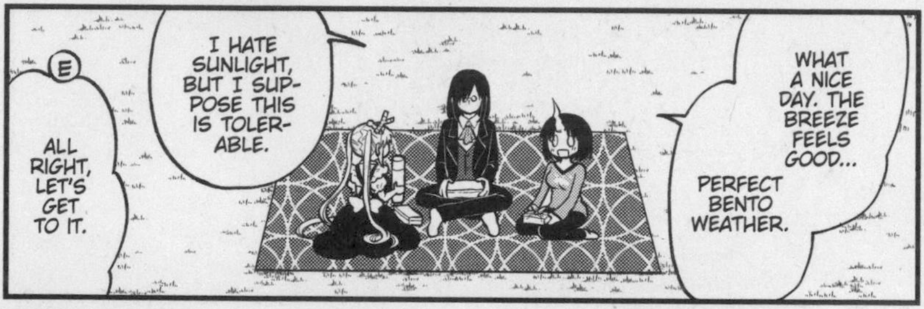
WHAT A NICE DAY. THE BREEZE FEELS GOOD... PERFECT BENTO WEATHER.
I HATE SUNLIGHT, BUT I SUP-POSE THIS IS TOLER-ABLE.
E
ALL RIGHT, LET'S GET TO IT.

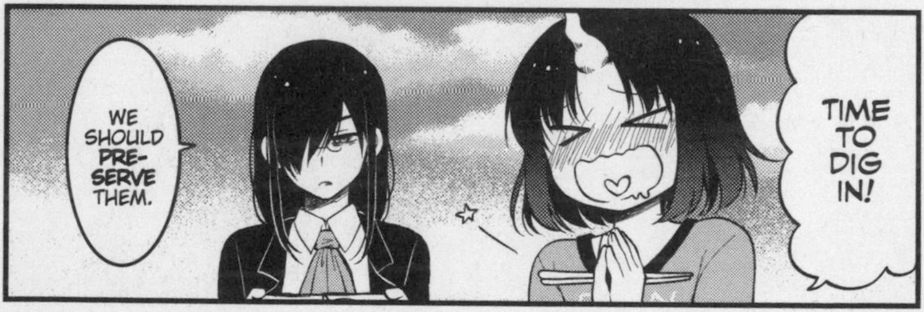
TIME TO DIG IN!
WE SHOULD PRE-SERVE THEM.

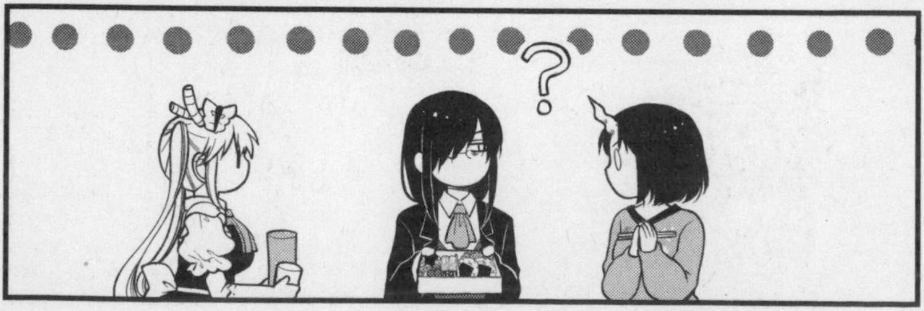
?

TAKIYA-SENPAI'S WISDOM

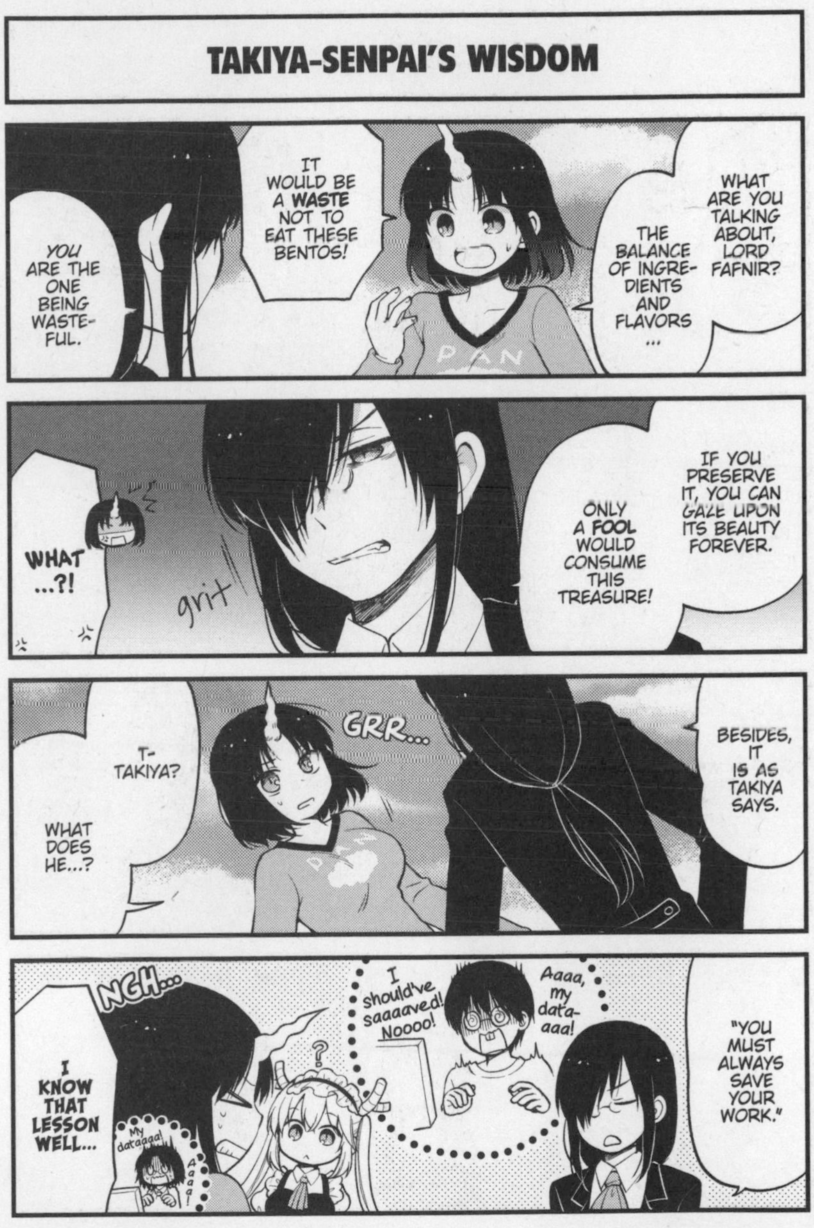
WHAT ARE YOU TALKING ABOUT, LORD FAFNIR?
THE BALANCE OF INGREDIENTS AND FLAVORS ...
IT WOULD BE A WASTE NOT TO EAT THESE BENTOS!
YOU ARE THE ONE BEING WASTEFUL.
IF YOU PRESERVE IT, YOU CAN GAZE UPON ITS BEAUTY FOREVER.
ONLY A FOOL WOULD CONSUME THIS TREASURE!
grit
WHAT ...?!
BESIDES, IT IS AS TAKIYA SAYS.
GRR...
T-TAKIYA?
WHAT DOES HE...?
"YOU MUST ALWAYS SAVE YOUR WORK."
Aaaa, my data-aaa!
I should've saaaaved! Noooo!
NGH...
I KNOW THAT LESSON WELL...
My dataaaa!
Aaaa!

ELMA'S WAY

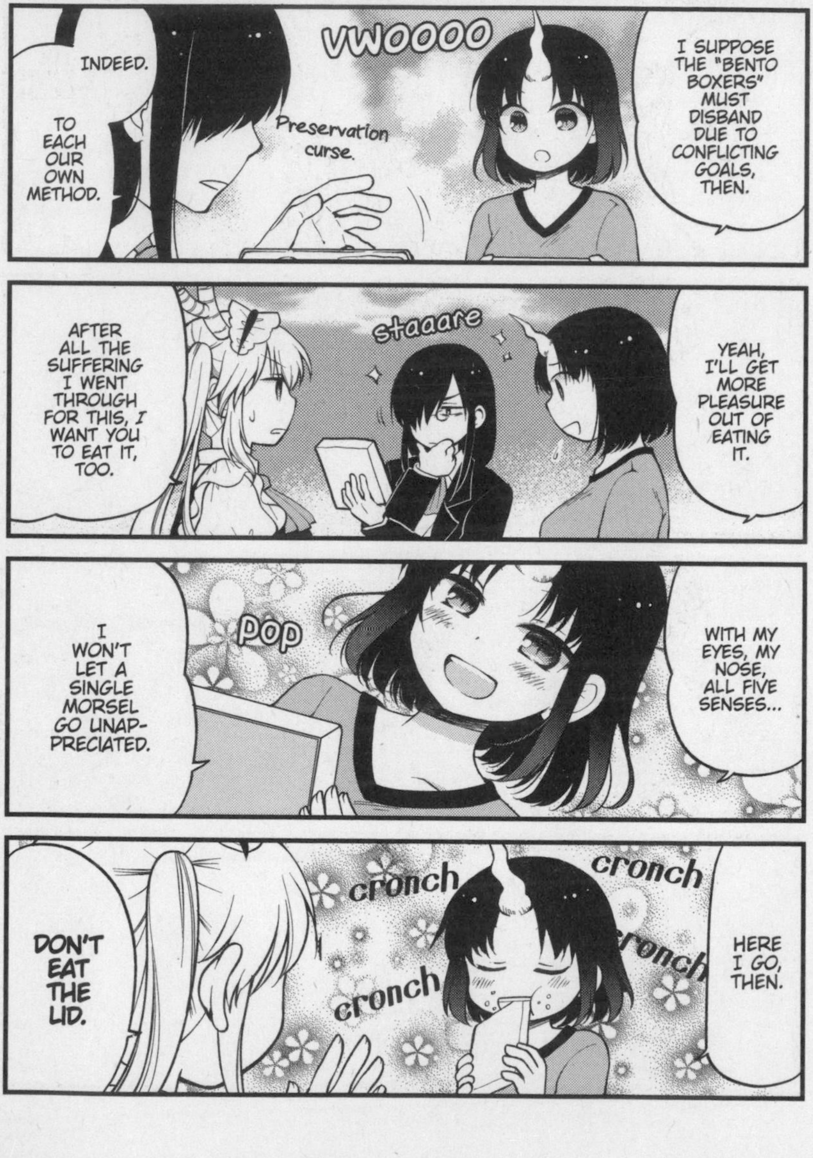
I SUPPOSE THE "BENTO BOXERS" MUST DISBAND DUE TO CONFLICTING GOALS, THEN.
VWOOOO
Preservation curse.
INDEED.
TO EACH OUR OWN METHOD.
YEAH, I'LL GET MORE PLEASURE OUT OF EATING IT.
staaare
AFTER ALL THE SUFFERING I WENT THROUGH FOR THIS, *I* WANT YOU TO EAT IT, TOO.
WITH MY EYES, MY NOSE, ALL FIVE SENSES...
pop
I WON'T LET A SINGLE MORSEL GO UNAPPRECIATED.
HERE I GO, THEN.
cronch
cronch
cronch
cronch
DON'T EAT THE LID.

THE POWER OF THE BOX LUNCH

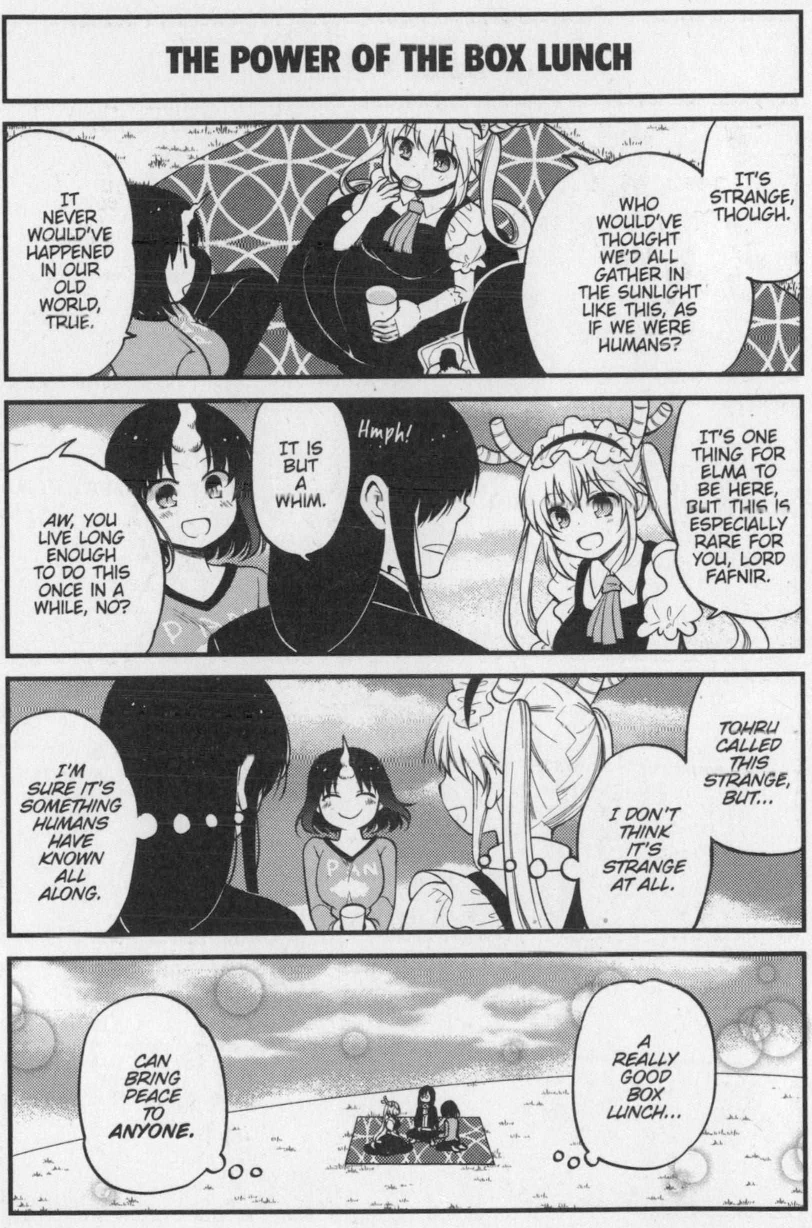
IT'S STRANGE, THOUGH.
WHO WOULD'VE THOUGHT WE'D ALL GATHER IN THE SUNLIGHT LIKE THIS, AS IF WE WERE HUMANS?
IT NEVER WOULD'VE HAPPENED IN OUR OLD WORLD, TRUE.
IT'S ONE THING FOR ELMA TO BE HERE, BUT THIS IS ESPECIALLY RARE FOR YOU, LORD FAFNIR.
Hmph!
IT IS BUT A WHIM.
AW, YOU LIVE LONG ENOUGH TO DO THIS ONCE IN A WHILE, NO?
TOHRU CALLED THIS STRANGE, BUT...
I DON'T THINK IT'S STRANGE AT ALL.
I'M SURE IT'S SOMETHING HUMANS HAVE KNOWN ALL ALONG.
A REALLY GOOD BOX LUNCH...
CAN BRING PEACE TO ANYONE.

REALITY

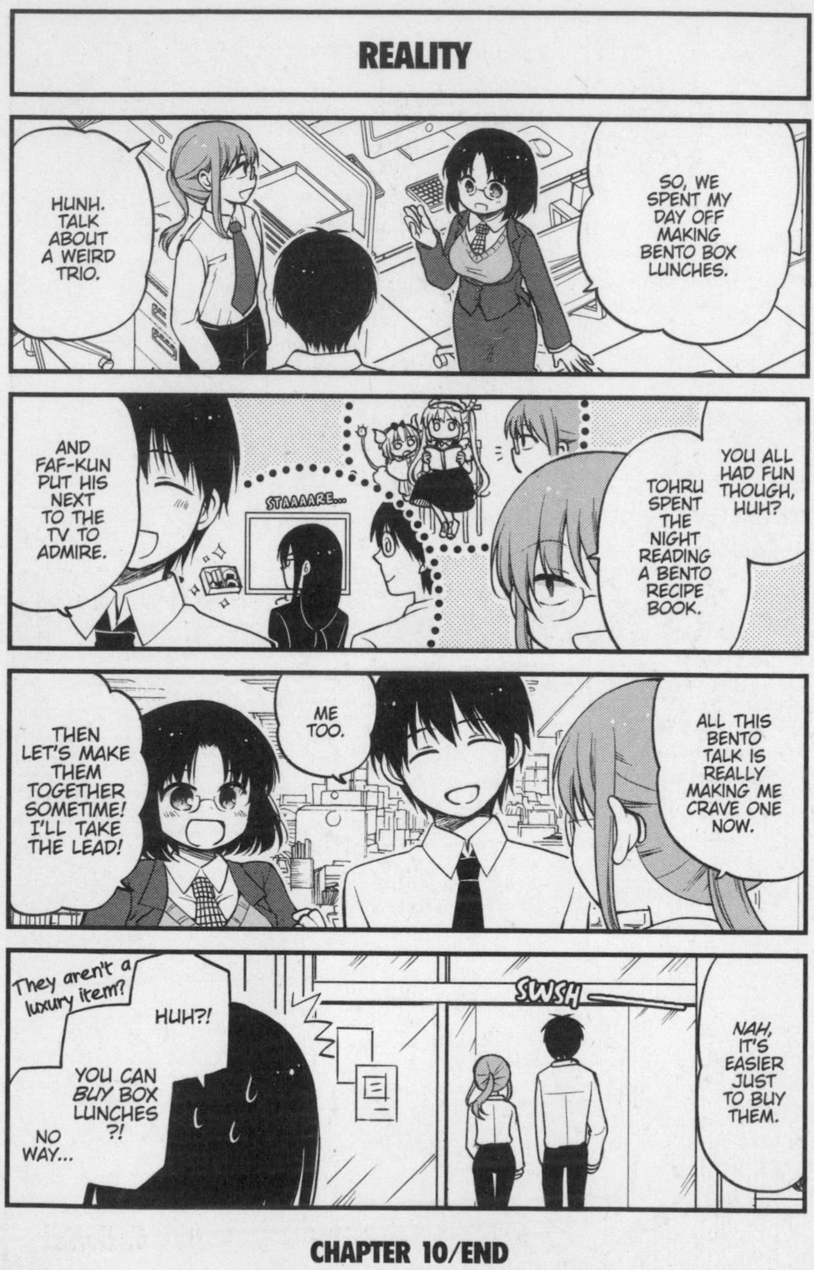
SO, WE SPENT MY DAY OFF MAKING BENTO BOX LUNCHES.
HUNH. TALK ABOUT A WEIRD TRIO.
YOU ALL HAD FUN THOUGH, HUH?
TOHRU SPENT THE NIGHT READING A BENTO RECIPE BOOK.
STAAAARE...
AND FAF-KUN PUT HIS NEXT TO THE TV TO ADMIRE.
ALL THIS BENTO TALK IS REALLY MAKING ME CRAVE ONE NOW.
ME TOO.
THEN LET'S MAKE THEM TOGETHER SOMETIME! I'LL TAKE THE LEAD!
NAH, IT'S EASIER JUST TO BUY THEM.
SWSH
HUH?!
YOU CAN *BUY* BOX LUNCHES ?!
They aren't a luxury item?
NO WAY...

CHAPTER 10/END

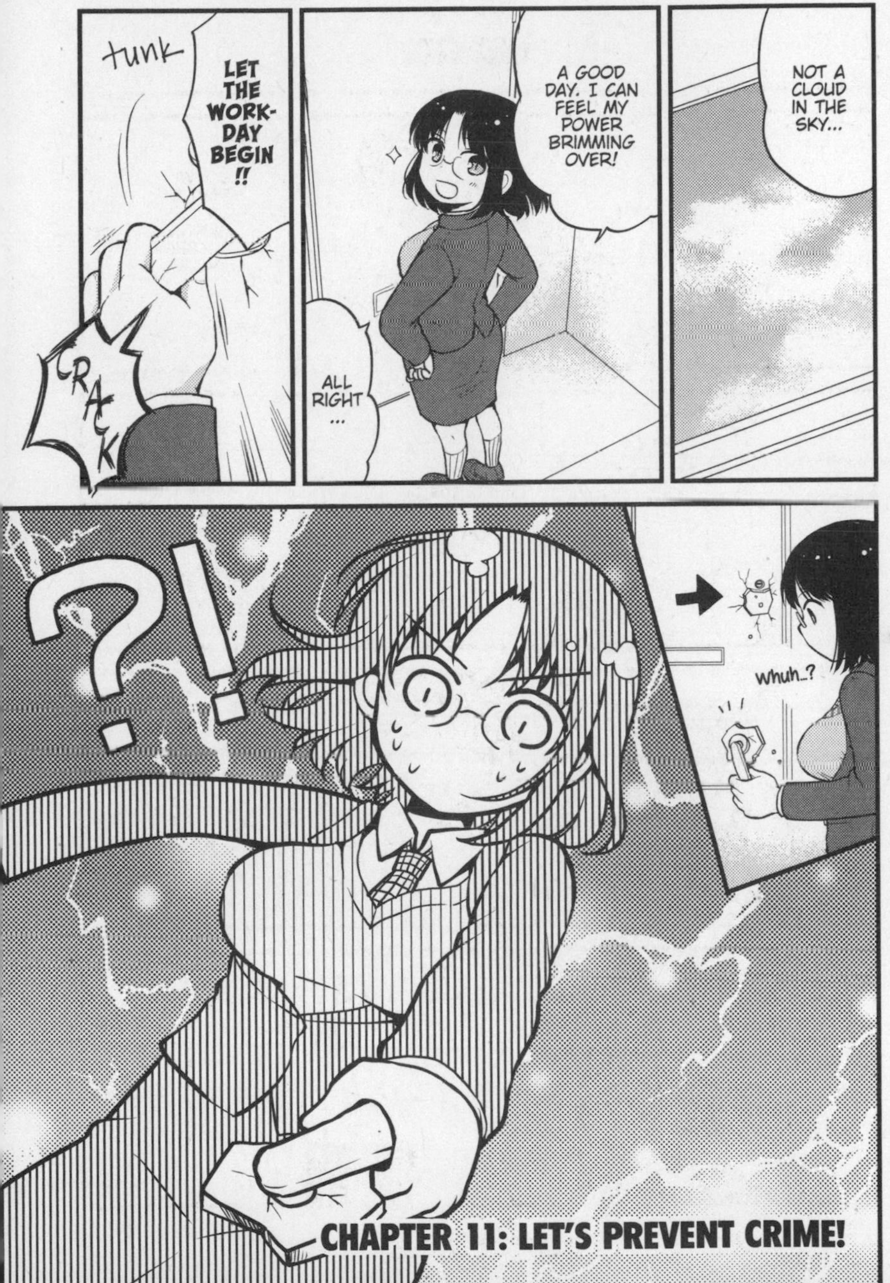
NOT A CLOUD IN THE SKY...
A GOOD DAY. I CAN FEEL MY POWER BRIMMING OVER!
ALL RIGHT...
tunk
LET THE WORK-DAY BEGIN!!
CRACK
whuh..?
?!

CHAPTER 11: LET'S PREVENT CRIME!

DEVOTED WORKER

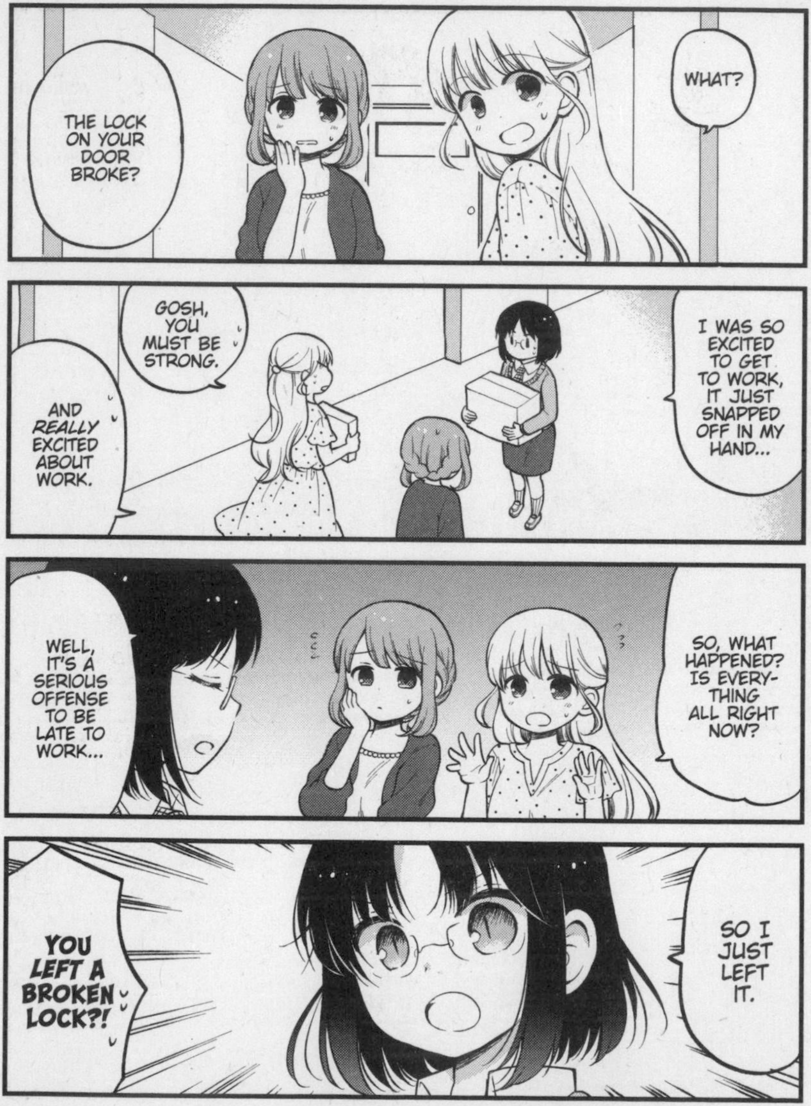
WHAT?
THE LOCK ON YOUR DOOR BROKE?
I WAS SO EXCITED TO GET TO WORK, IT JUST SNAPPED OFF IN MY HAND...
GOSH, YOU MUST BE STRONG.
AND *REALLY* EXCITED ABOUT WORK.
SO, WHAT HAPPENED? IS EVERY-THING ALL RIGHT NOW?
WELL, IT'S A SERIOUS OFFENSE TO BE LATE TO WORK...
SO I JUST LEFT IT.
YOU *LEFT* A BROKEN LOCK?!

THIS WORLD'S DANGEROUS, TOO...

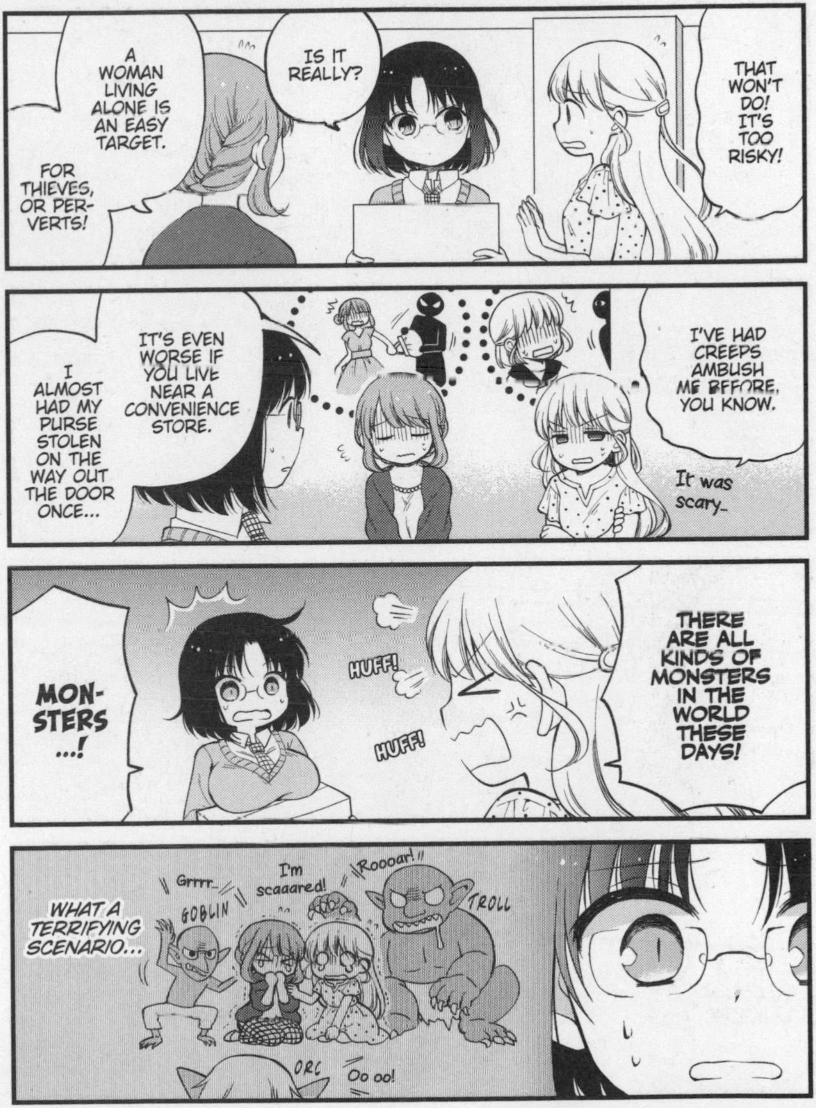
THAT WON'T DO! IT'S TOO RISKY!
IS IT REALLY?
A WOMAN LIVING ALONE IS AN EASY TARGET.
FOR THIEVES, OR PERVERTS!
I'VE HAD CREEPS AMBUSH ME BEFORE, YOU KNOW.
It was scary..
IT'S EVEN WORSE IF YOU LIVE NEAR A CONVENIENCE STORE.
I ALMOST HAD MY PURSE STOLEN ON THE WAY OUT THE DOOR ONCE...
THERE ARE ALL KINDS OF MONSTERS IN THE WORLD THESE DAYS!
HUFF!
HUFF!
MONSTERS...!
Roooar!
TROLL
I'm scaaared!
Grrrr..
GOBLIN
WHAT A TERRIFYING SCENARIO...
ORC
Oo oo!

SAFETY FIRST

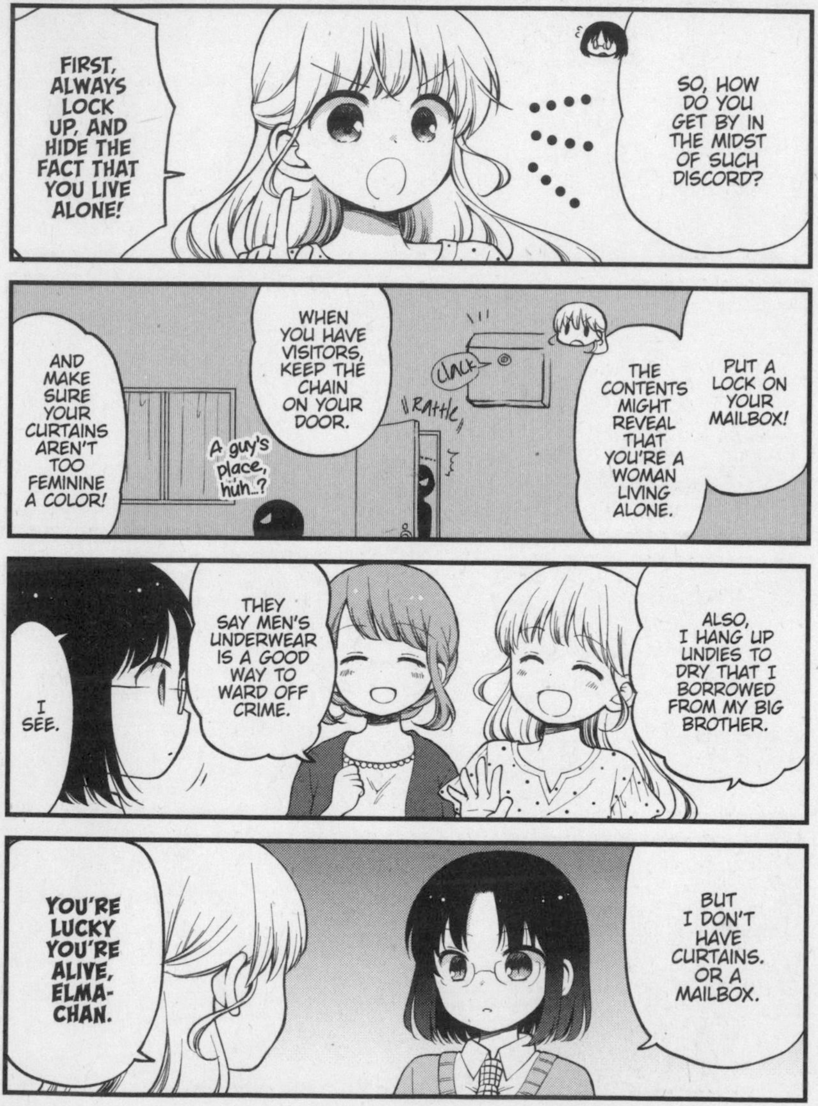
SO, HOW DO YOU GET BY IN THE MIDST OF SUCH DISCORD?
......
FIRST, ALWAYS LOCK UP, AND HIDE THE FACT THAT YOU LIVE ALONE!
PUT A LOCK ON YOUR MAILBOX!
THE CONTENTS MIGHT REVEAL THAT YOU'RE A WOMAN LIVING ALONE.
CLICK
Rattle
WHEN YOU HAVE VISITORS, KEEP THE CHAIN ON YOUR DOOR.
A guy's place, huh...?
AND MAKE SURE YOUR CURTAINS AREN'T TOO FEMININE A COLOR!
ALSO, I HANG UP UNDIES TO DRY THAT I BORROWED FROM MY BIG BROTHER.
THEY SAY MEN'S UNDERWEAR IS A GOOD WAY TO WARD OFF CRIME.
I SEE.
BUT I DON'T HAVE CURTAINS. OR A MAILBOX.
YOU'RE LUCKY YOU'RE ALIVE, ELMA-CHAN.

POWERFUL GUARDIANS

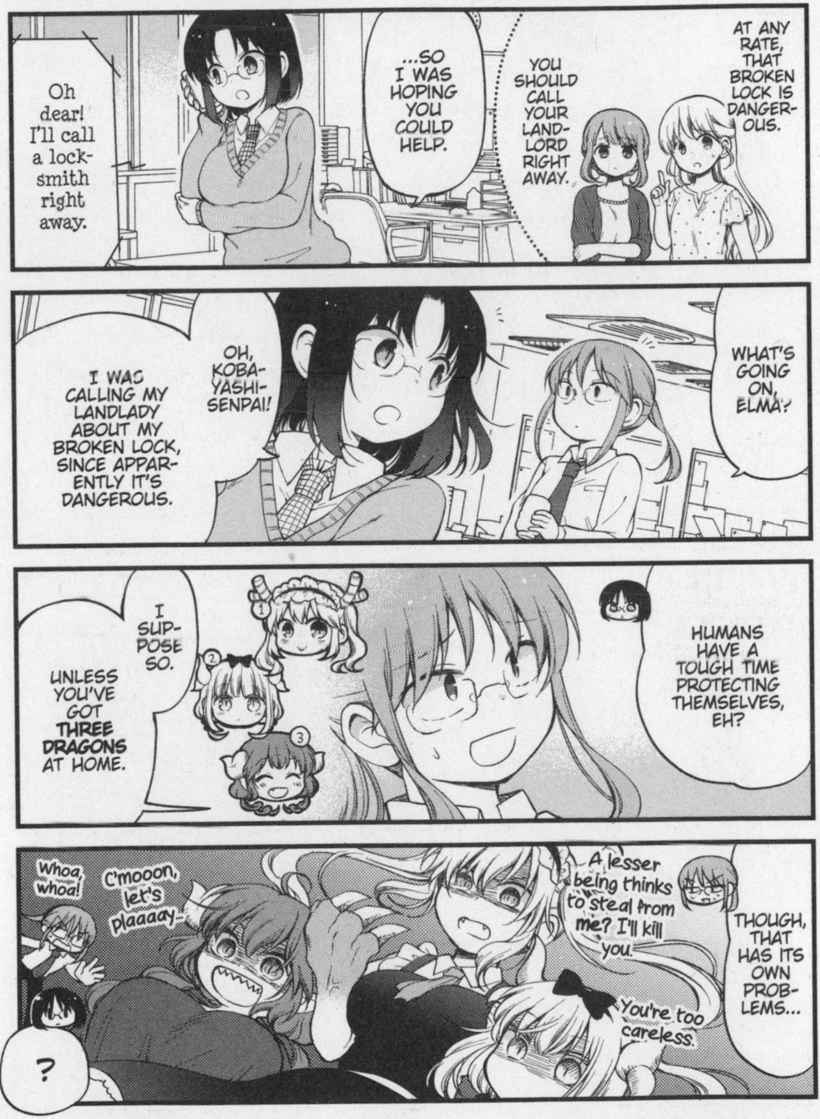
AT ANY RATE, THAT BROKEN LOCK IS DANGEROUS.
YOU SHOULD CALL YOUR LANDLORD RIGHT AWAY.
...SO I WAS HOPING YOU COULD HELP.
Oh dear! I'll call a locksmith right away.
WHAT'S GOING ON, ELMA?
OH, KOBAYASHI-SENPAI!
I WAS CALLING MY LANDLADY ABOUT MY BROKEN LOCK, SINCE APPARENTLY IT'S DANGEROUS.
HUMANS HAVE A TOUGH TIME PROTECTING THEMSELVES, EH?
I SUPPOSE SO.
1
2
3
UNLESS YOU'VE GOT **THREE DRAGONS** AT HOME.
THOUGH, THAT HAS ITS OWN PROBLEMS...
A lesser being thinks to steal from me? I'll kill you.
You're too careless.
C'mooon, let's plaaaay...
Whoa, whoa!
?

AFTER THE FACT

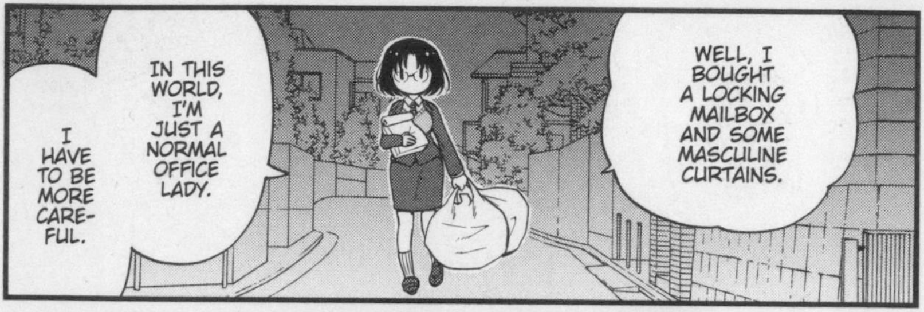
WELL, I BOUGHT A LOCKING MAILBOX AND SOME MASCULINE CURTAINS.
IN THIS WORLD, I'M JUST A NORMAL OFFICE LADY.
I HAVE TO BE MORE CARE-FUL.

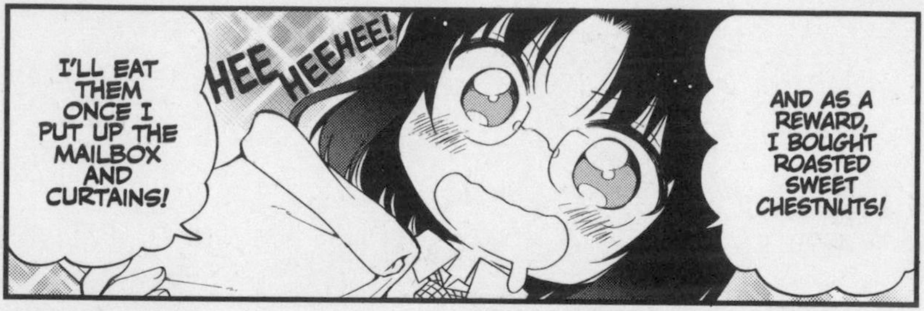
AND AS A REWARD, I BOUGHT ROASTED SWEET CHESTNUTS!
HEE HEEHEE!
I'LL EAT THEM ONCE I PUT UP THE MAILBOX AND CURTAINS!

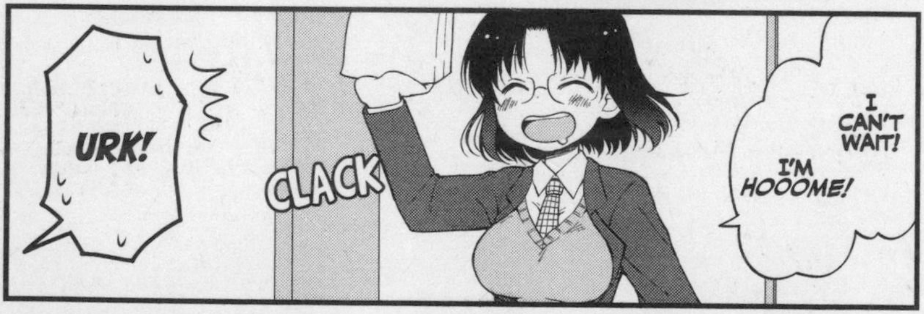
I CAN'T WAIT!
I'M HOOOME!
CLACK
URK!

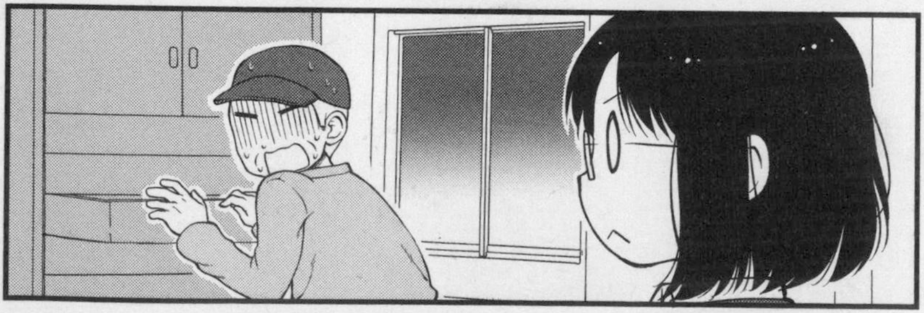

AN OFFICE WORKER'S WELCOME

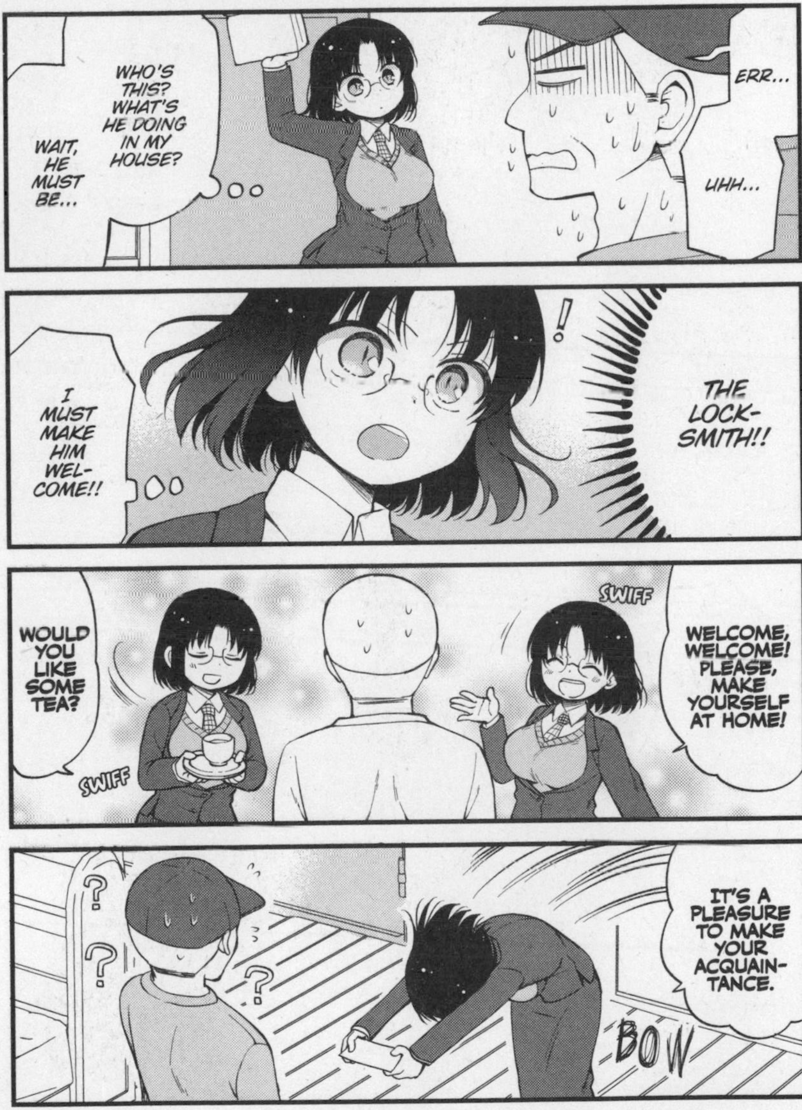
ERR...
UHH...
WHO'S THIS? WHAT'S HE DOING IN MY HOUSE?
WAIT, HE MUST BE...
!
THE LOCKSMITH!!
I MUST MAKE HIM WELCOME!!
SWIFF
WELCOME, WELCOME! PLEASE, MAKE YOURSELF AT HOME!
WOULD YOU LIKE SOME TEA?
SWIFF
IT'S A PLEASURE TO MAKE YOUR ACQUAINTANCE.
BOW

SHE GETS IT

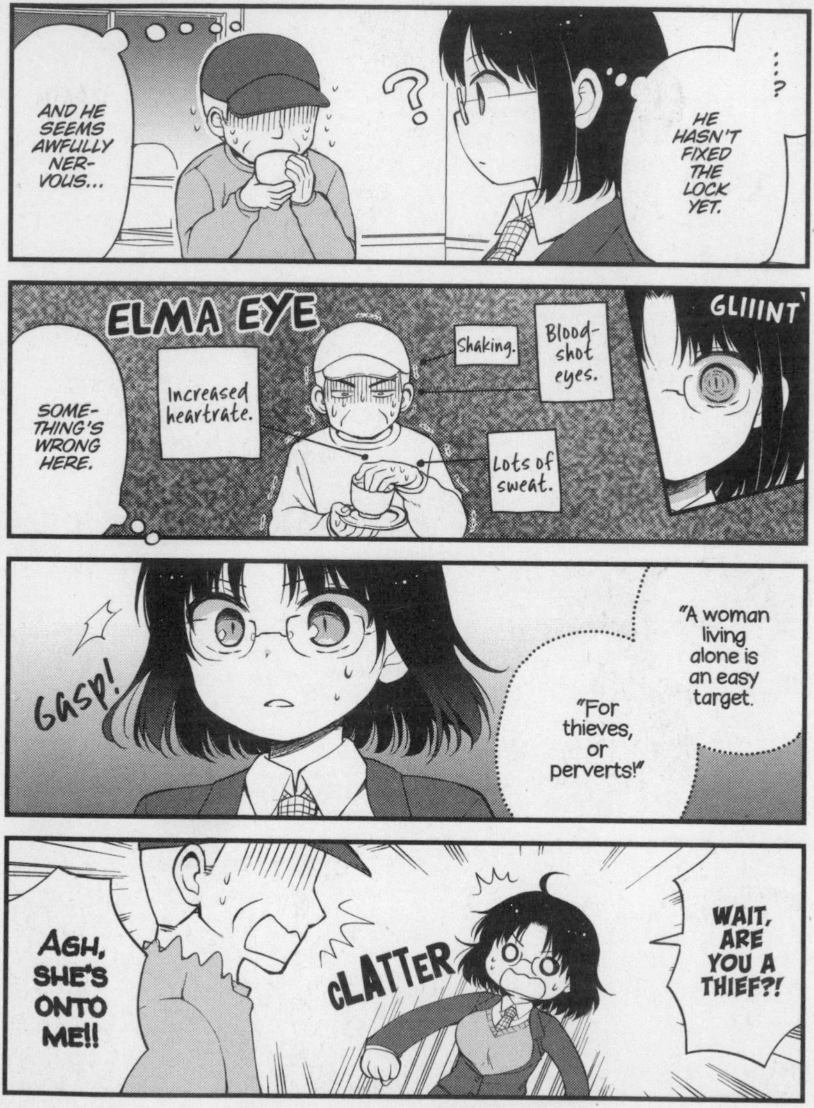

...?
HE HASN'T FIXED THE LOCK YET.
?
AND HE SEEMS AWFULLY NER-VOUS...
GLIIINT
Blood-shot eyes.
Shaking.
ELMA EYE
Increased heartrate.
Lots of sweat.
SOME-THING'S WRONG HERE.
"A woman living alone is an easy target.
"For thieves, or perverts!"
Gasp!
WAIT, ARE YOU A THIEF?!
CLATTER
AGH, SHE'S ONTO ME!!

WRONG IDEA

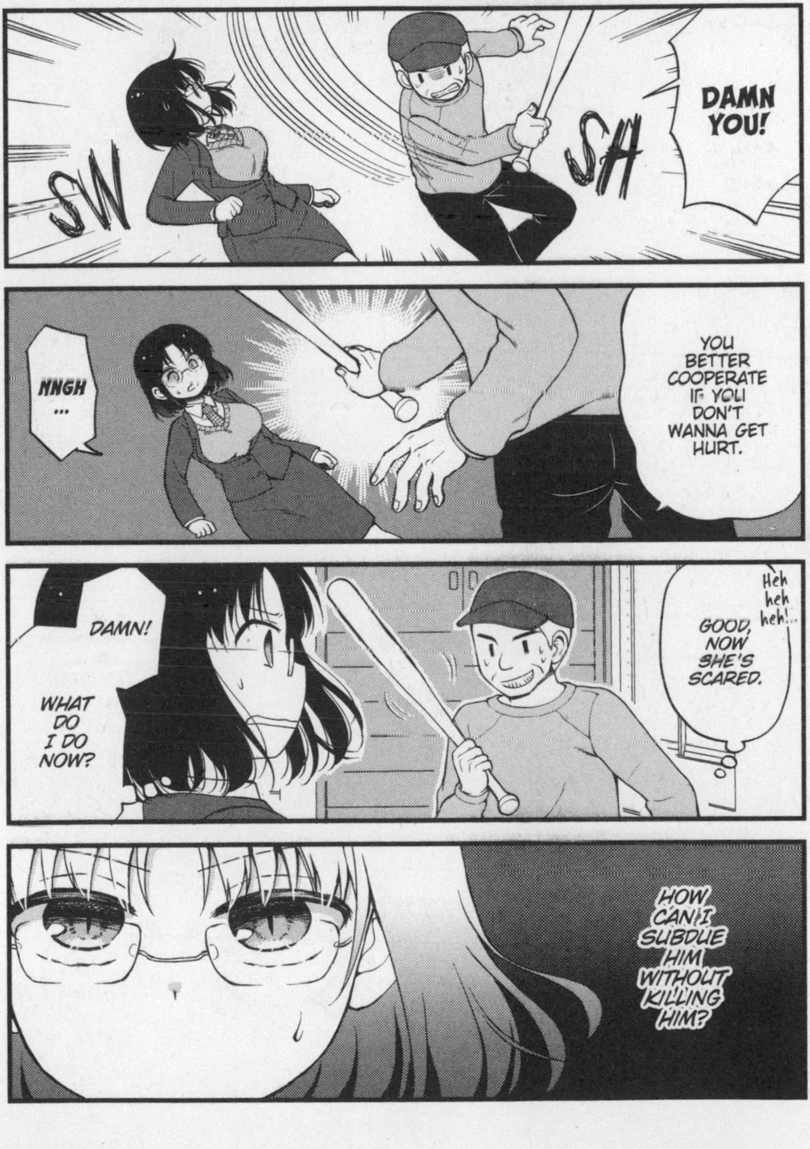
DAMN YOU!
SH
SW
YOU BETTER COOPERATE IF YOU DON'T WANNA GET HURT.
NNGH ...
Heh heh heh!...
GOOD, NOW SHE'S SCARED.
DAMN!
WHAT DO I DO NOW?
HOW CAN I SUBDUE HIM WITHOUT KILLING HIM?

UNUSUAL

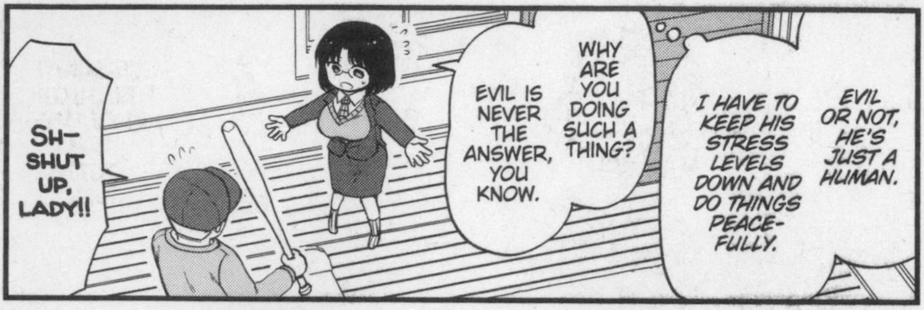
EVIL OR NOT, HE'S JUST A HUMAN.
I HAVE TO KEEP HIS STRESS LEVELS DOWN AND DO THINGS PEACE-FULLY.
WHY ARE YOU DOING SUCH A THING?
EVIL IS NEVER THE ANSWER, YOU KNOW.
SH-SHUT UP, LADY!!

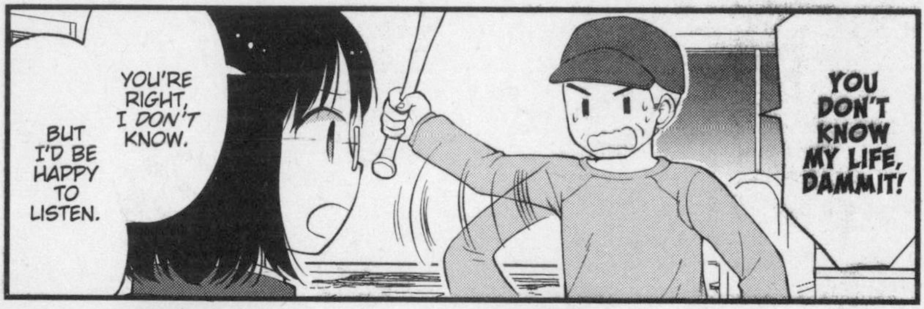
YOU DON'T KNOW MY LIFE, DAMMIT!
YOU'RE RIGHT, I *DON'T* KNOW.
BUT I'D BE HAPPY TO LISTEN.

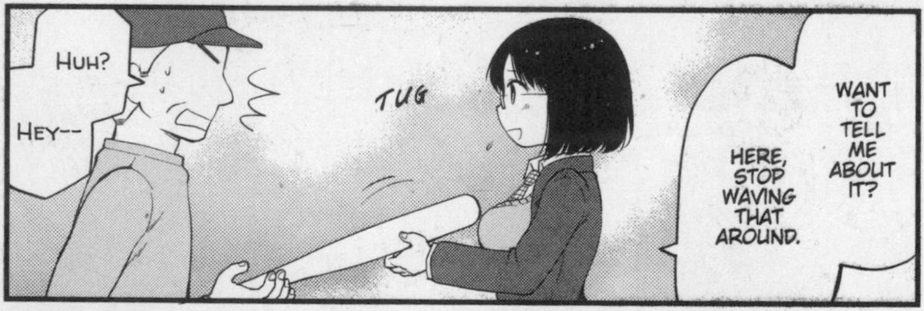
WANT TO TELL ME ABOUT IT?
HERE, STOP WAVING THAT AROUND.
TUG
HUH?
HEY--

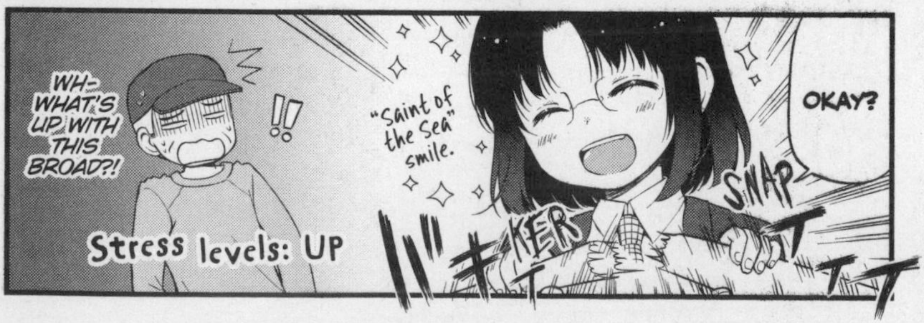
OKAY?
SNAP
KER
"Saint of the Sea" smile.
!!
WH-WHAT'S UP WITH THIS BROAD?!
Stress levels: UP

HIT A NERVE

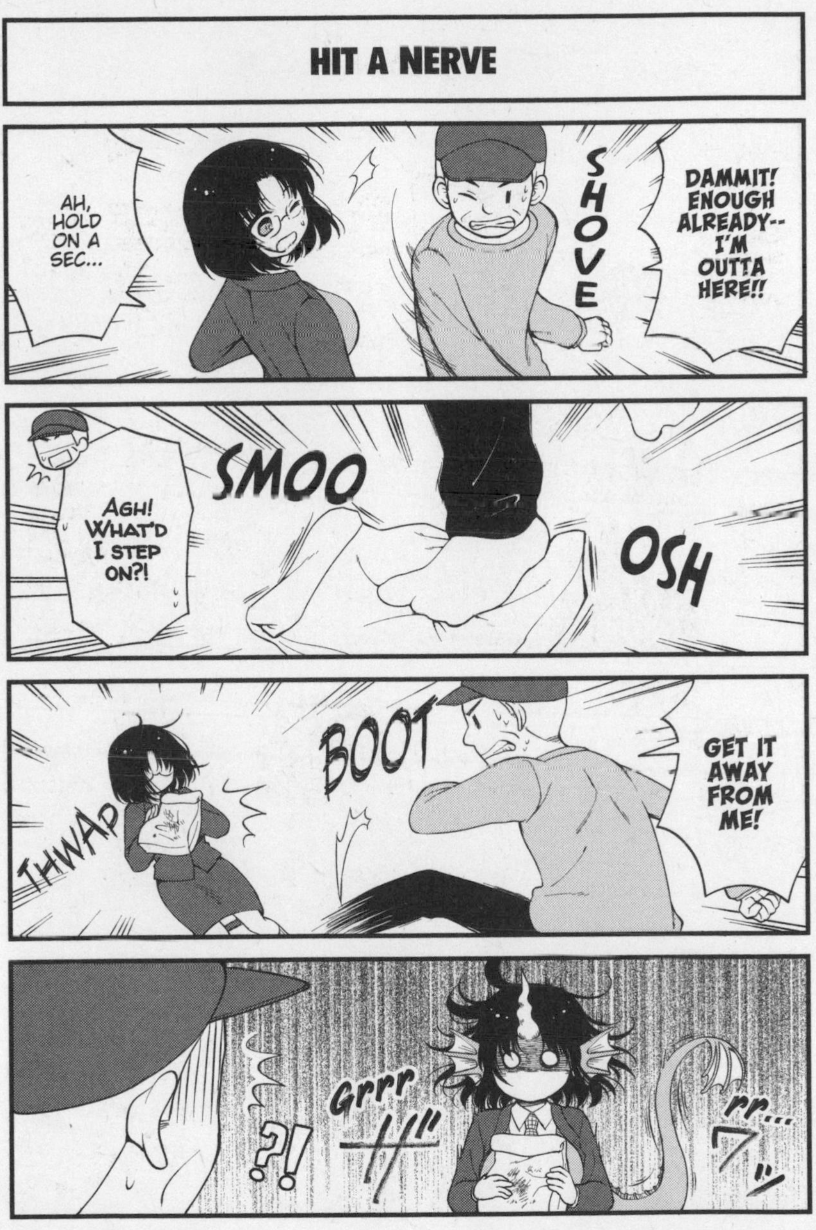
DAMMIT! ENOUGH ALREADY-- I'M OUTTA HERE!!
SHOVE
AH, HOLD ON A SEC...
SMOO
OSH
AGH! WHAT'D I STEP ON?!
GET IT AWAY FROM ME!
BOOT
THWAP
rr...
Grrr
?!

TAIYAKI TO THE RESCUE

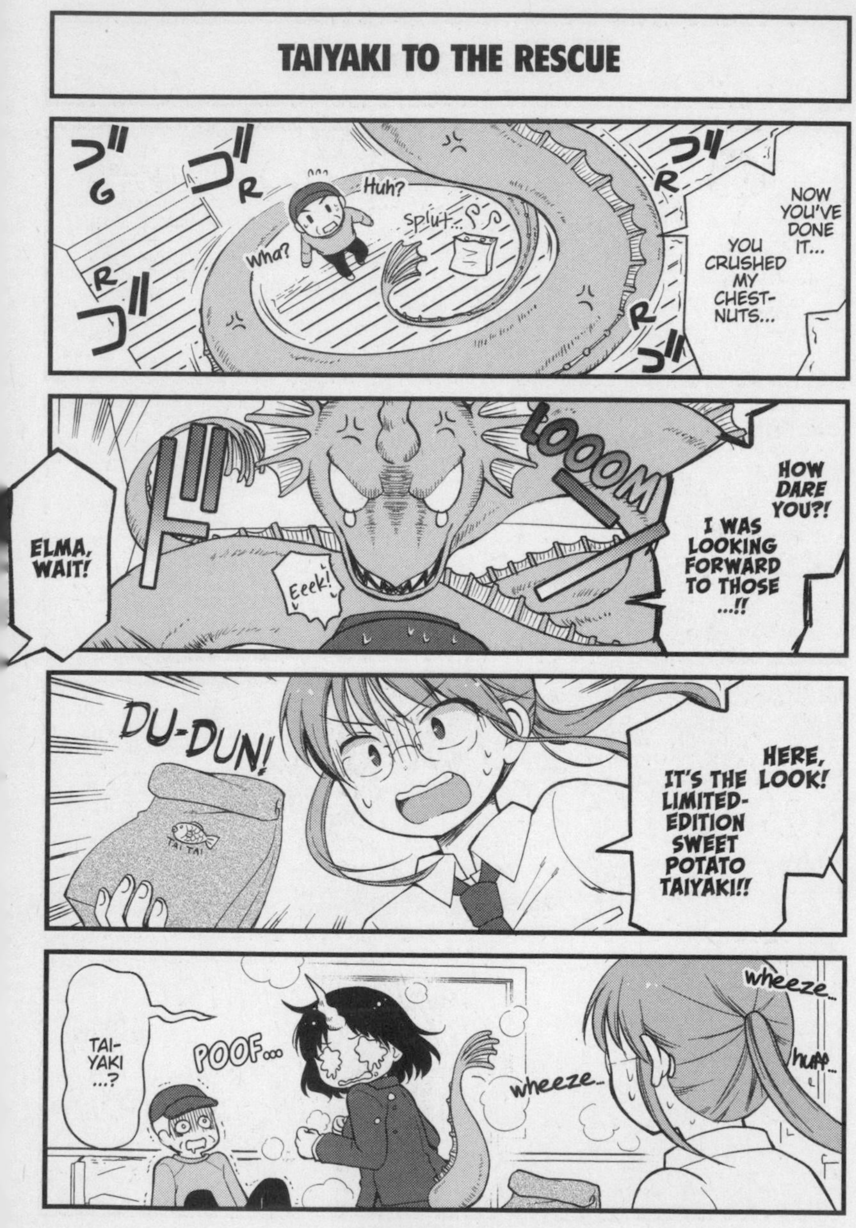
NOW YOU'VE DONE IT...
YOU CRUSHED MY CHEST-NUTS...
R
R
Huh?
splut...
G
R
wha?
R
HOW DARE YOU?!
I WAS LOOKING FORWARD TO THOSE ...!!
LOOOM
Eeek!
ELMA, WAIT!
HERE, LOOK!
IT'S THE LIMITED-EDITION SWEET POTATO TAIYAKI!!
DU-DUN!
TAI TAI
wheeze...
huff...
wheeze...
POOF...
TAI-YAKI ...?

RESOLUTION

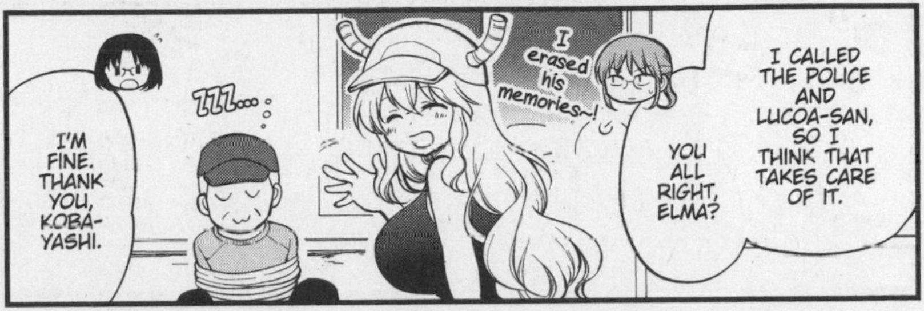
I CALLED THE POLICE AND LUCOA-SAN, SO I THINK THAT TAKES CARE OF IT.
YOU ALL RIGHT, ELMA?
I erased his memories~!
ZZZ...
I'M FINE. THANK YOU, KOBA-YASHI.

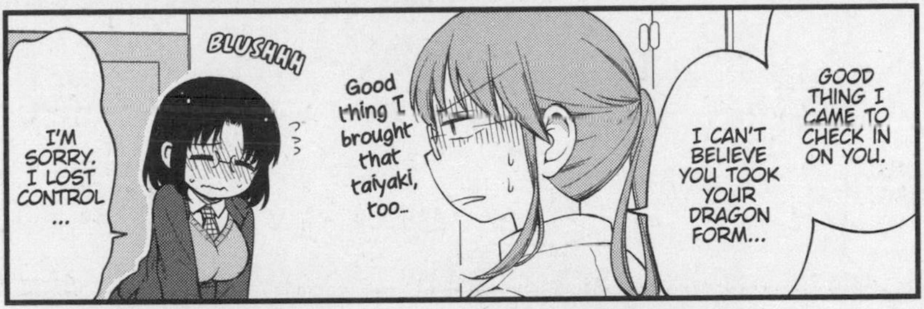
GOOD THING I CAME TO CHECK IN ON YOU.
I CAN'T BELIEVE YOU TOOK YOUR DRAGON FORM...
Good thing I brought that taiyaki, too..
BLUSHHH
I'M SORRY. I LOST CONTROL ...

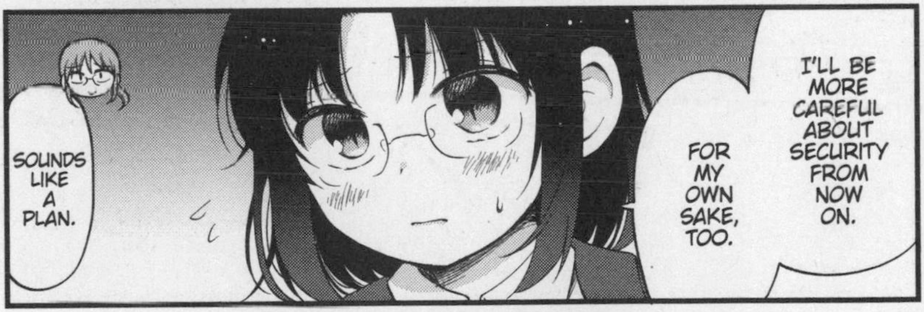
I'LL BE MORE CAREFUL ABOUT SECURITY FROM NOW ON.
FOR MY OWN SAKE, TOO.
SOUNDS LIKE A PLAN.

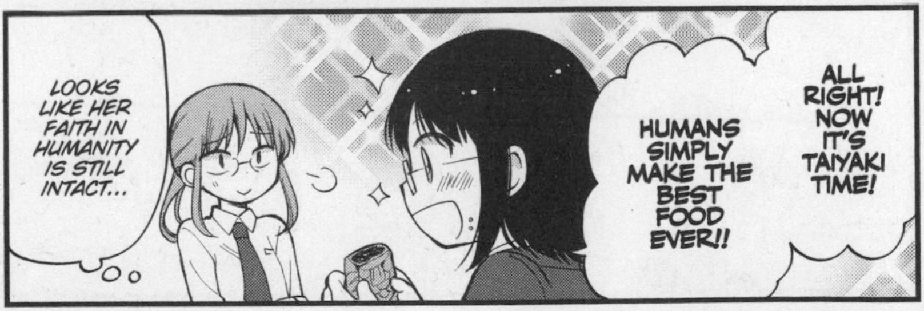
ALL RIGHT! NOW IT'S TAIYAKI TIME!
HUMANS SIMPLY MAKE THE BEST FOOD EVER!!
LOOKS LIKE HER FAITH IN HUMANITY IS STILL INTACT...

GUARDIAN SPIRIT

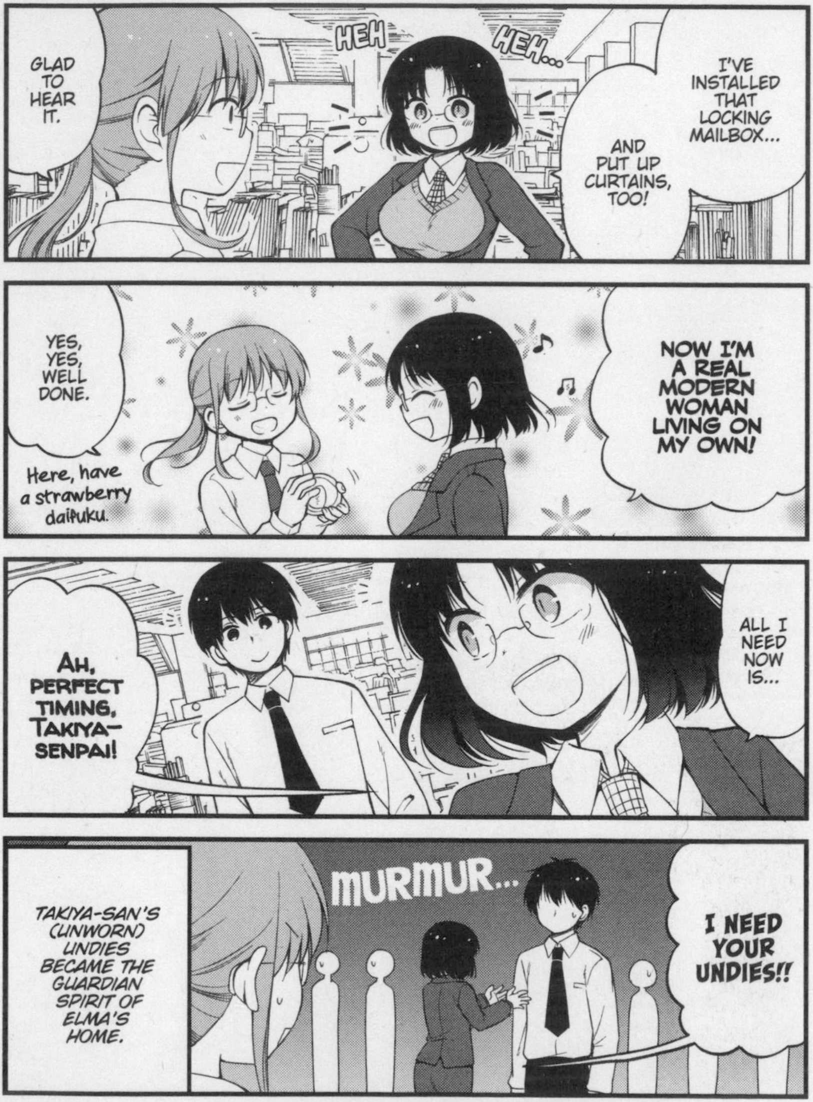
HEH HEH...
I'VE INSTALLED THAT LOCKING MAILBOX...
AND PUT UP CURTAINS, TOO!
GLAD TO HEAR IT.
NOW I'M A REAL MODERN WOMAN LIVING ON MY OWN!
YES, YES, WELL DONE.
Here, have a strawberry daifuku.
ALL I NEED NOW IS...
AH, PERFECT TIMING, TAKIYA-SENPAI!
I NEED YOUR UNDIES!!
MURMUR...
TAKIYA-SAN'S (UNWORN) UNDIES BECAME THE GUARDIAN SPIRIT OF ELMA'S HOME.

CHAPTER 11/END

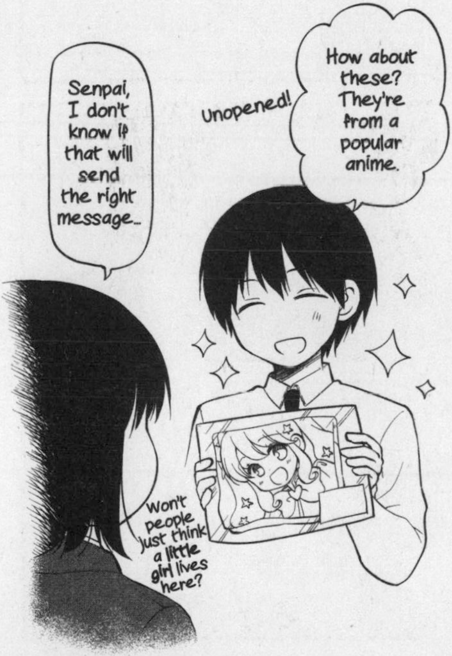
How about these? They're from a popular anime.
Unopened!
Senpai, I don't know if that will send the right message...
Won't people just think a little girl lives here?

Miss Kobayashi's Dragon Maid
Elma's Office Lady Diary

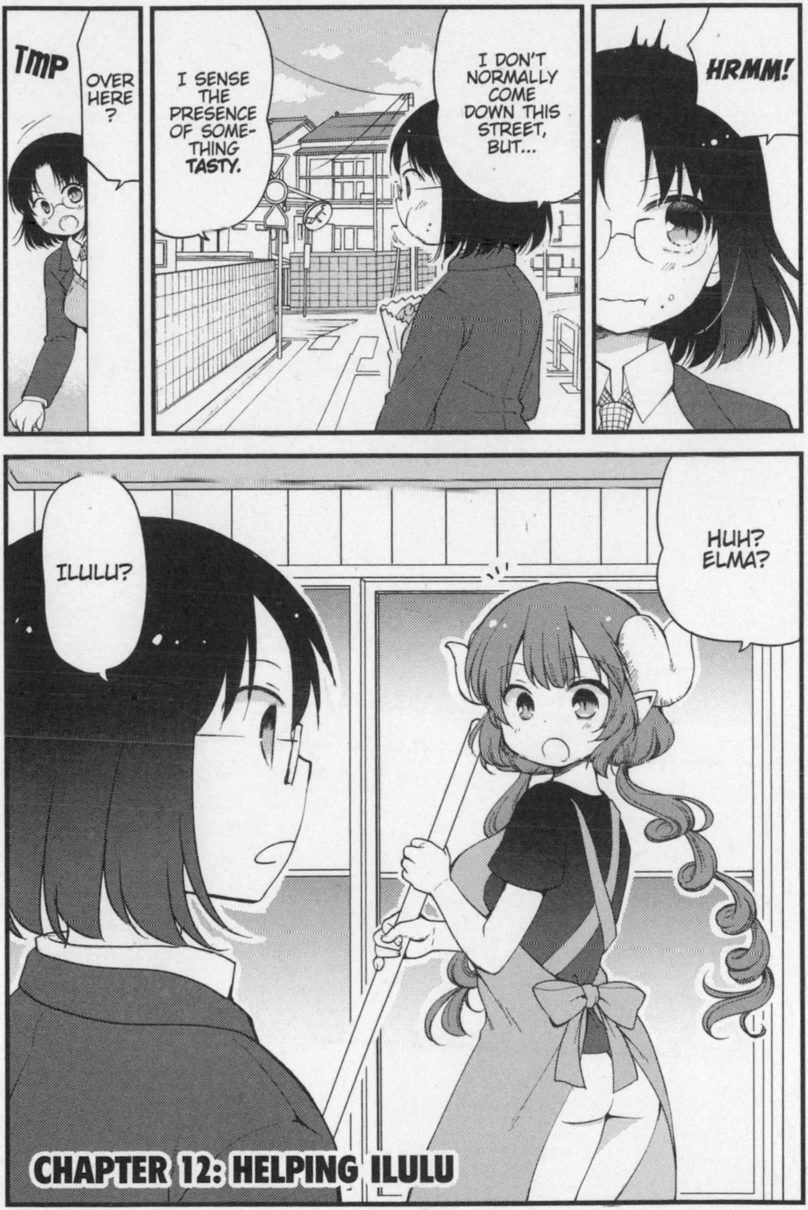
HRMM!
I DON'T NORMALLY COME DOWN THIS STREET, BUT...
I SENSE THE PRESENCE OF SOME-THING TASTY.
OVER HERE ?
TMP
HUH? ELMA?
ILULU?
CHAPTER 12: HELPING ILULU

EXTREMIST

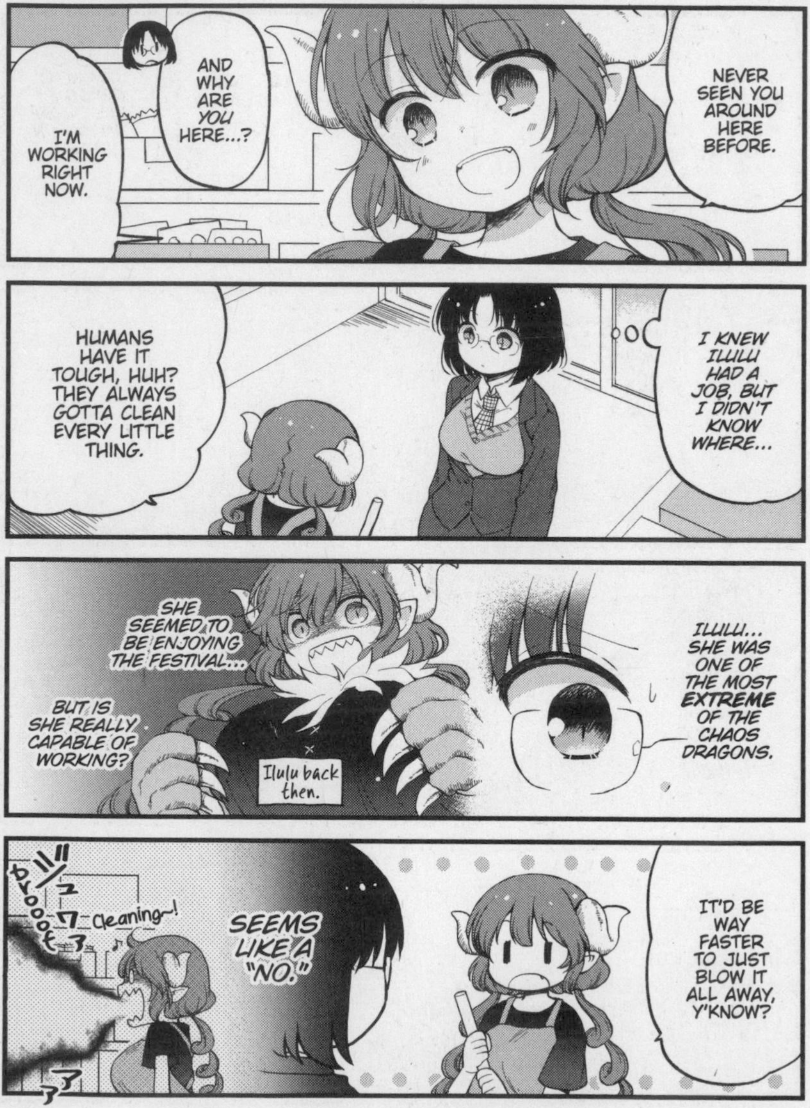
NEVER SEEN YOU AROUND HERE BEFORE.
AND WHY ARE YOU HERE...?
I'M WORKING RIGHT NOW.
I KNEW ILULU HAD A JOB, BUT I DIDN'T KNOW WHERE...
HUMANS HAVE IT TOUGH, HUH? THEY ALWAYS GOTTA CLEAN EVERY LITTLE THING.
ILULU... SHE WAS ONE OF THE MOST EXTREME OF THE CHAOS DRAGONS.
SHE SEEMED TO BE ENJOYING THE FESTIVAL...
BUT IS SHE REALLY CAPABLE OF WORKING?
Ilulu back then.
IT'D BE WAY FASTER TO JUST BLOW IT ALL AWAY, Y'KNOW?
SEEMS LIKE A "NO."
Cleaning~!
broooot

PEERLESS PEAKS

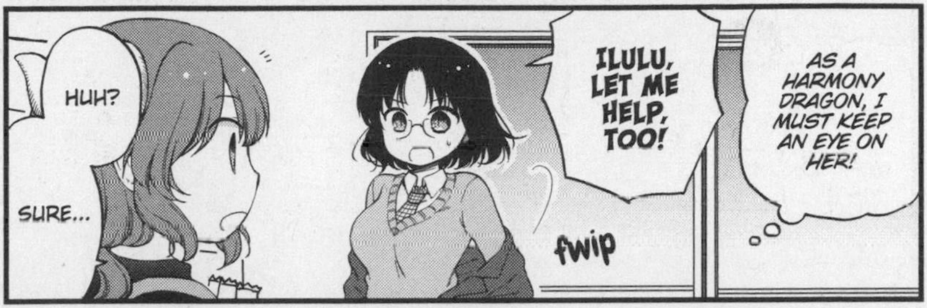
AS A HARMONY DRAGON, I MUST KEEP AN EYE ON HER!
ILULU, LET ME HELP, TOO!
fwip
HUH?
SURE...

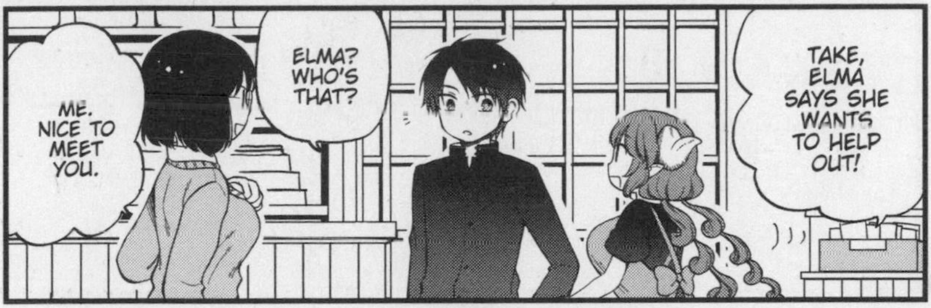
TAKE, ELMA SAYS SHE WANTS TO HELP OUT!
ELMA? WHO'S THAT?
ME. NICE TO MEET YOU.

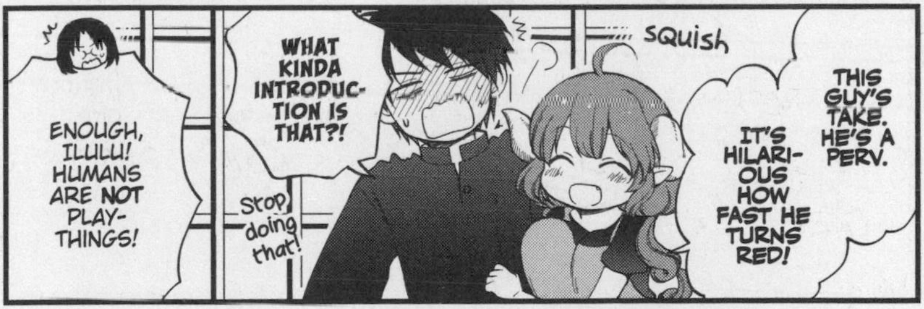
THIS GUY'S TAKE. HE'S A PERV.
IT'S HILARI-OUS HOW FAST HE TURNS RED!
SQUISH
WHAT KINDA INTRODUC-TION IS THAT?!
Stop doing that!
ENOUGH, ILULU! HUMANS ARE NOT PLAY-THINGS!

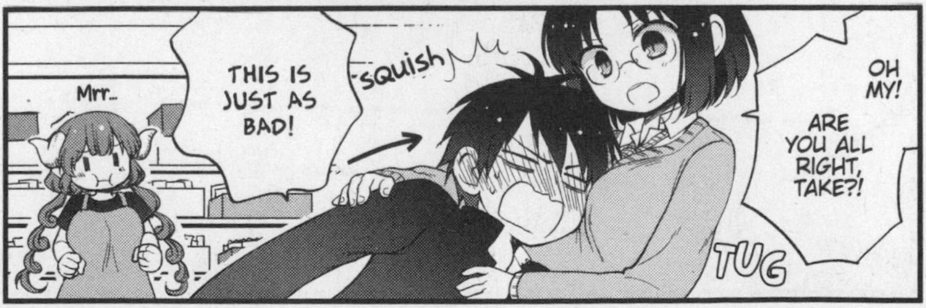
OH MY!
ARE YOU ALL RIGHT, TAKE?!
TUG
SQUISH
THIS IS JUST AS BAD!
Mrr..

FIRE-TYPE DRAGON

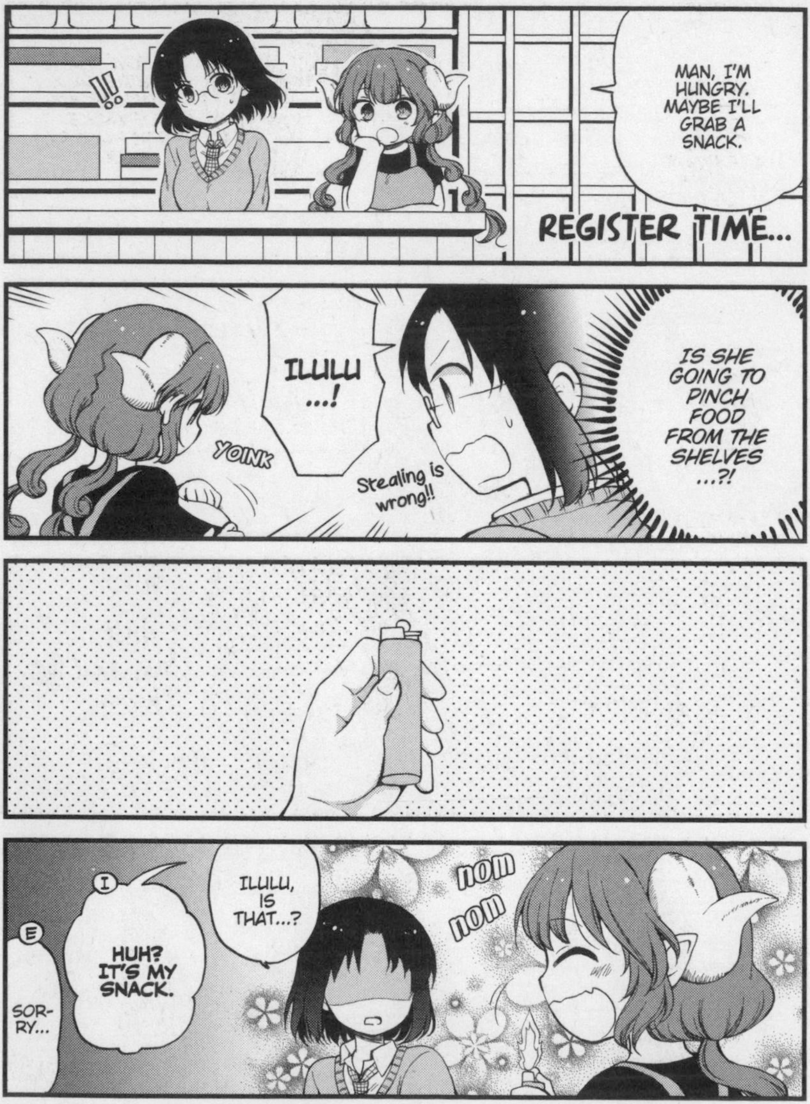
MAN, I'M HUNGRY. MAYBE I'LL GRAB A SNACK.
REGISTER TIME...
!!
IS SHE GOING TO PINCH FOOD FROM THE SHELVES ...?!
ILULU ...!
Stealing is wrong!!
YOINK
nom nom
ILULU, IS THAT...?
HUH? IT'S MY SNACK.
I
E
SOR-RY...

ROLE REVERSAL

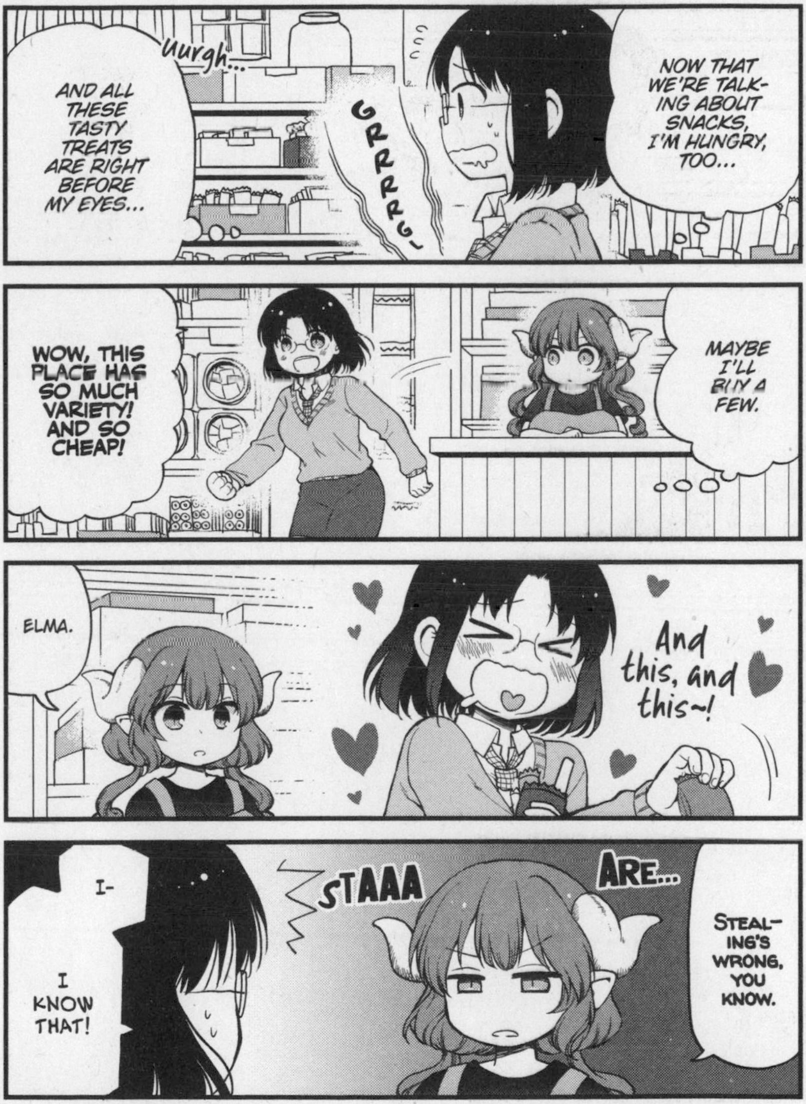
NOW THAT WE'RE TALK-ING ABOUT SNACKS, I'M HUNGRY, TOO...
GRRRRGL
Uurgh...
AND ALL THESE TASTY TREATS ARE RIGHT BEFORE MY EYES...
MAYBE I'LL BUY A FEW.
WOW, THIS PLACE HAS SO MUCH VARIETY! AND SO CHEAP!
And this, and this~!
ELMA.
STAAA ARE...
STEAL-ING'S WRONG, YOU KNOW.
I-
I KNOW THAT!

HER REPUTATION PRECEDES HER

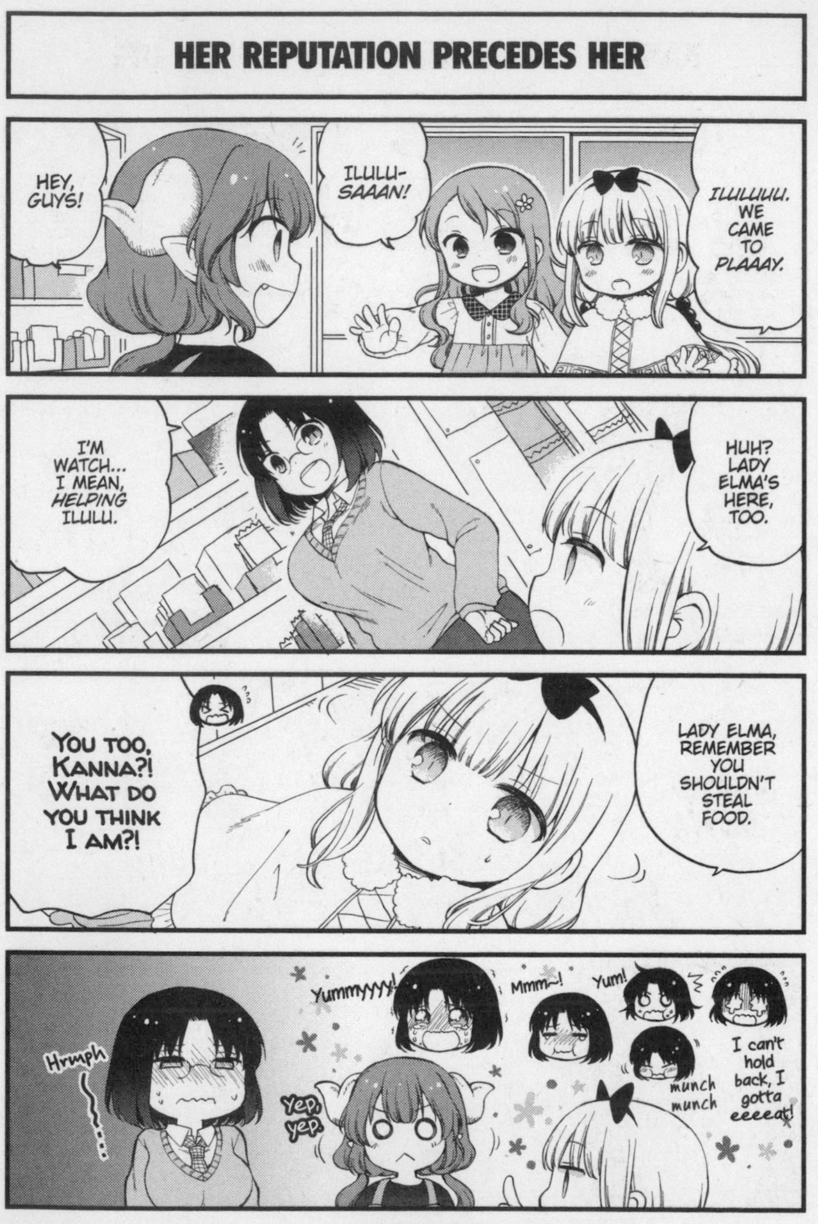
ILULUUU. WE CAME TO PLAAAY.
ILULU-SAAAN!
HEY, GUYS!
HUH? LADY ELMA'S HERE, TOO.
I'M WATCH... I MEAN, HELPING ILULU.
LADY ELMA, REMEMBER YOU SHOULDN'T STEAL FOOD.
YOU TOO, KANNA?! WHAT DO YOU THINK I AM?!
Yum!
Mmm~!
Yummyyyy!
I can't hold back, I gotta eeeeat!
munch munch
Yep, yep.
Hrmph ~~...

KANNA AND SAIKAWA-SAN'S DAILY LIFE

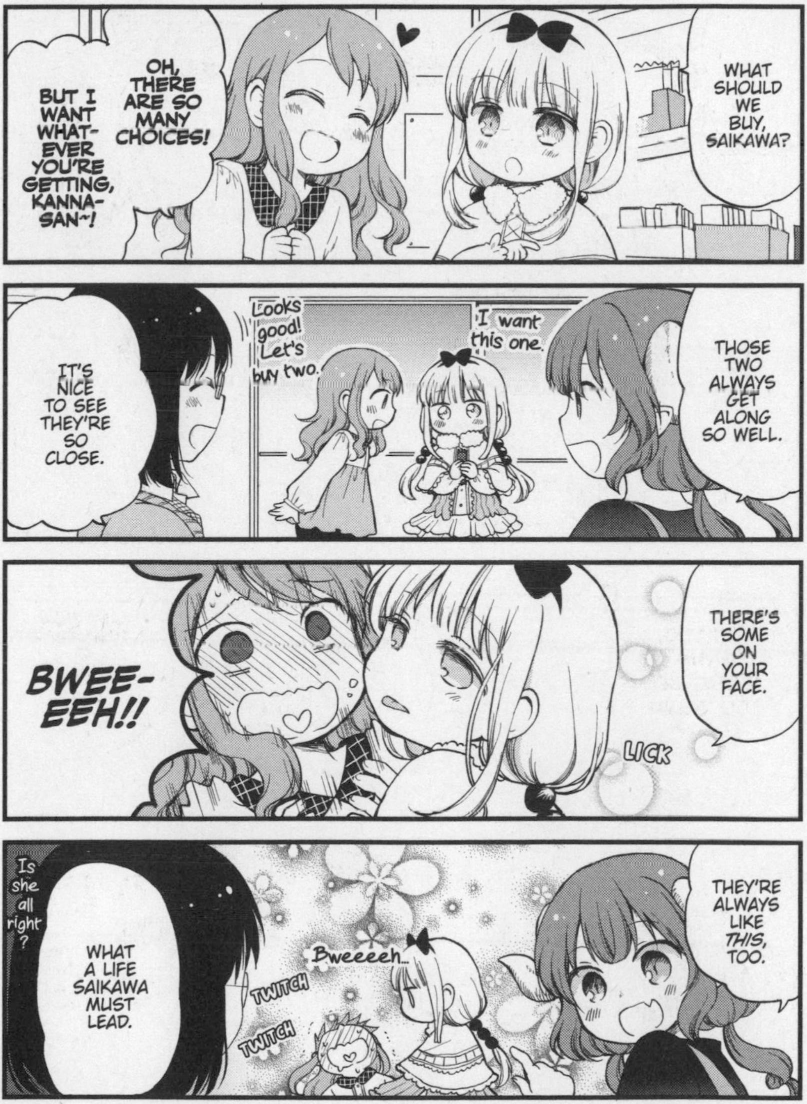
WHAT SHOULD WE BUY, SAIKAWA?
OH, THERE ARE SO MANY CHOICES!
BUT I WANT WHAT-EVER YOU'RE GETTING, KANNA-SAN~!
THOSE TWO ALWAYS GET ALONG SO WELL.
I want this one.
Looks good! Let's buy two.
IT'S NICE TO SEE THEY'RE SO CLOSE.
THERE'S SOME ON YOUR FACE.
LICK
BWEE-EEH!!
THEY'RE ALWAYS LIKE *THIS*, TOO.
Bweeeeh...
TWITCH
TWITCH
WHAT A LIFE SAIKAWA MUST LEAD.
Is she all right?

THE SECRETS OF A SALESWOMAN

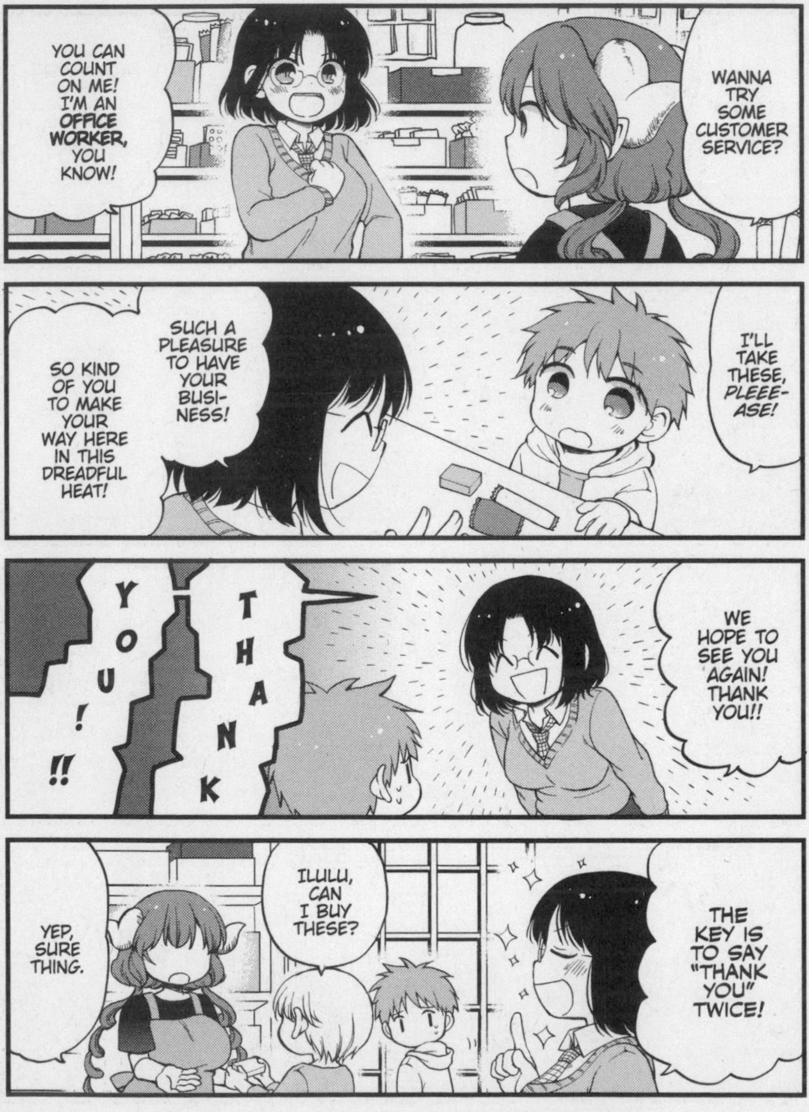
WANNA TRY SOME CUSTOMER SERVICE?
YOU CAN COUNT ON ME! I'M AN OFFICE WORKER, YOU KNOW!
I'LL TAKE THESE, PLEEE-ASE!
SUCH A PLEASURE TO HAVE YOUR BUSI-NESS!
SO KIND OF YOU TO MAKE YOUR WAY HERE IN THIS DREADFUL HEAT!
WE HOPE TO SEE YOU AGAIN! THANK YOU!!
THANK YOU!!!
THE KEY IS TO SAY "THANK YOU" TWICE!
ILULU, CAN I BUY THESE?
YEP, SURE THING.

FLARE-UP

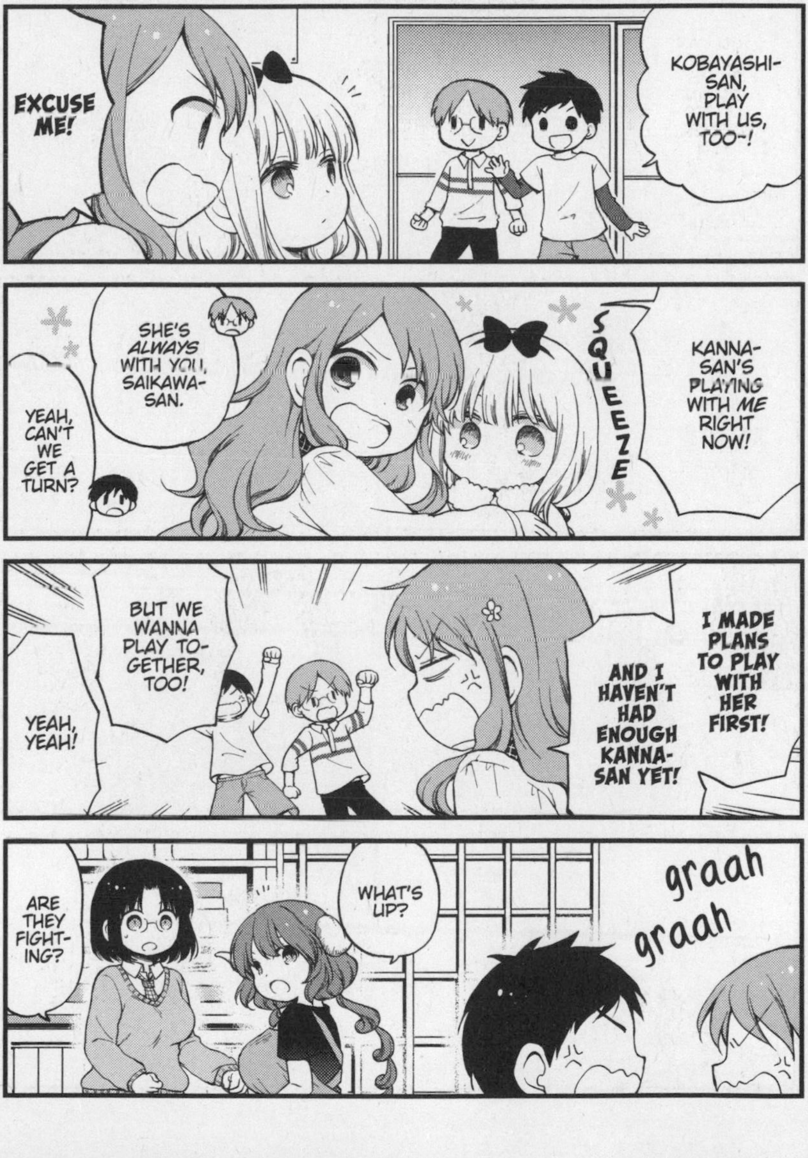
KOBAYASHI-SAN, PLAY WITH US, TOO~!
EXCUSE ME!
SQUEEZE
KANNA-SAN'S PLAYING WITH *ME* RIGHT NOW!
SHE'S *ALWAYS* WITH YOU, SAIKAWA-SAN.
YEAH, CAN'T WE GET A TURN?
I MADE PLANS TO PLAY WITH HER FIRST!
AND I HAVEN'T HAD ENOUGH KANNA-SAN YET!
BUT WE WANNA PLAY TOGETHER, TOO!
YEAH, YEAH!
graah graah
WHAT'S UP?
ARE THEY FIGHTING?

MEDIATOR

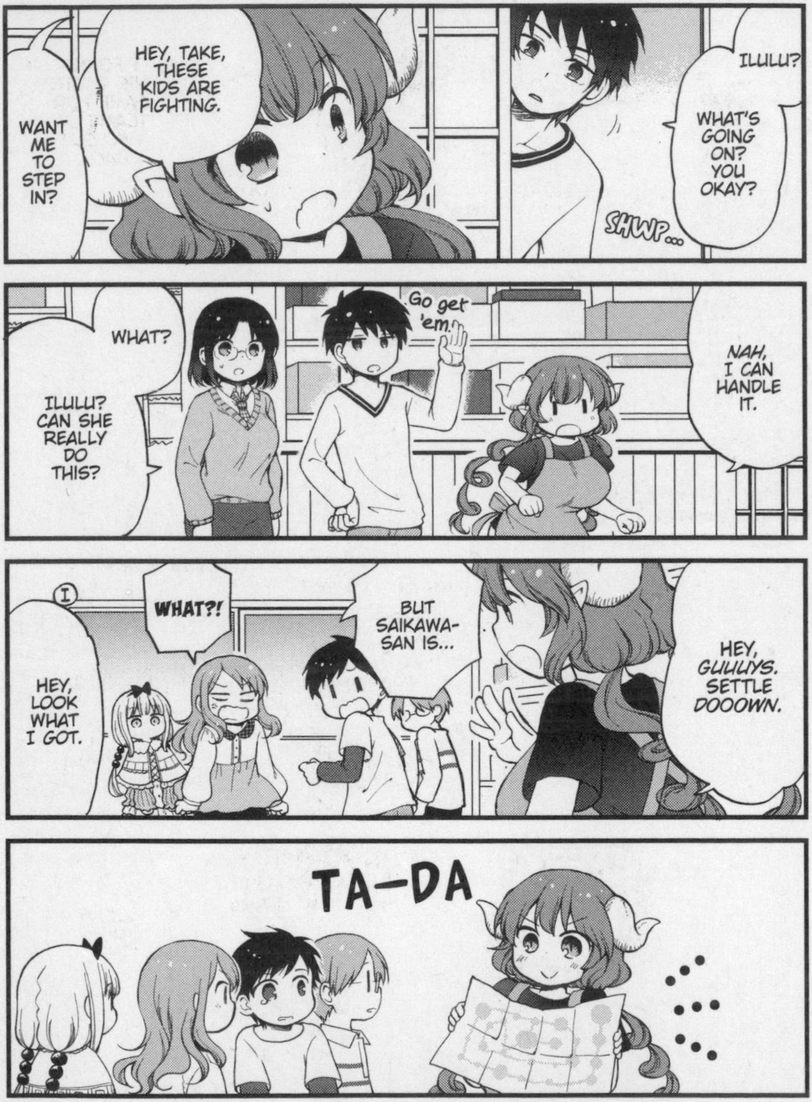
ILULU?
WHAT'S GOING ON? YOU OKAY?
SHWP...
HEY, TAKE, THESE KIDS ARE FIGHTING.
WANT ME TO STEP IN?
NAH, I CAN HANDLE IT.
Go get 'em.
WHAT?
ILULU? CAN SHE REALLY DO THIS?
HEY, GUUUYS. SETTLE DOOOWN.
BUT SAIKAWA-SAN IS...
WHAT?!
I
HEY, LOOK WHAT I GOT.
TA-DA

SOLUTION

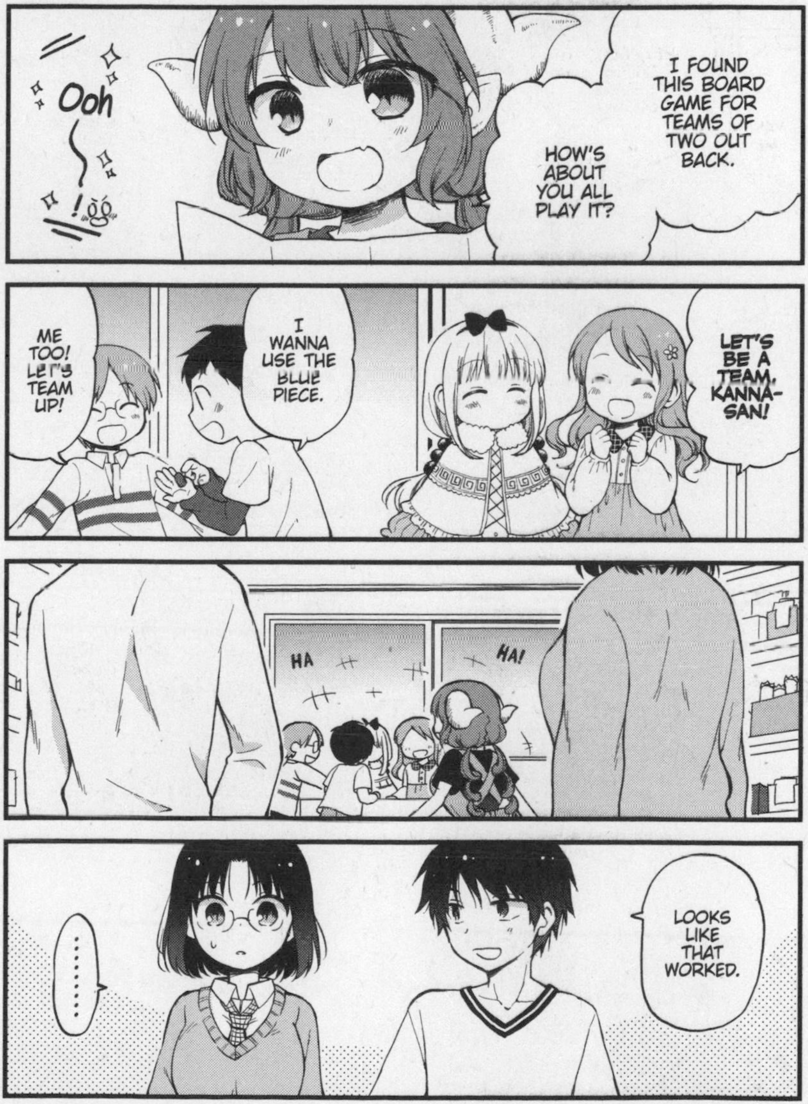
I FOUND THIS BOARD GAME FOR TEAMS OF TWO OUT BACK.
HOW'S ABOUT YOU ALL PLAY IT?
Ooh~!
LET'S BE A TEAM, KANNA-SAN!
I WANNA USE THE BLUE PIECE.
ME TOO! LET'S TEAM UP!
HA!
HA
LOOKS LIKE THAT WORKED.
......

CLUELESS

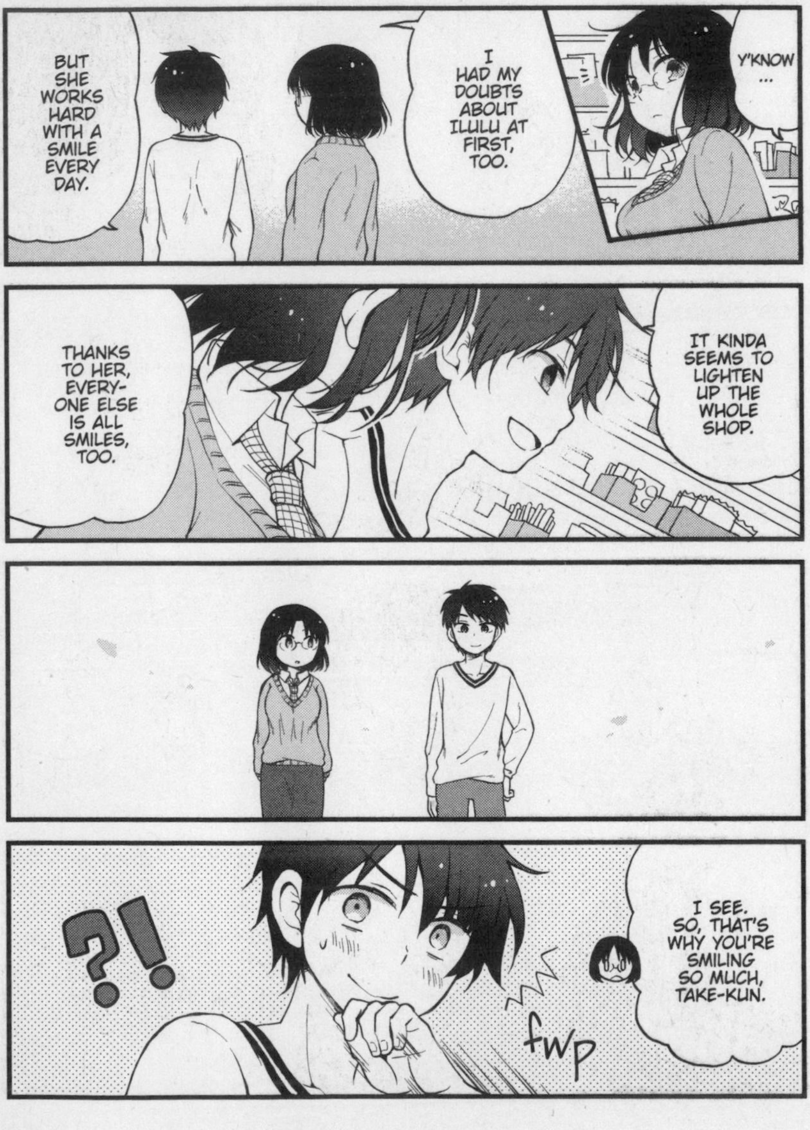
Y'KNOW ...
I HAD MY DOUBTS ABOUT ILULU AT FIRST, TOO.
BUT SHE WORKS HARD WITH A SMILE EVERY DAY.
IT KINDA SEEMS TO LIGHTEN UP THE WHOLE SHOP.
THANKS TO HER, EVERY-ONE ELSE IS ALL SMILES, TOO.
I SEE. SO, THAT'S WHY YOU'RE SMILING SO MUCH, TAKE-KUN.
fwp
?!

TIT FOR TAT

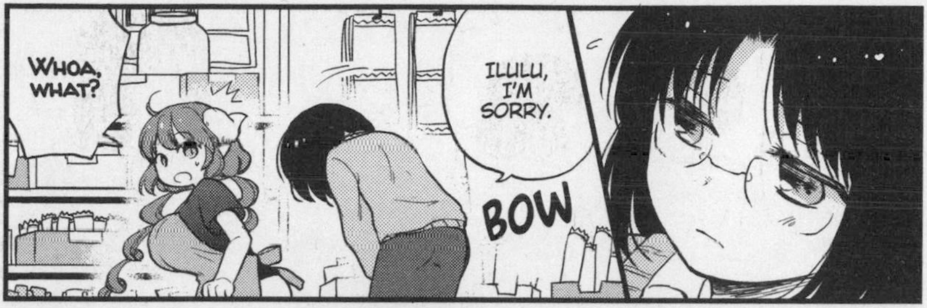
ILULU, I'M SORRY.
BOW
WHOA, WHAT?

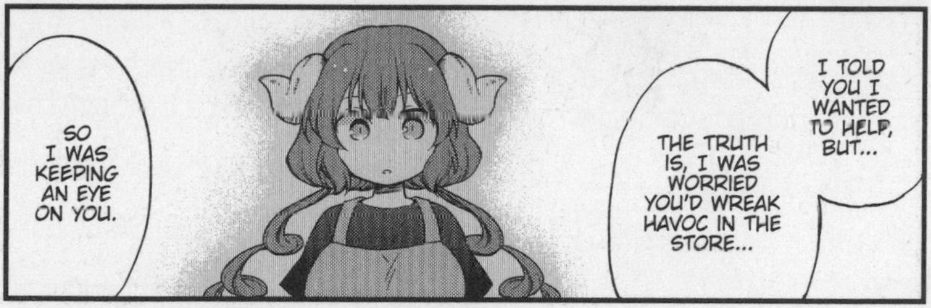
I TOLD YOU I WANTED TO HELP, BUT...
THE TRUTH IS, I WAS WORRIED YOU'D WREAK HAVOC IN THE STORE...
SO I WAS KEEPING AN EYE ON YOU.

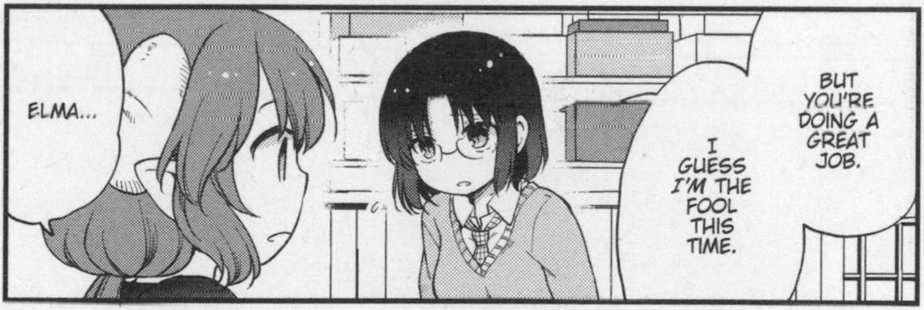
BUT YOU'RE DOING A GREAT JOB.
I GUESS *I'M* THE FOOL THIS TIME.
ELMA...

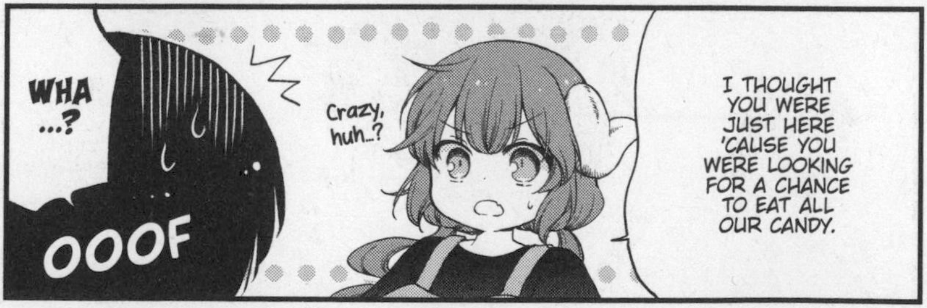
I THOUGHT YOU WERE JUST HERE 'CAUSE YOU WERE LOOKING FOR A CHANCE TO EAT ALL OUR CANDY.
Crazy, huh..?
WHA ...?
OOOF

LET'S GET ALONG

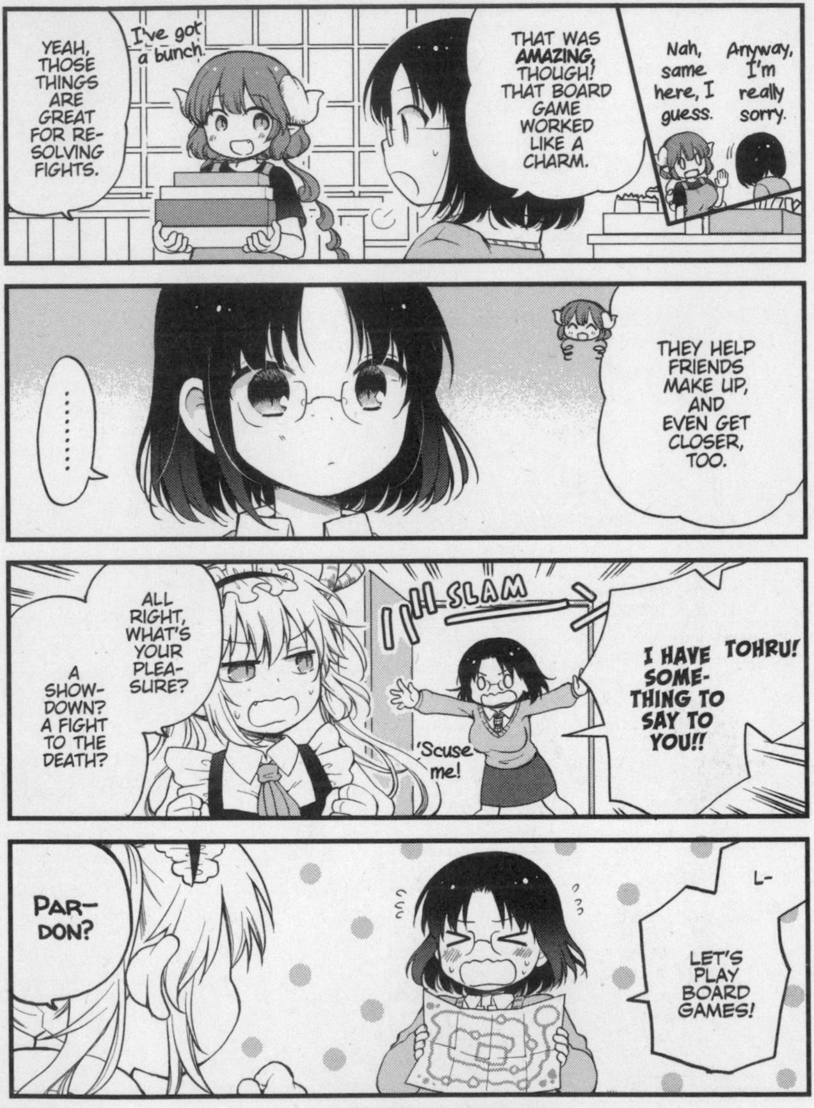
Anyway, I'm really sorry.
Nah, same here, I guess.
THAT WAS AMAZING, THOUGH! THAT BOARD GAME WORKED LIKE A CHARM.
I've got a bunch.
YEAH, THOSE THINGS ARE GREAT FOR RE-SOLVING FIGHTS.
THEY HELP FRIENDS MAKE UP, AND EVEN GET CLOSER, TOO.
....
TOHRU!
I HAVE SOMETHING TO SAY TO YOU!!
SLAM
'Scuse me!
ALL RIGHT, WHAT'S YOUR PLEASURE?
A SHOWDOWN? A FIGHT TO THE DEATH?
L-
LET'S PLAY BOARD GAMES!
PARDON?

CHAPTER 12/END

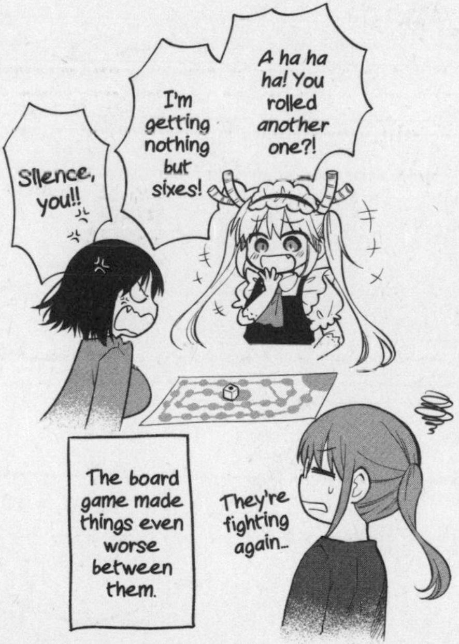
A ha ha ha! You rolled another one?!
I'm getting nothing but sixes!
Silence, you!!
They're fighting again...
The board game made things even worse between them.

Miss Kobayashi's Dragon Maid
Elma's Office Lady Diary

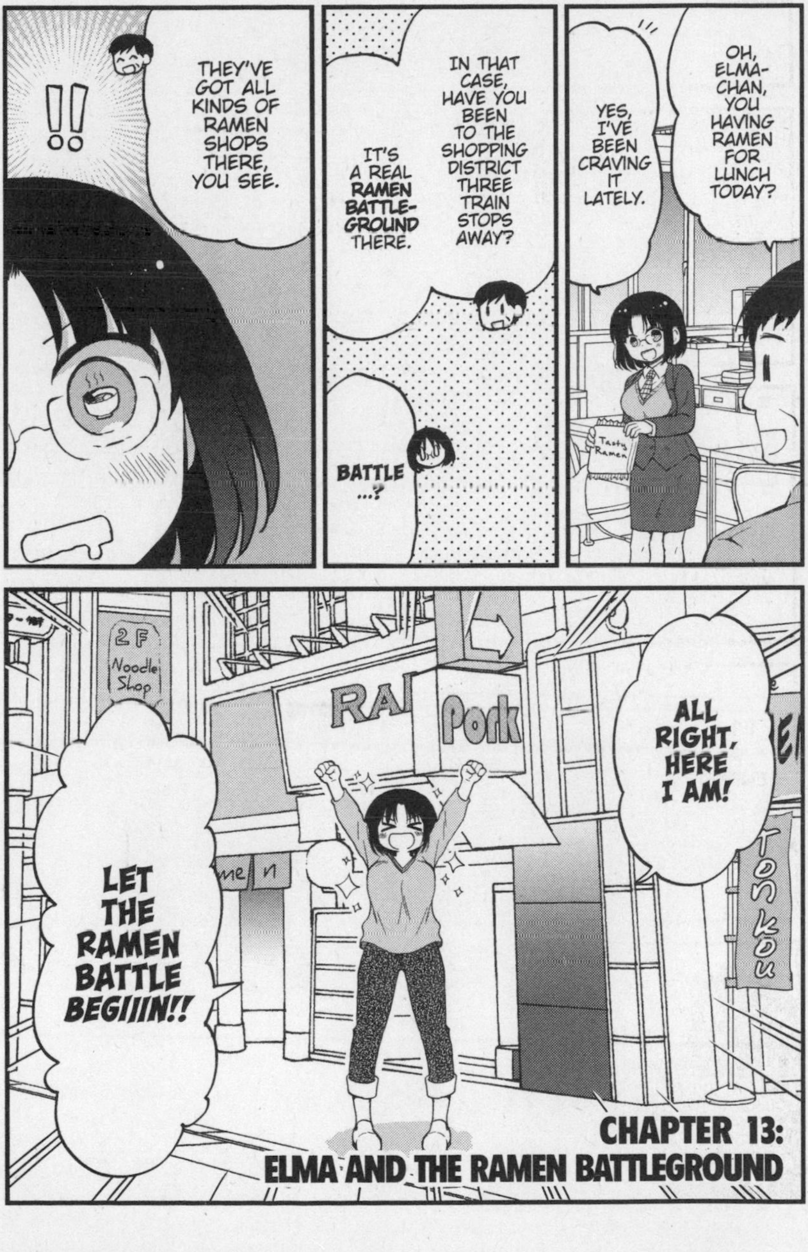
OH, ELMA-CHAN, YOU HAVING RAMEN FOR LUNCH TODAY?
YES, I'VE BEEN CRAVING IT LATELY.
Tasty Ramen
IN THAT CASE, HAVE YOU BEEN TO THE SHOPPING DISTRICT THREE TRAIN STOPS AWAY?
IT'S A REAL RAMEN BATTLE-GROUND THERE.
BATTLE ...?
THEY'VE GOT ALL KINDS OF RAMEN SHOPS THERE, YOU SEE.
!!
ALL RIGHT, HERE I AM!
2 F Noodle Shop
Pork
Tonkou
LET THE RAMEN BATTLE BEGIIIN!!
CHAPTER 13:
ELMA AND THE RAMEN BATTLEGROUND

CHANCE MEETING

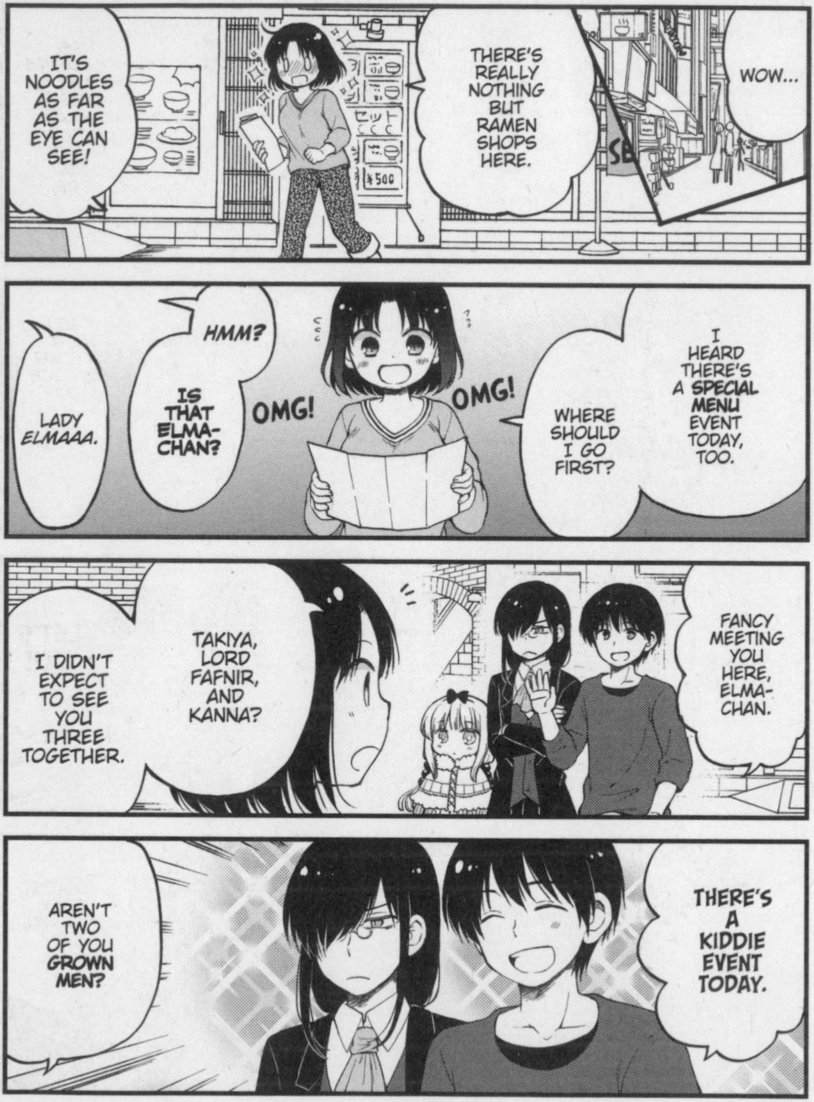
WOW...
THERE'S REALLY NOTHING BUT RAMEN SHOPS HERE.
セット
¥500
IT'S NOODLES AS FAR AS THE EYE CAN SEE!
I HEARD THERE'S A SPECIAL MENU EVENT TODAY, TOO.
WHERE SHOULD I GO FIRST?
OMG!
OMG!
HMM?
IS THAT ELMA-CHAN?
LADY ELMAAA.
FANCY MEETING YOU HERE, ELMA-CHAN.
TAKIYA, LORD FAFNIR, AND KANNA?
I DIDN'T EXPECT TO SEE YOU THREE TOGETHER.
THERE'S A KIDDIE EVENT TODAY.
AREN'T TWO OF YOU GROWN MEN?

ELMA'S WORLD

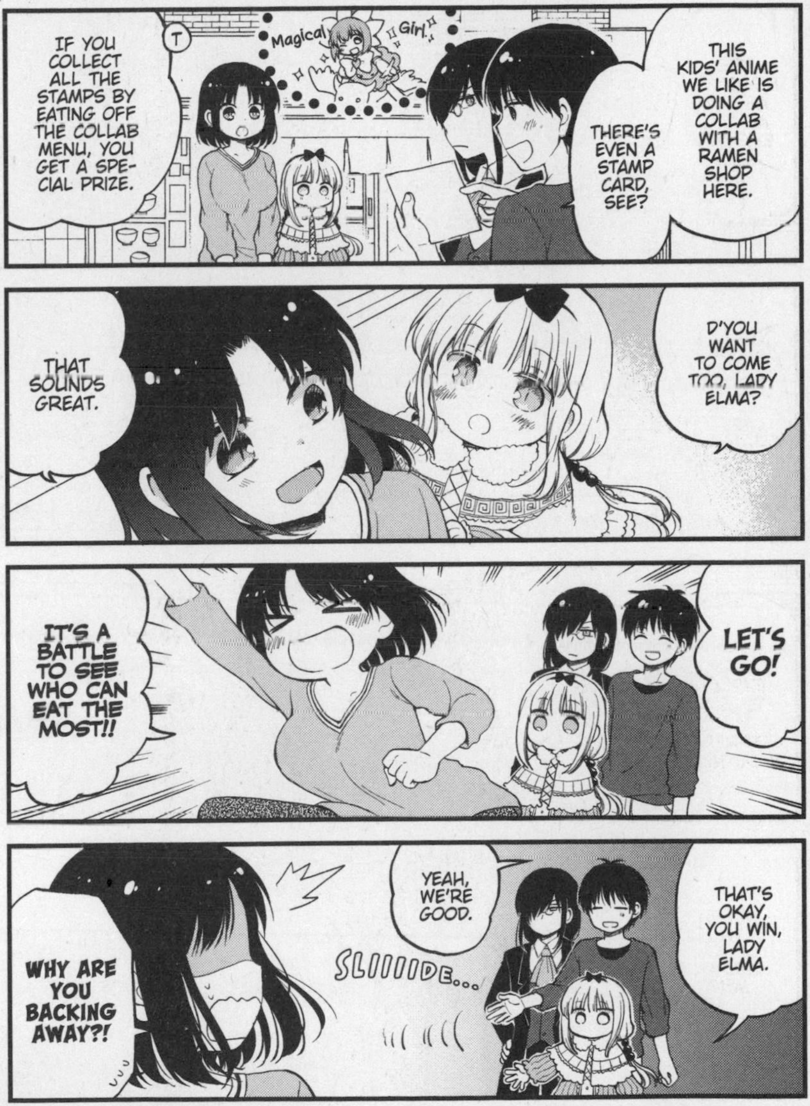
THIS KIDS' ANIME WE LIKE IS DOING A COLLAB WITH A RAMEN SHOP HERE.
THERE'S EVEN A STAMP CARD, SEE?
Magical Girl
IF YOU COLLECT ALL THE STAMPS BY EATING OFF THE COLLAB MENU, YOU GET A SPE-CIAL PRIZE.
D'YOU WANT TO COME TOO, LADY ELMA?
THAT SOUNDS GREAT.
LET'S GO!
IT'S A BATTLE TO SEE WHO CAN EAT THE MOST!!
THAT'S OKAY, YOU WIN, LADY ELMA.
YEAH, WE'RE GOOD.
SLIIIIIDE...
WHY ARE YOU BACKING AWAY?!

TAKIYA-SENPAI'S EATING HABITS

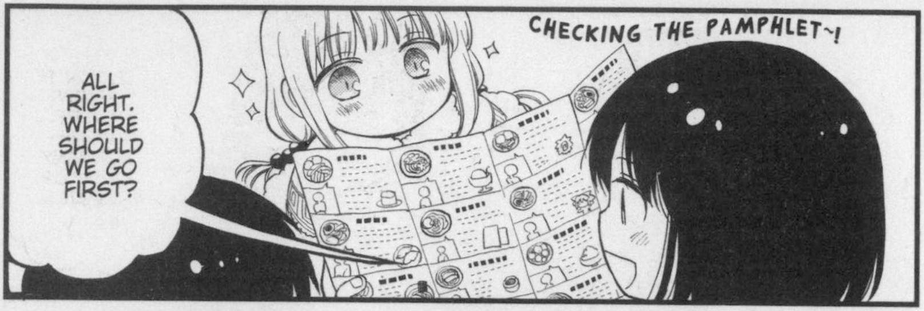
CHECKING THE PAMPHLET~!
ALL RIGHT. WHERE SHOULD WE GO FIRST?

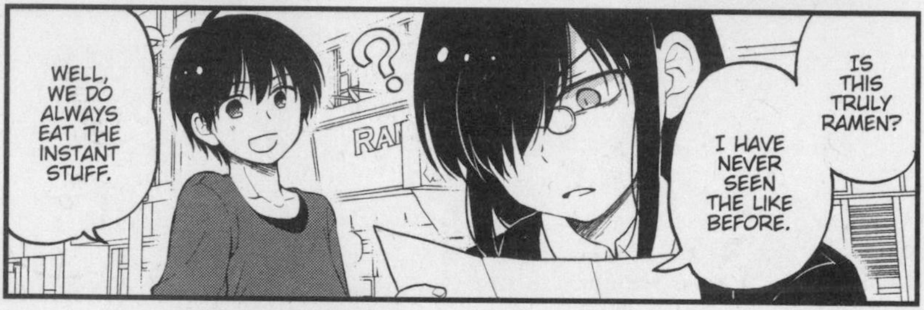
IS THIS TRULY RAMEN?
I HAVE NEVER SEEN THE LIKE BEFORE.
WELL, WE DO ALWAYS EAT THE INSTANT STUFF.

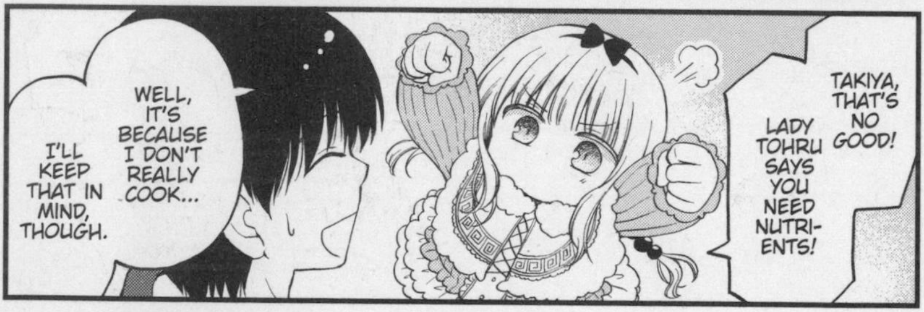
TAKIYA, THAT'S NO GOOD!
LADY TOHRU SAYS YOU NEED NUTRIENTS!
WELL, IT'S BECAUSE I DON'T REALLY COOK...
I'LL KEEP THAT IN MIND, THOUGH.

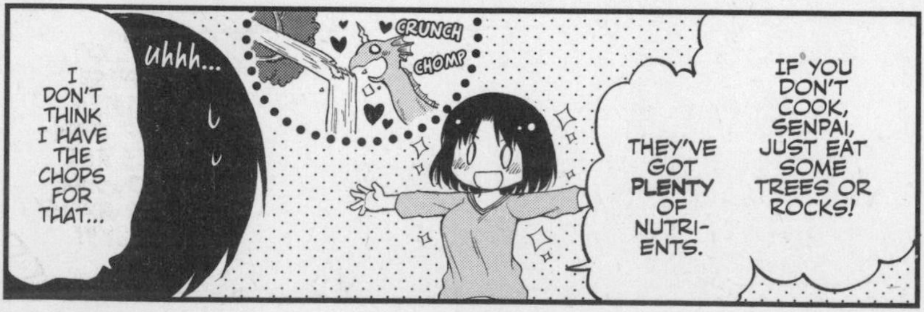
IF YOU DON'T COOK, SENPAI, JUST EAT SOME TREES OR ROCKS!
THEY'VE GOT PLENTY OF NUTRIENTS.
CRUNCH
CHOMP
uhhh...
I DON'T THINK I HAVE THE CHOPS FOR THAT...

MYSTERIOUS

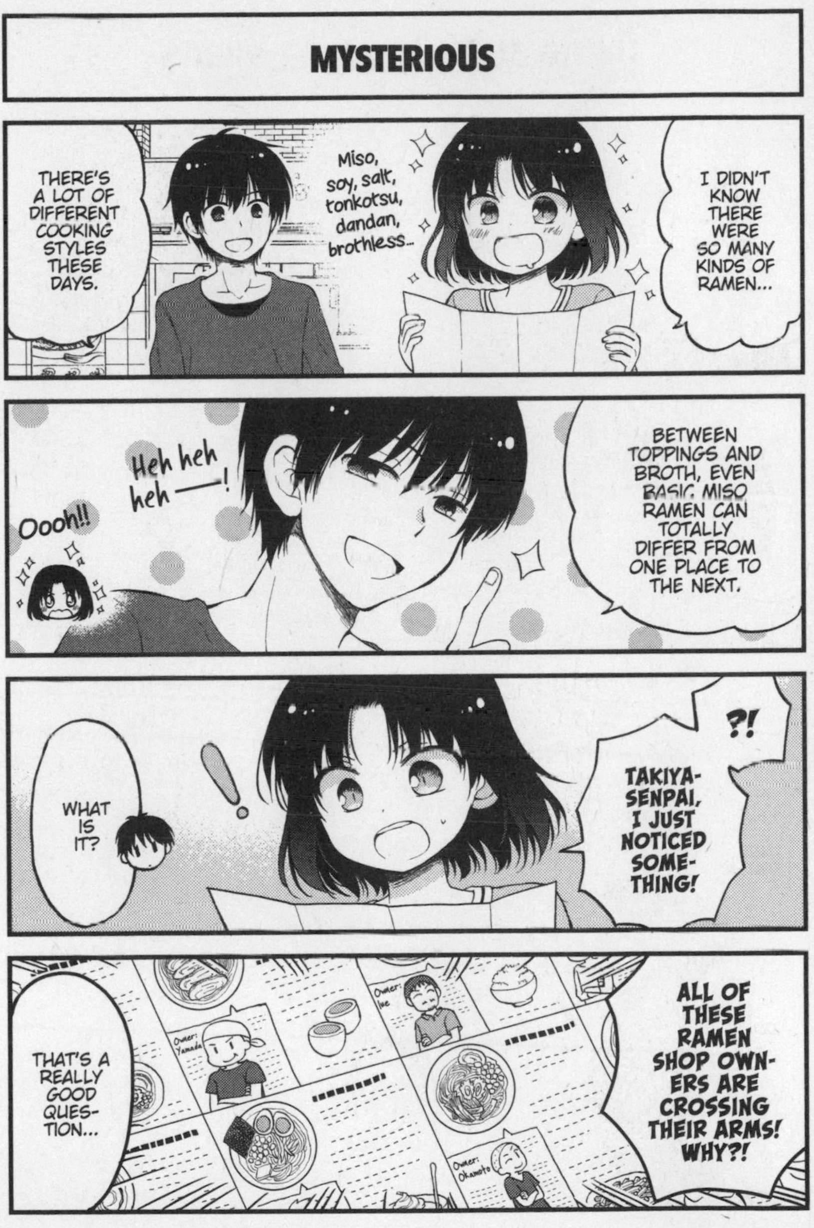
I DIDN'T KNOW THERE WERE SO MANY KINDS OF RAMEN...
Miso, soy, salt, tonkotsu, dandan, brothless...
THERE'S A LOT OF DIFFERENT COOKING STYLES THESE DAYS.
BETWEEN TOPPINGS AND BROTH, EVEN BASIC MISO RAMEN CAN TOTALLY DIFFER FROM ONE PLACE TO THE NEXT.
Heh heh heh——!
Oooh!!
?!
TAKIYA-SENPAI, I JUST NOTICED SOMETHING!
WHAT IS IT?
ALL OF THESE RAMEN SHOP OWNERS ARE CROSSING THEIR ARMS! WHY?!
Owner: Ike
Owner: Yamada
Owner: Okamoto
THAT'S A REALLY GOOD QUESTION...

UNCLEAR COMPARISON

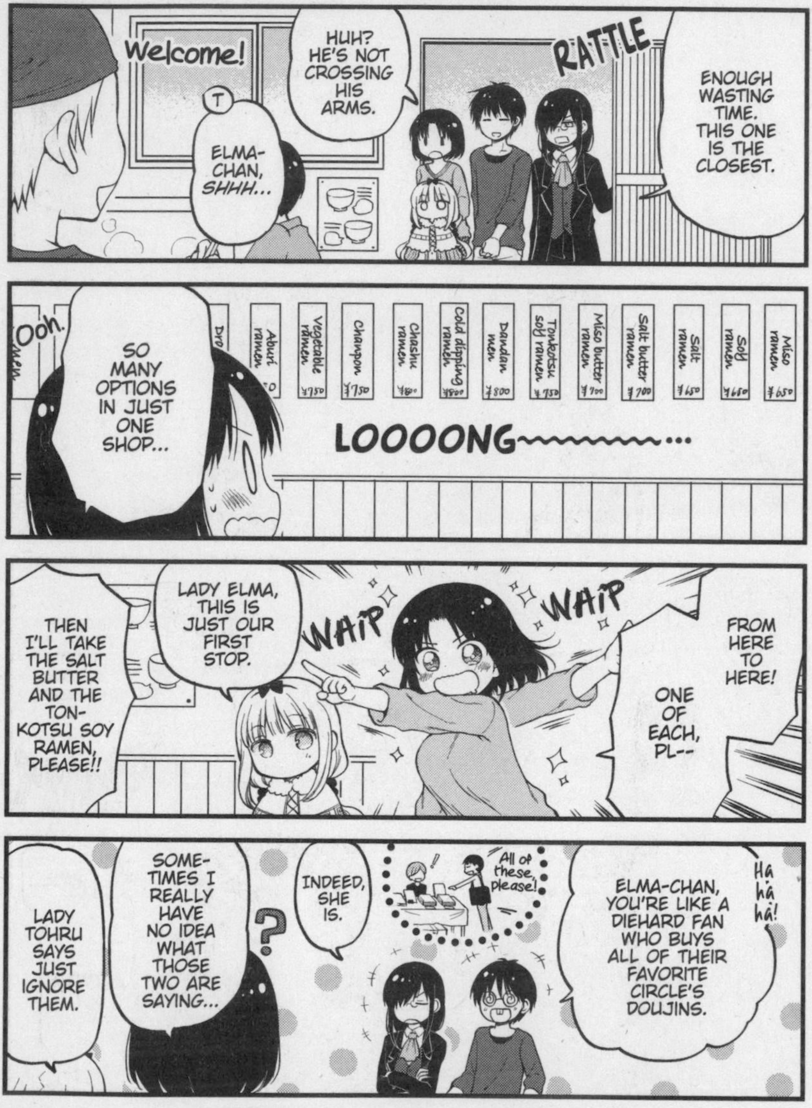
RATTLE
ENOUGH WASTING TIME. THIS ONE IS THE CLOSEST.
HUH? HE'S NOT CROSSING HIS ARMS.
Welcome!
T
ELMA-CHAN, SHHH...
Miso ramen ¥650
Soy ramen ¥650
Salt ramen ¥650
Salt butter ramen ¥700
Miso butter ramen ¥700
Tonkotsu soy ramen ¥750
Dandan men ¥800
Cold dipping ramen ¥800
Chashu ramen
Champon ¥750
Vegetable ramen ¥750
Aburi ramen
LOOOONG~~~~~~~...
SO MANY OPTIONS IN JUST ONE SHOP...
Ooh.
FROM HERE TO HERE!
ONE OF EACH, PL--
WAIP WAIP
LADY ELMA, THIS IS JUST OUR FIRST STOP.
THEN I'LL TAKE THE SALT BUTTER AND THE TON-KOTSU SOY RAMEN, PLEASE!!
Ha ha ha!
ELMA-CHAN, YOU'RE LIKE A DIEHARD FAN WHO BUYS ALL OF THEIR FAVORITE CIRCLE'S DOUJINS.
All of these, please!
INDEED, SHE IS.
?
SOME-TIMES I REALLY HAVE NO IDEA WHAT THOSE TWO ARE SAYING...
LADY TOHRU SAYS JUST IGNORE THEM.

LET'S SHARE THESE FEELINGS

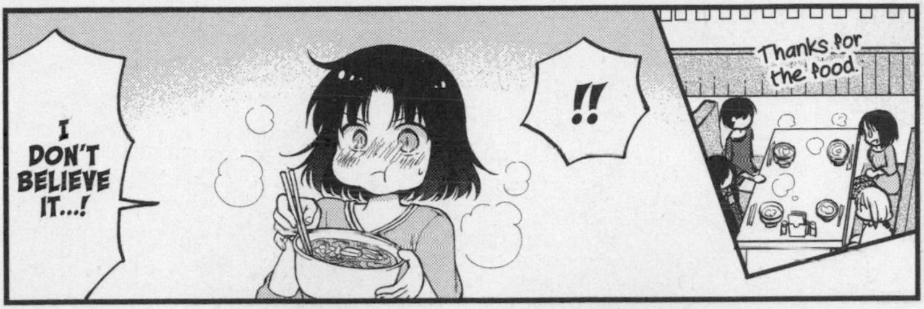
Thanks for the food.
!!
I DON'T BELIEVE IT...!

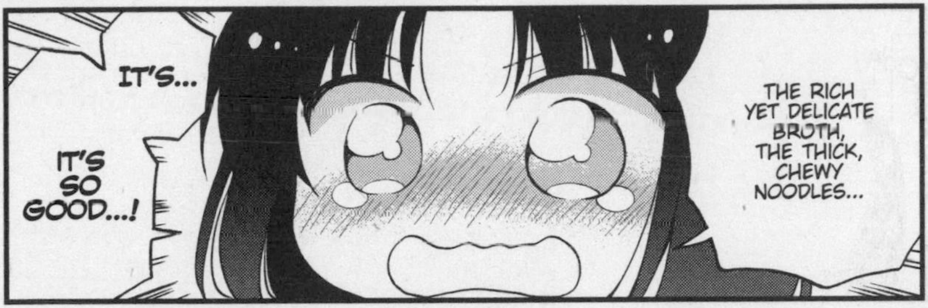
THE RICH YET DELICATE BROTH, THE THICK, CHEWY NOODLES...
IT'S...
IT'S SO GOOD...!

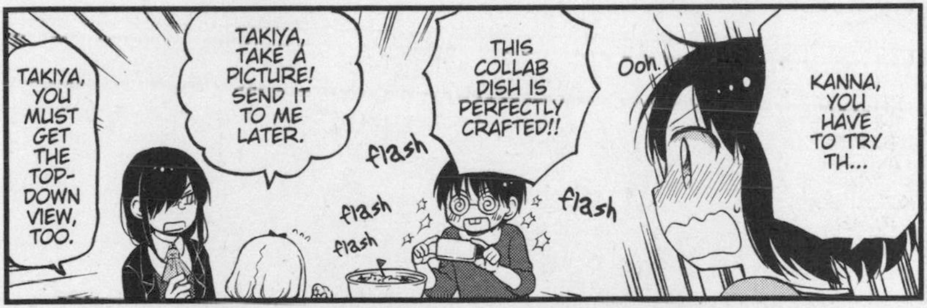
KANNA, YOU HAVE TO TRY TH...
Ooh.
THIS COLLAB DISH IS PERFECTLY CRAFTED!!
flash
flash
flash
flash
TAKIYA, TAKE A PICTURE! SEND IT TO ME LATER.
TAKIYA, YOU MUST GET THE TOP-DOWN VIEW, TOO.

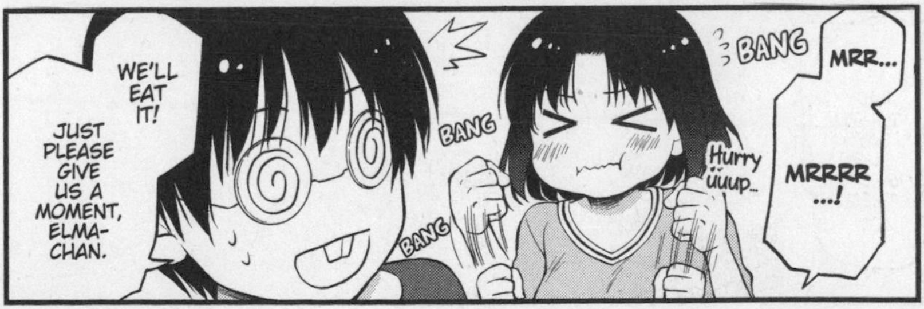
MRR...
MRRRR...!
BANG
Hurry üuup...
BANG
BANG
WE'LL EAT IT!
JUST PLEASE GIVE US A MOMENT, ELMA-CHAN.

KNOWLEDGEABLE

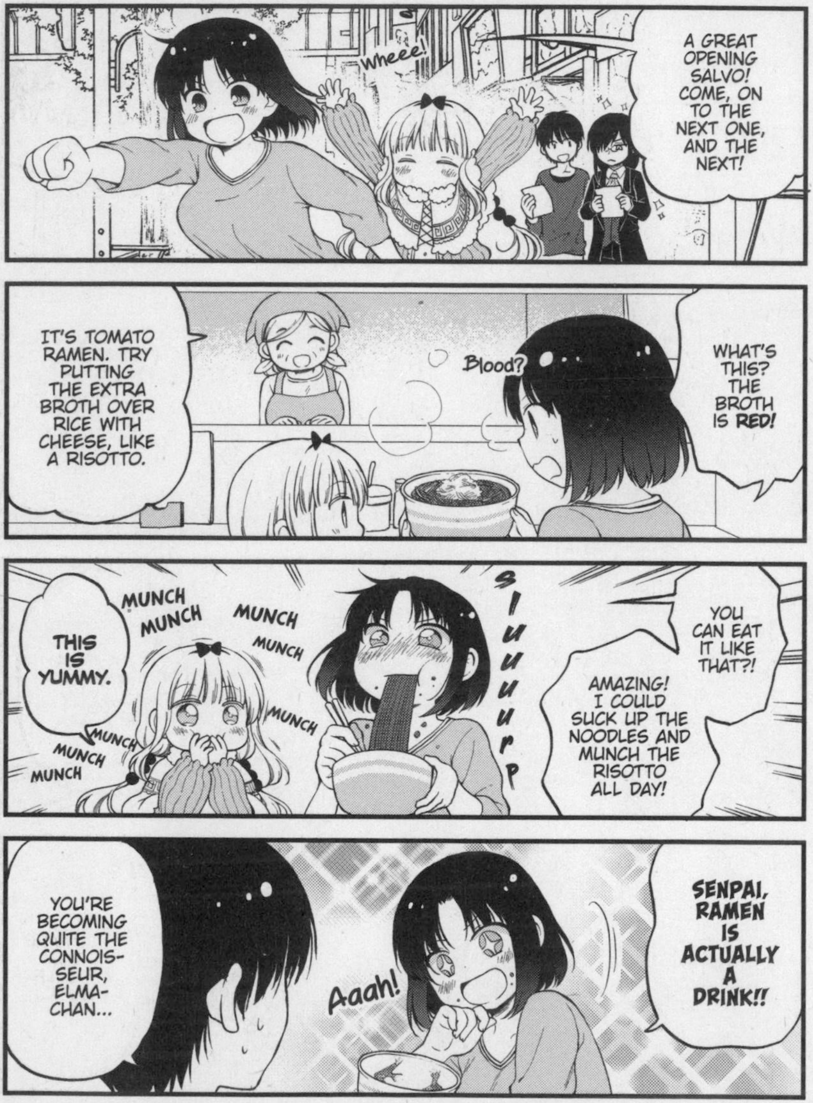
A GREAT OPENING SALVO! COME, ON TO THE NEXT ONE, AND THE NEXT!
Wheee!
WHAT'S THIS? THE BROTH IS RED!
Blood?
IT'S TOMATO RAMEN. TRY PUTTING THE EXTRA BROTH OVER RICE WITH CHEESE, LIKE A RISOTTO.
YOU CAN EAT IT LIKE THAT?!
AMAZING! I COULD SUCK UP THE NOODLES AND MUNCH THE RISOTTO ALL DAY!
SLUUUURP
MUNCH MUNCH MUNCH MUNCH MUNCH
MUNCH MUNCH MUNCH
THIS IS YUMMY.
SENPAI, RAMEN IS ACTUALLY A DRINK!!
Aaah!
YOU'RE BECOMING QUITE THE CONNOISSEUR, ELMA-CHAN...

EXPERT OPINION

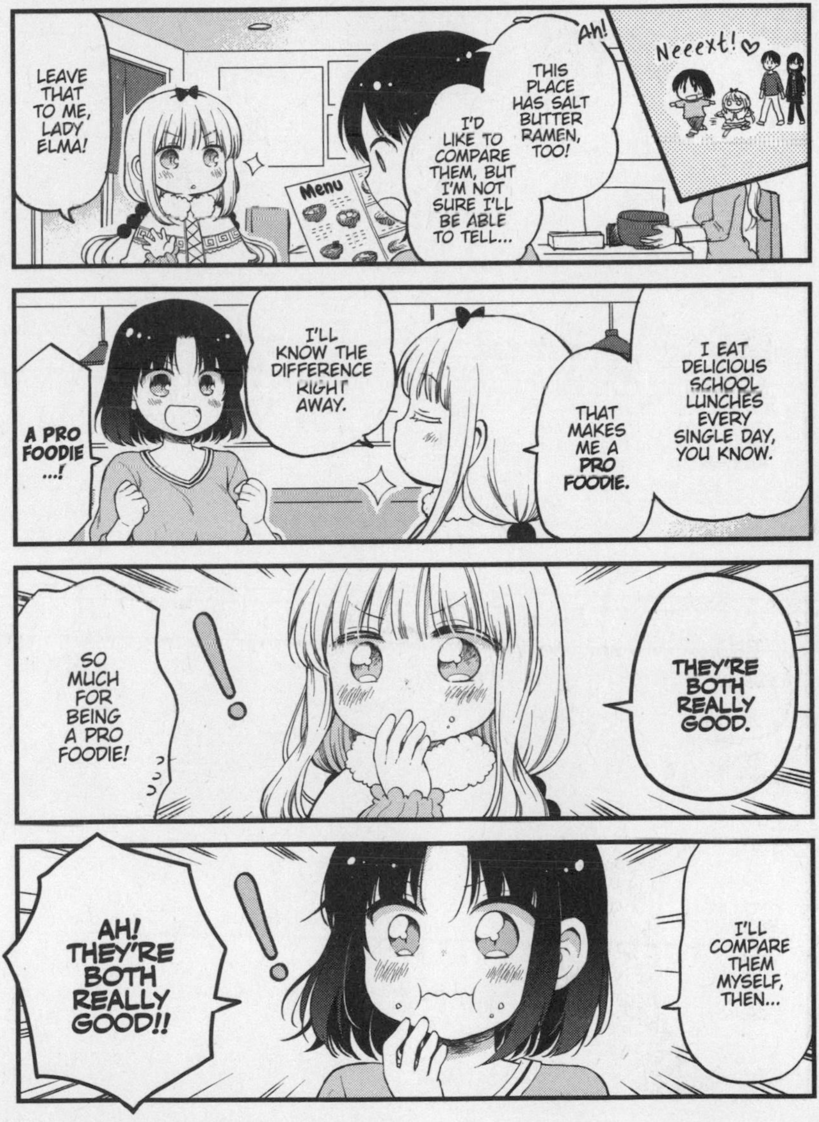
Neeext!
Ah!
THIS PLACE HAS SALT BUTTER RAMEN, TOO!
I'D LIKE TO COMPARE THEM, BUT I'M NOT SURE I'LL BE ABLE TO TELL...
Menu
LEAVE THAT TO ME, LADY ELMA!
I EAT DELICIOUS SCHOOL LUNCHES EVERY SINGLE DAY, YOU KNOW.
THAT MAKES ME A PRO FOODIE.
I'LL KNOW THE DIFFERENCE RIGHT AWAY.
A PRO FOODIE ...!
THEY'RE BOTH REALLY GOOD.
SO MUCH FOR BEING A PRO FOODIE!
I'LL COMPARE THEM MYSELF, THEN...
AH! THEY'RE BOTH REALLY GOOD!!

A DRAGON'S STAMINA

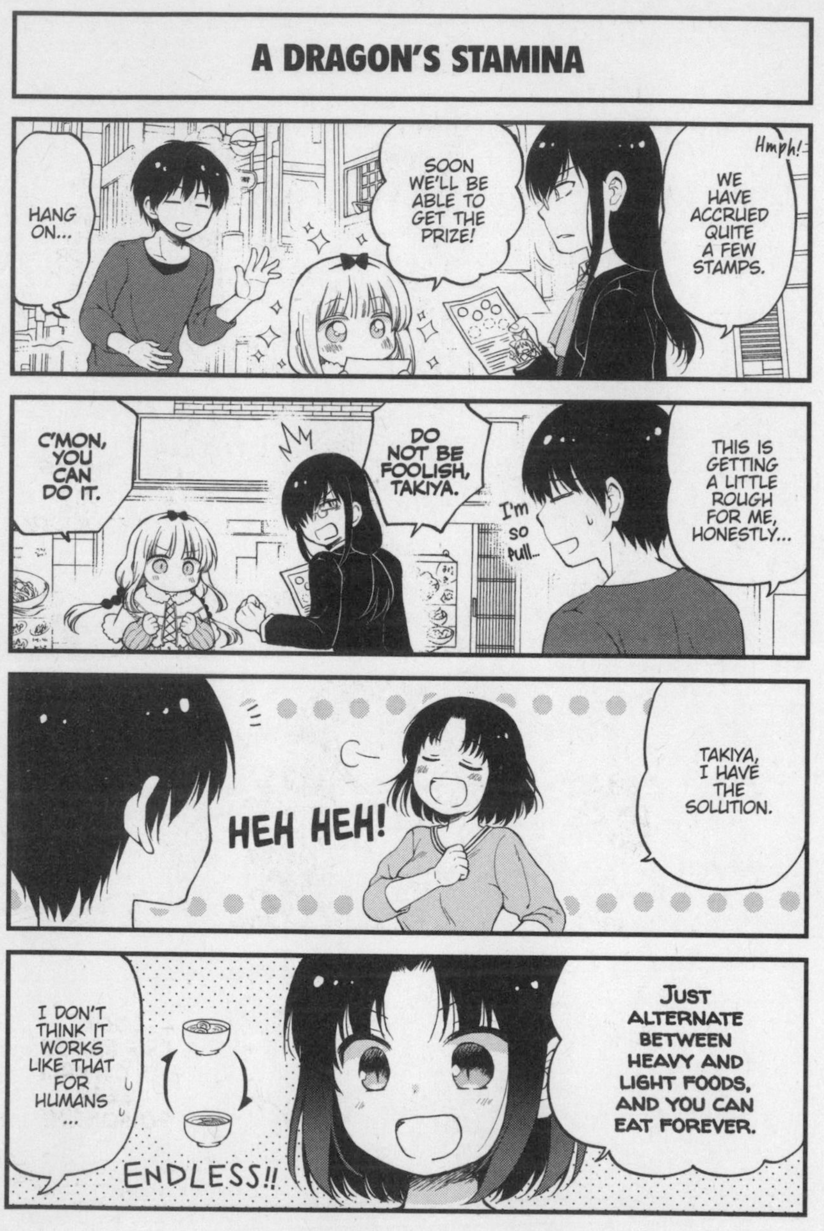
Hmph!
WE HAVE ACCRUED QUITE A FEW STAMPS.
SOON WE'LL BE ABLE TO GET THE PRIZE!
HANG ON...
THIS IS GETTING A LITTLE ROUGH FOR ME, HONESTLY...
I'm so full...
DO NOT BE FOOLISH, TAKIYA.
C'MON, YOU CAN DO IT.
TAKIYA, I HAVE THE SOLUTION.
HEH HEH!
JUST ALTERNATE BETWEEN HEAVY AND LIGHT FOODS, AND YOU CAN EAT FOREVER.
ENDLESS!!
I DON'T THINK IT WORKS LIKE THAT FOR HUMANS...

NO ORDINARY RAMEN

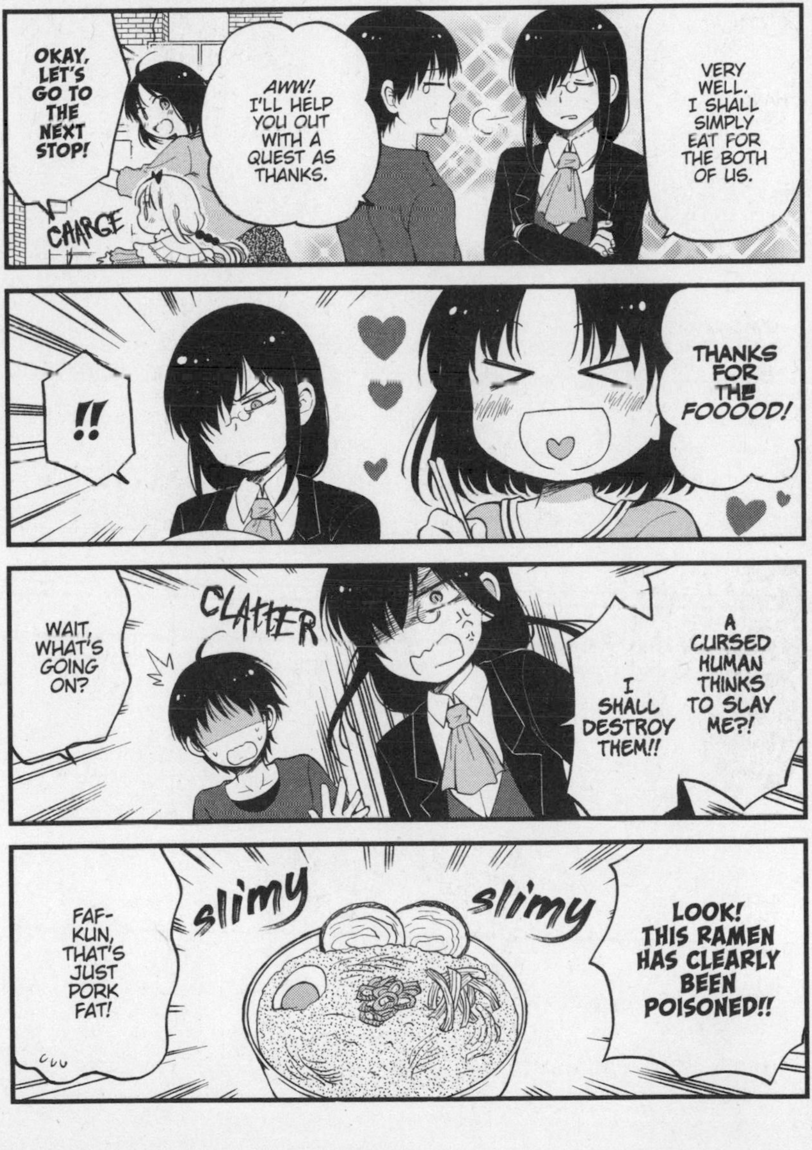
VERY WELL. I SHALL SIMPLY EAT FOR THE BOTH OF US.
AWW! I'LL HELP YOU OUT WITH A QUEST AS THANKS.
OKAY, LET'S GO TO THE NEXT STOP!
CHARGE
THANKS FOR THE FOOOOD!
!!
A CURSED HUMAN THINKS TO SLAY ME?!
I SHALL DESTROY THEM!!
CLATTER
WAIT, WHAT'S GOING ON?
LOOK! THIS RAMEN HAS CLEARLY BEEN POISONED!!
slimy
slimy
FAF-KUN, THAT'S JUST PORK FAT!

VICTORY!!

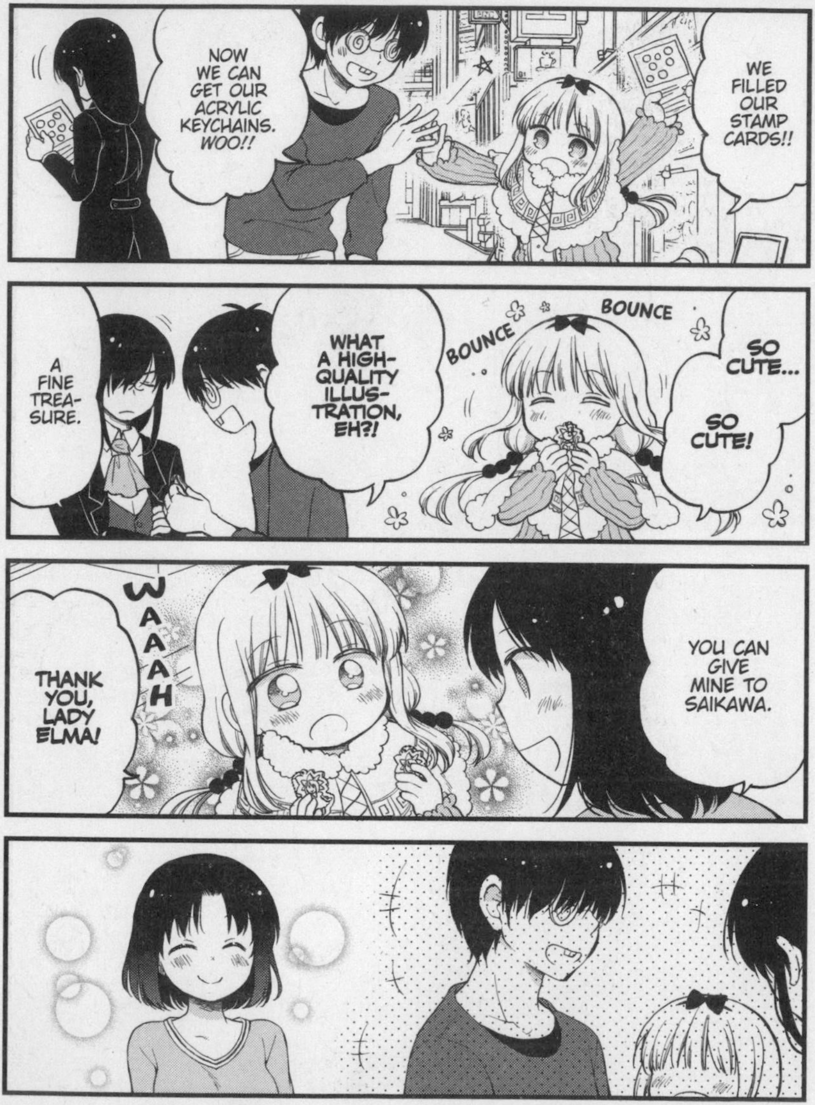
WE FILLED OUR STAMP CARDS!!
NOW WE CAN GET OUR ACRYLIC KEYCHAINS. WOO!!
SO CUTE...
SO CUTE!
BOUNCE
BOUNCE
WHAT A HIGH-QUALITY ILLUSTRATION, EH?!
A FINE TREASURE.
YOU CAN GIVE MINE TO SAIKAWA.
WAAAH
THANK YOU, LADY ELMA!

MORE THAN ENOUGH

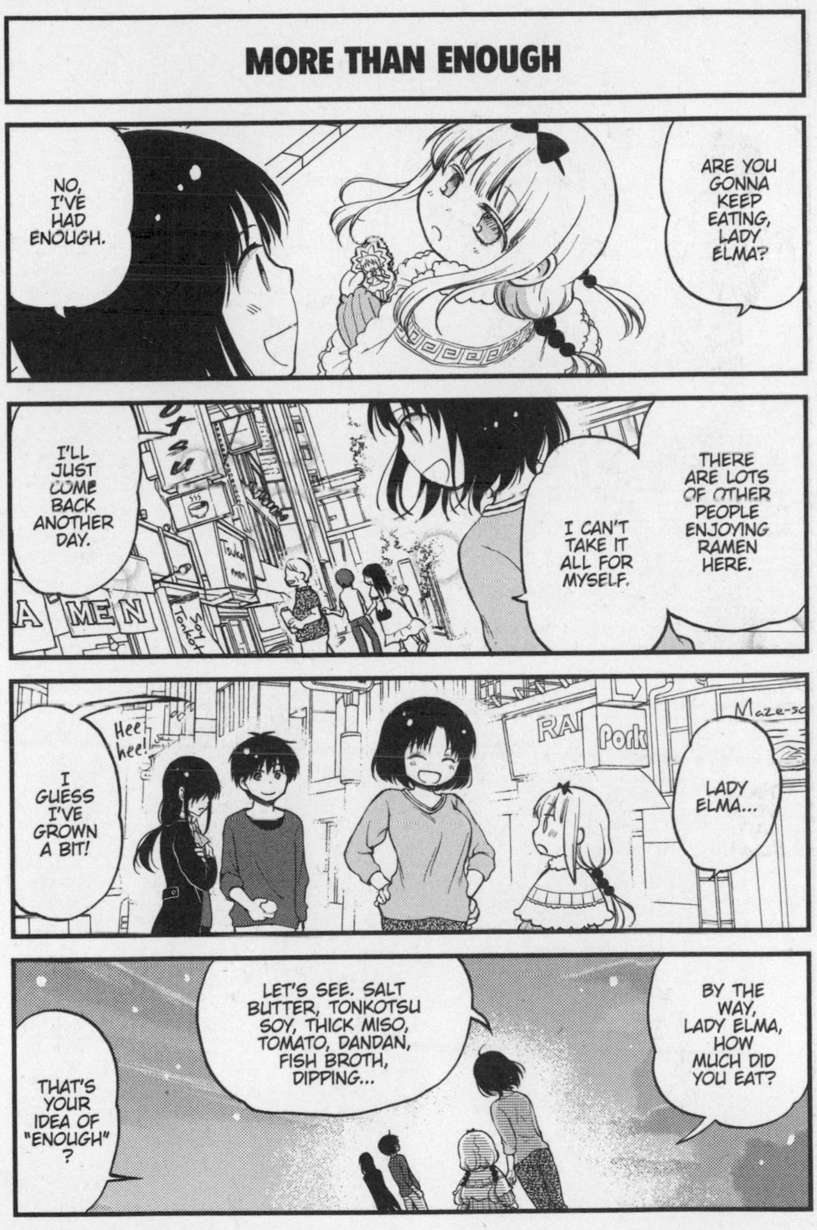
ARE YOU GONNA KEEP EATING, LADY ELMA?
NO, I'VE HAD ENOUGH.
THERE ARE LOTS OF OTHER PEOPLE ENJOYING RAMEN HERE.
I CAN'T TAKE IT ALL FOR MYSELF.
I'LL JUST COME BACK ANOTHER DAY.
LADY ELMA...
Pork
Hee hee!
I GUESS I'VE GROWN A BIT!
BY THE WAY, LADY ELMA, HOW MUCH DID YOU EAT?
LET'S SEE. SALT BUTTER, TONKOTSU SOY, THICK MISO, TOMATO, DANDAN, FISH BROTH, DIPPING...
THAT'S YOUR IDEA OF "ENOUGH"?

AFTER THE BATTLE

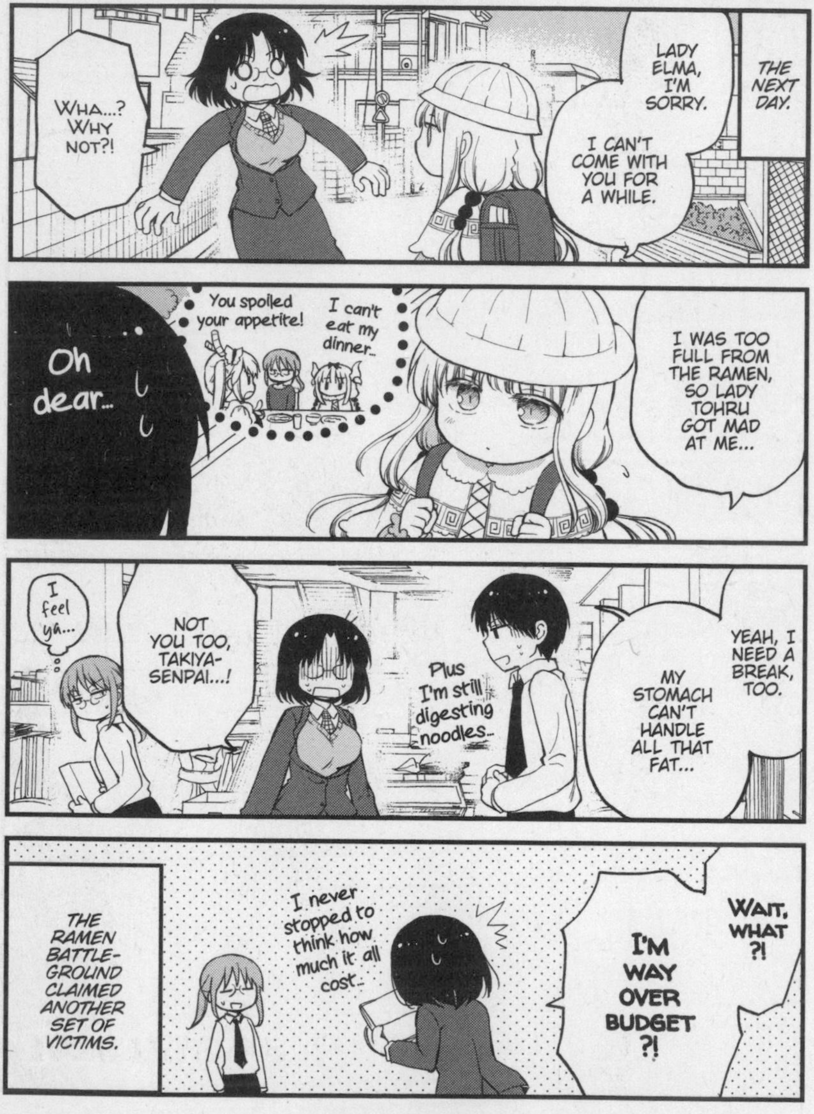
THE NEXT DAY.
LADY ELMA, I'M SORRY.
I CAN'T COME WITH YOU FOR A WHILE.
WHA...? WHY NOT?!
I WAS TOO FULL FROM THE RAMEN, SO LADY TOHRU GOT MAD AT ME...
I can't eat my dinner...
You spoiled your appetite!
Oh dear...
YEAH, I NEED A BREAK, TOO.
MY STOMACH CAN'T HANDLE ALL THAT FAT...
Plus I'm still digesting noodles...
NOT YOU TOO, TAKIYA-SENPAI...!
I feel ya...
WAIT, WHAT?!
I'M WAY OVER BUDGET?!
I never stopped to think how much it all cost...
THE RAMEN BATTLE-GROUND CLAIMED ANOTHER SET OF VICTIMS.

CHAPTER 13/END

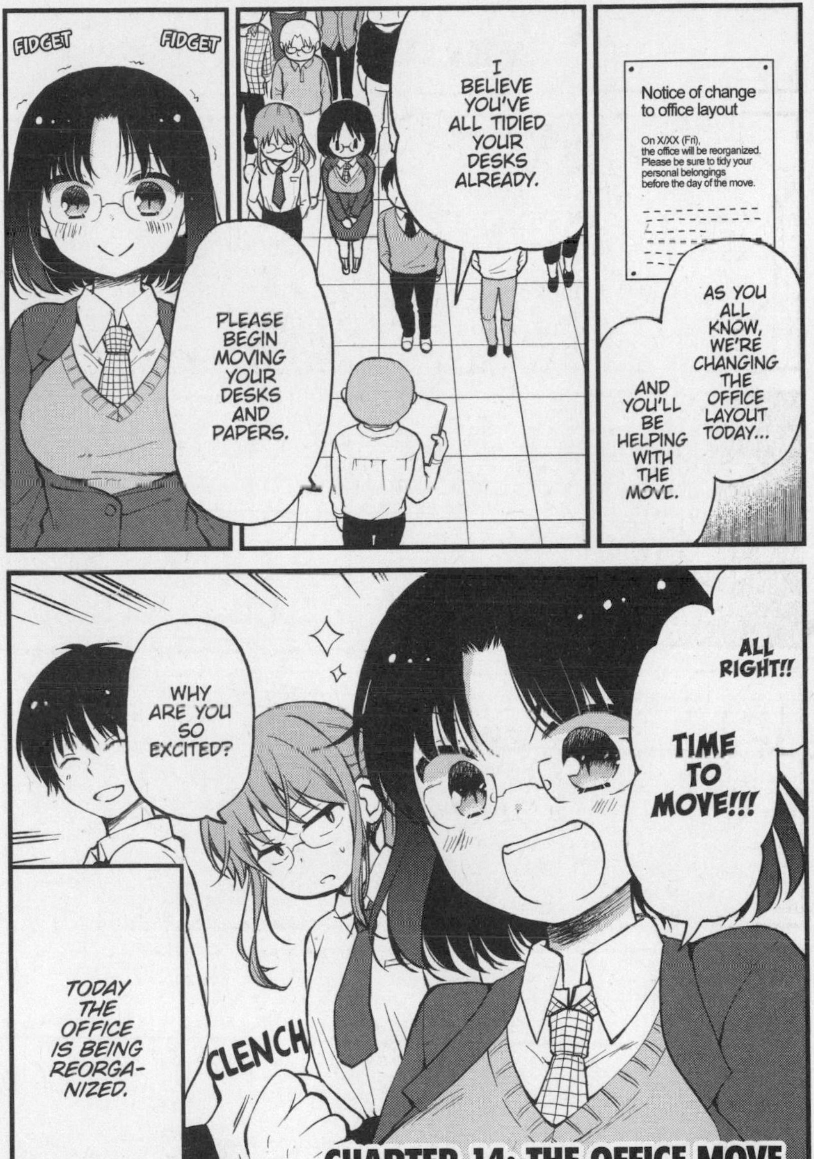
Notice of change to office layout
On X/XX (Fri), the office will be reorganized. Please be sure to tidy your personal belongings before the day of the move.
AS YOU ALL KNOW, WE'RE CHANGING THE OFFICE LAYOUT TODAY...
AND YOU'LL BE HELPING WITH THE MOVE.
I BELIEVE YOU'VE ALL TIDIED YOUR DESKS ALREADY.
PLEASE BEGIN MOVING YOUR DESKS AND PAPERS.
FIDGET
FIDGET
ALL RIGHT!!
TIME TO MOVE!!!
WHY ARE YOU SO EXCITED?
TODAY THE OFFICE IS BEING REORGA-NIZED.
CLENCH
CHAPTER 14: THE OFFICE MOVE

ELMA'S MOTIVATION

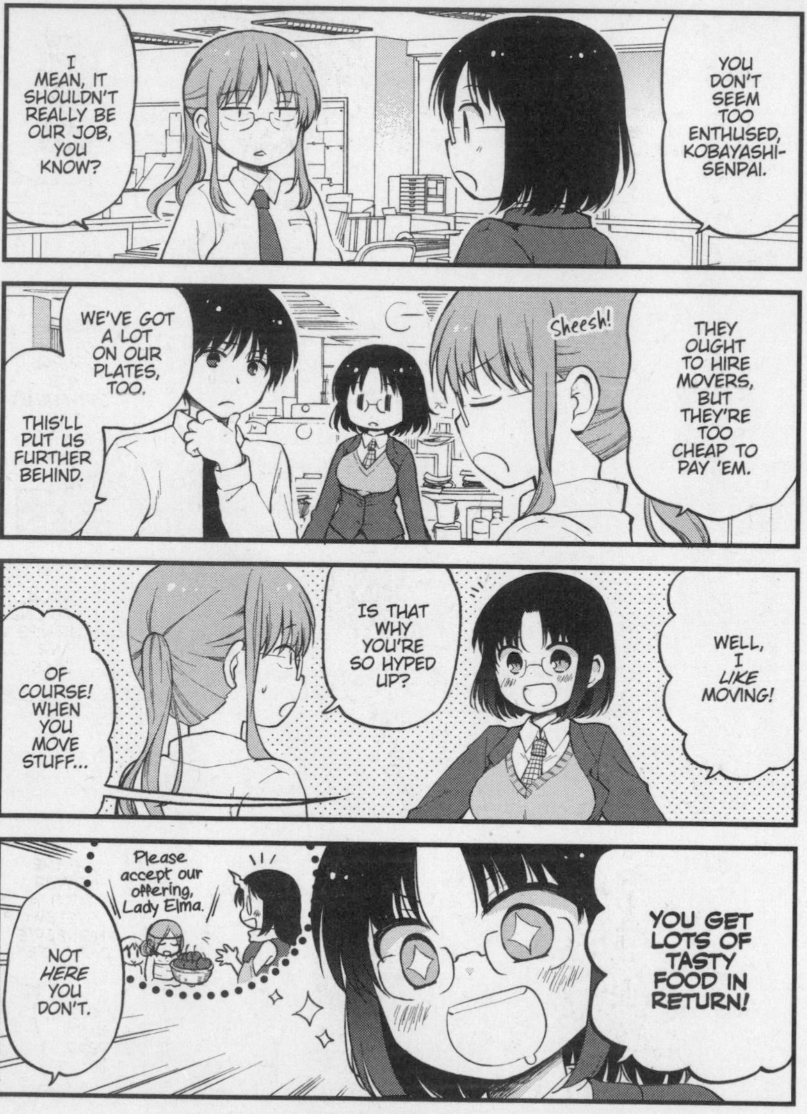
YOU DON'T SEEM TOO ENTHUSED, KOBAYASHI-SENPAI.
I MEAN, IT SHOULDN'T REALLY BE OUR JOB, YOU KNOW?
Sheesh!
THEY OUGHT TO HIRE MOVERS, BUT THEY'RE TOO CHEAP TO PAY 'EM.
WE'VE GOT A LOT ON OUR PLATES, TOO.
THIS'LL PUT US FURTHER BEHIND.
WELL, I *LIKE* MOVING!
IS THAT WHY YOU'RE SO HYPED UP?
OF COURSE! WHEN YOU MOVE STUFF...
YOU GET LOTS OF TASTY FOOD IN RETURN!
Please accept our offering, Lady Elma.
NOT *HERE* YOU DON'T.

STAY ON TARGET!

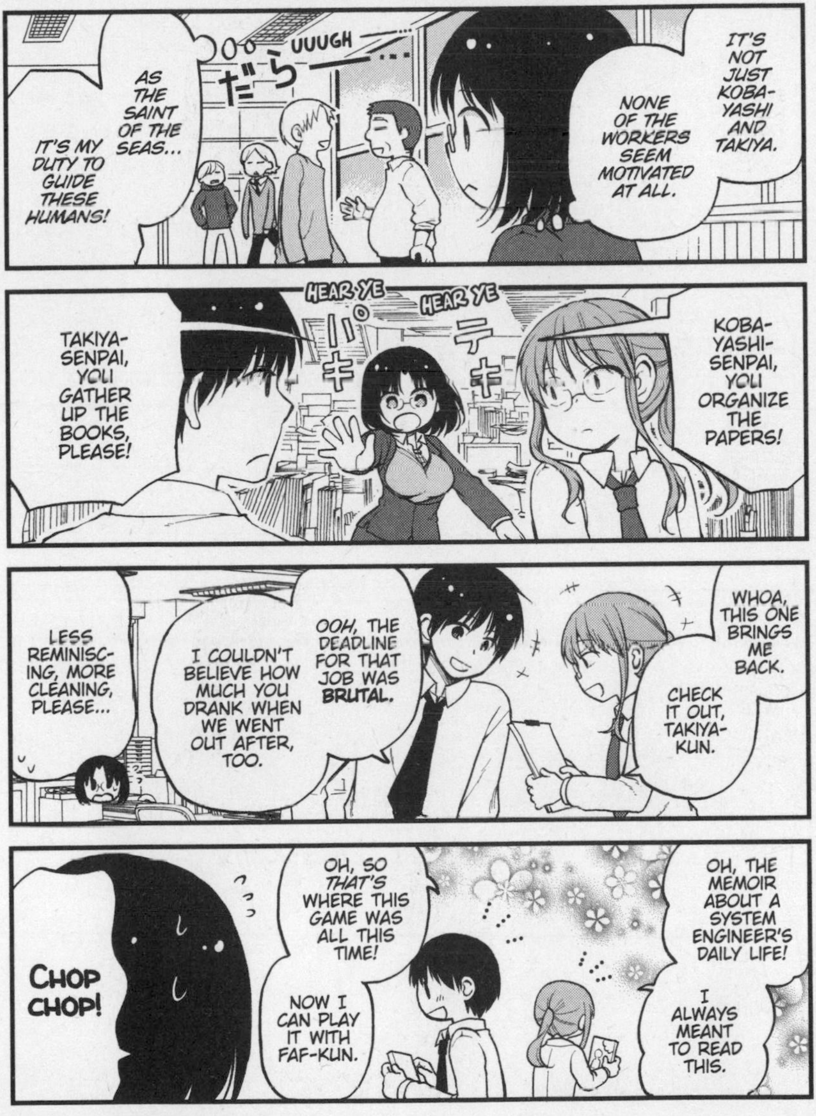
IT'S NOT JUST KOBA-YASHI AND TAKIYA.
NONE OF THE WORKERS SEEM MOTIVATED AT ALL.
UUUGH
だら
AS THE SAINT OF THE SEAS...
IT'S MY DUTY TO GUIDE THESE HUMANS!
KOBA-YASHI-SENPAI, YOU ORGANIZE THE PAPERS!
HEAR YE
テキ
HEAR YE
パキ
TAKIYA-SENPAI, YOU GATHER UP THE BOOKS, PLEASE!
WHOA, THIS ONE BRINGS ME BACK.
CHECK IT OUT, TAKIYA-KUN.
OOH, THE DEADLINE FOR THAT JOB WAS BRUTAL.
I COULDN'T BELIEVE HOW MUCH YOU DRANK WHEN WE WENT OUT AFTER, TOO.
LESS REMINISC-ING, MORE CLEANING, PLEASE...
OH, THE MEMOIR ABOUT A SYSTEM ENGINEER'S DAILY LIFE!
I ALWAYS MEANT TO READ THIS.
OH, SO THAT'S WHERE THIS GAME WAS ALL THIS TIME!
NOW I CAN PLAY IT WITH FAF-KUN.
CHOP CHOP!

HOW TO TRAIN YOUR DRAGON

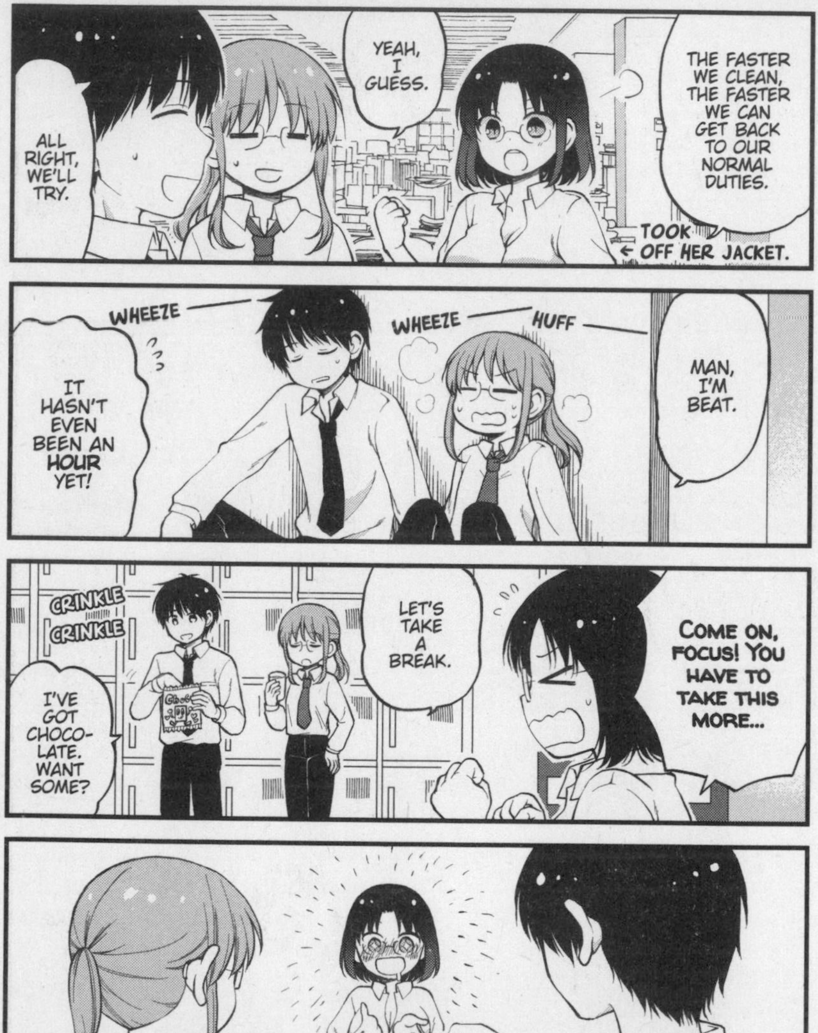
THE FASTER WE CLEAN, THE FASTER WE CAN GET BACK TO OUR NORMAL DUTIES.
TOOK OFF HER JACKET.
YEAH, I GUESS.
ALL RIGHT, WE'LL TRY.
MAN, I'M BEAT.
HUFF
WHEEZE
WHEEZE
IT HASN'T EVEN BEEN AN HOUR YET!
COME ON, FOCUS! YOU HAVE TO TAKE THIS MORE...
LET'S TAKE A BREAK.
CRINKLE
CRINKLE
I'VE GOT CHOCO-LATE. WANT SOME?

EFFORTLESS

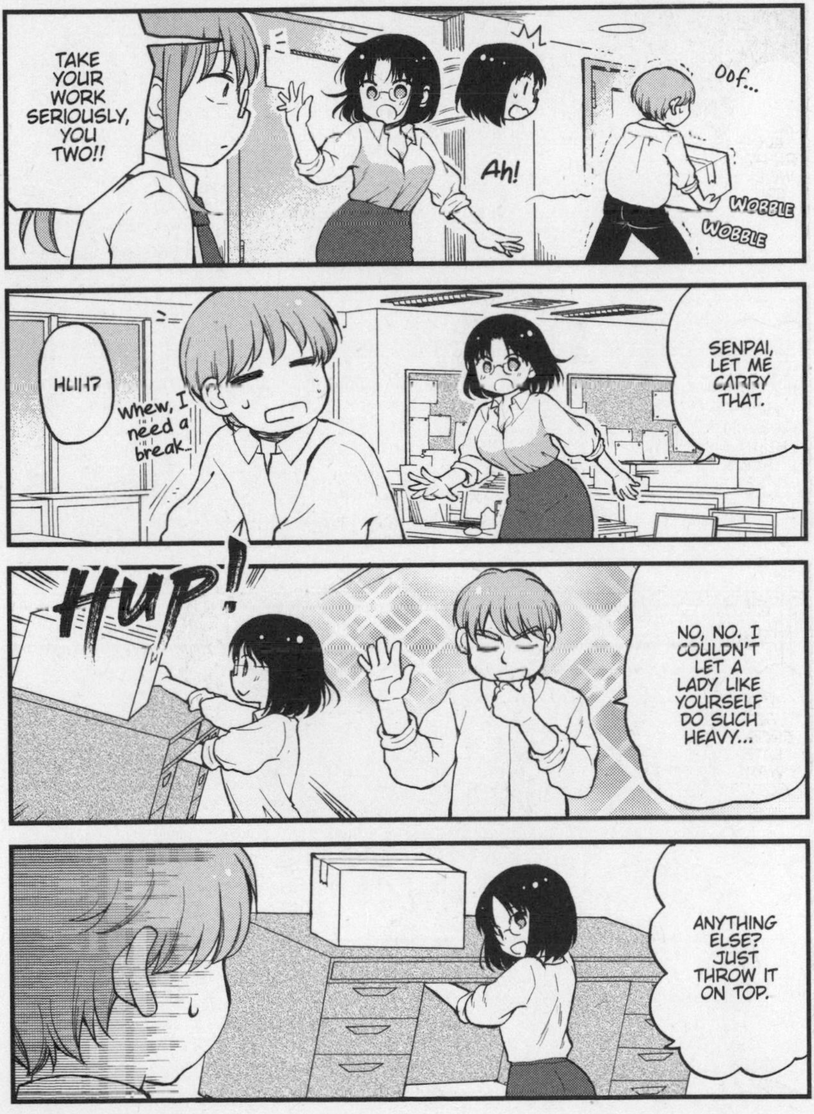
Oof...
WOBBLE WOBBLE
Ah!
TAKE YOUR WORK SERIOUSLY, YOU TWO!!
SENPAI, LET ME CARRY THAT.
Whew, I need a break...
HUH?
NO, NO. I COULDN'T LET A LADY LIKE YOURSELF DO SUCH HEAVY...
HUP!
ANYTHING ELSE? JUST THROW IT ON TOP.

LUCKY ♪

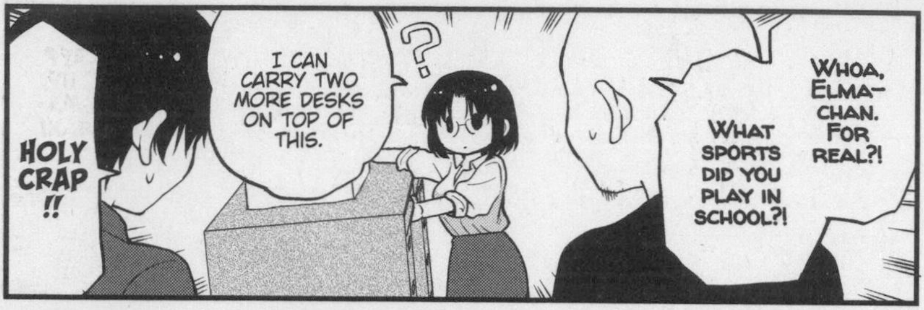
WHOA, ELMA-CHAN. FOR REAL?!
WHAT SPORTS DID YOU PLAY IN SCHOOL?!
?
I CAN CARRY TWO MORE DESKS ON TOP OF THIS.
HOLY CRAP!!

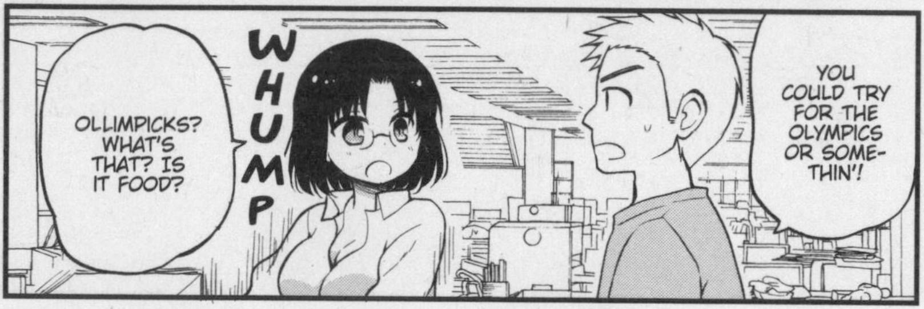
YOU COULD TRY FOR THE OLYMPICS OR SOMETHIN'!
WHUMP
OLLIMPICKS? WHAT'S THAT? IS IT FOOD?

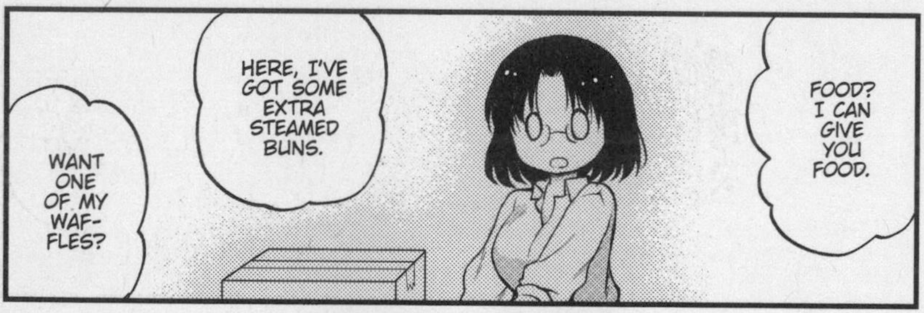
FOOD? I CAN GIVE YOU FOOD.
HERE, I'VE GOT SOME EXTRA STEAMED BUNS.
WANT ONE OF MY WAFFLES?

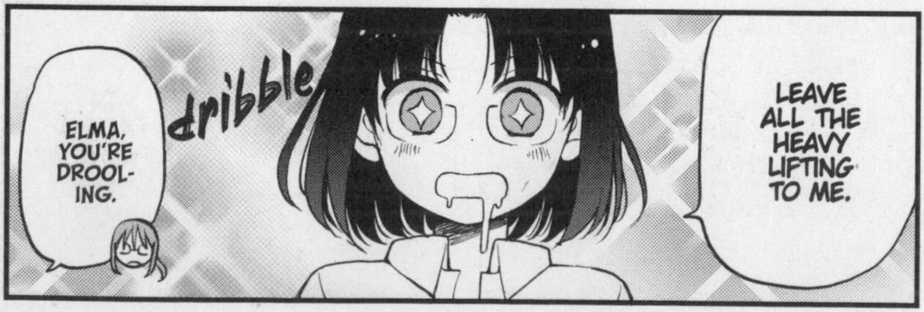
LEAVE ALL THE HEAVY LIFTING TO ME.
dribble
ELMA, YOU'RE DROOLING.

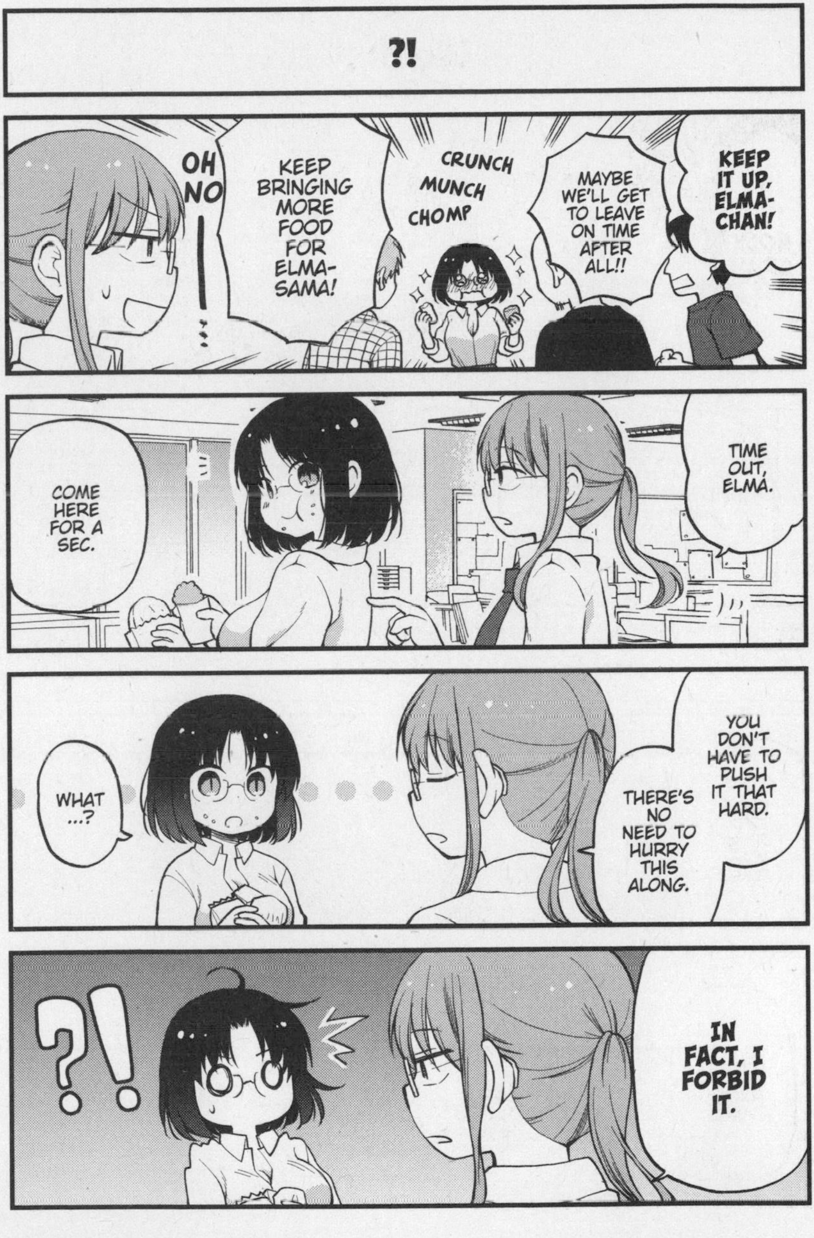
?!
KEEP IT UP, ELMA-CHAN!
MAYBE WE'LL GET TO LEAVE ON TIME AFTER ALL!!
CRUNCH
MUNCH
CHOMP
KEEP BRINGING MORE FOOD FOR ELMA-SAMA!
OH NO
TIME OUT, ELMA.
COME HERE FOR A SEC.
YOU DON'T HAVE TO PUSH IT THAT HARD.
THERE'S NO NEED TO HURRY THIS ALONG.
WHAT ...?
IN FACT, I FORBID IT.
?!

THE BIG PICTURE

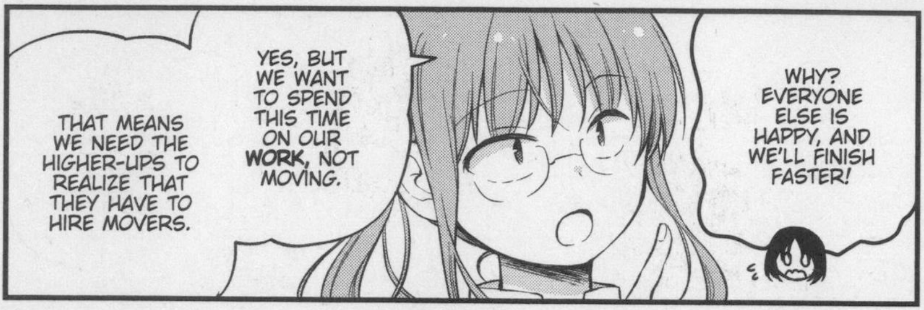
WHY? EVERYONE ELSE IS HAPPY, AND WE'LL FINISH FASTER!
YES, BUT WE WANT TO SPEND THIS TIME ON OUR **WORK**, NOT MOVING.
THAT MEANS WE NEED THE HIGHER-UPS TO REALIZE THAT THEY HAVE TO HIRE MOVERS.

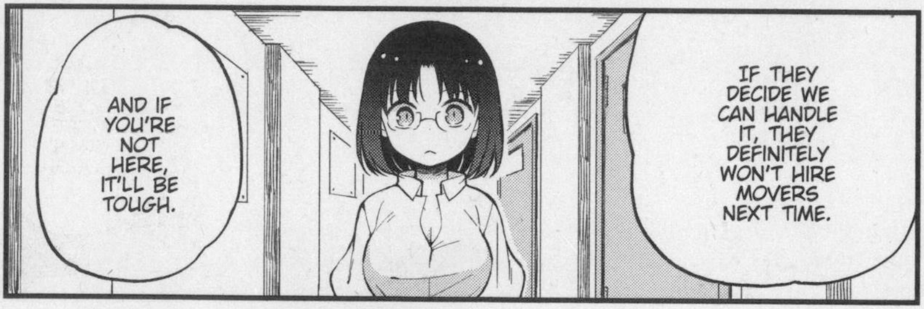
IF THEY DECIDE WE CAN HANDLE IT, THEY DEFINITELY WON'T HIRE MOVERS NEXT TIME.
AND IF YOU'RE NOT HERE, IT'LL BE TOUGH.

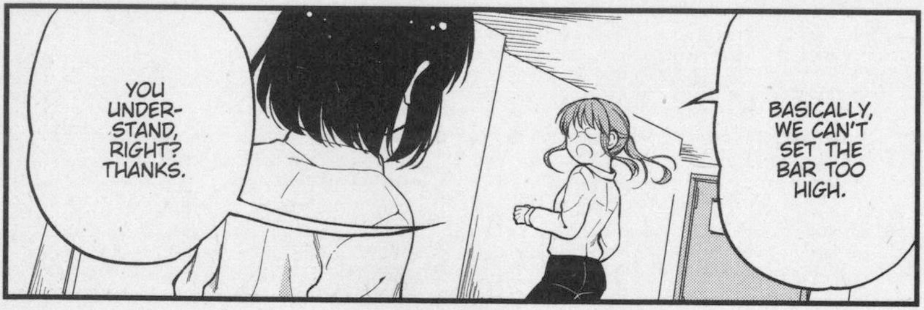
BASICALLY, WE CAN'T SET THE BAR TOO HIGH.
YOU UNDER-STAND, RIGHT? THANKS.

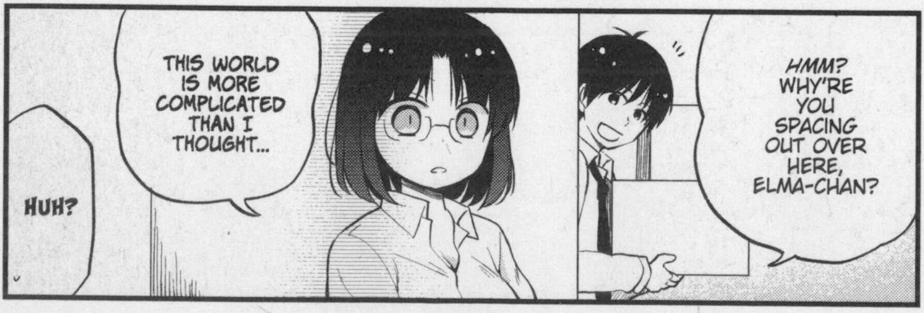
HMM? WHY'RE YOU SPACING OUT OVER HERE, ELMA-CHAN?
THIS WORLD IS MORE COMPLICATED THAN I THOUGHT...
HUH?

STRESS

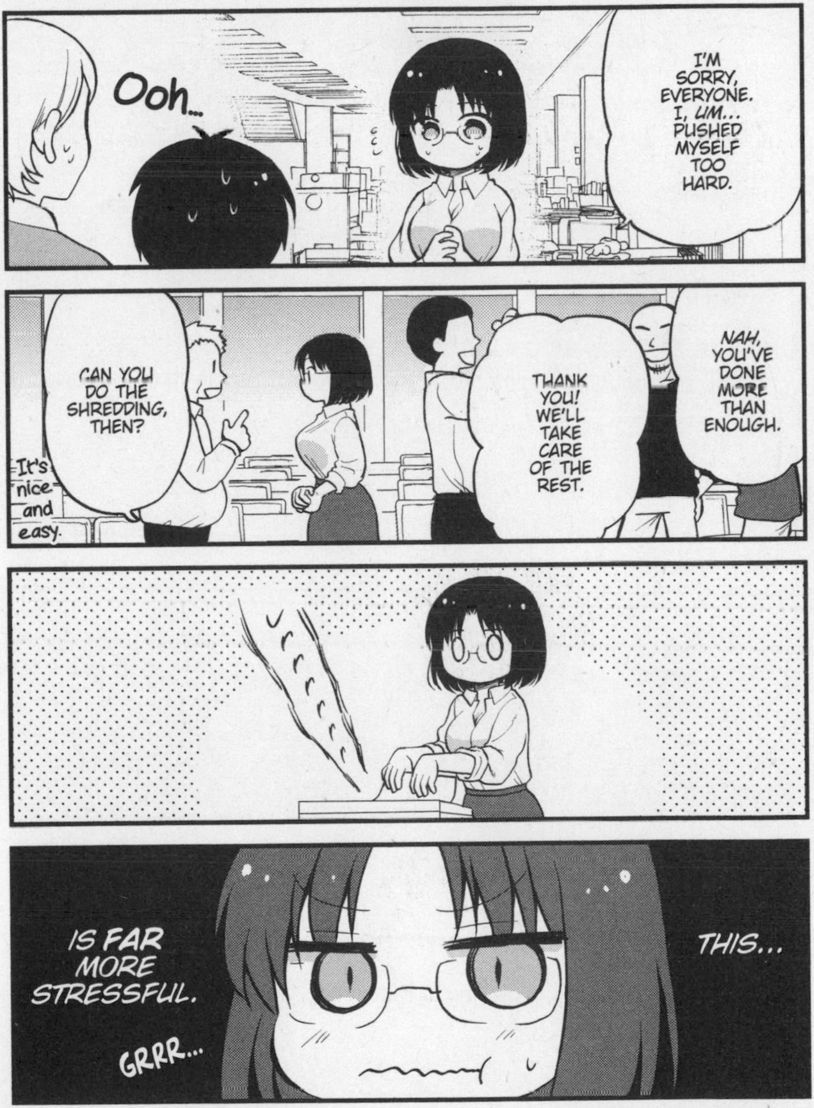
I'M SORRY, EVERYONE. I, UM... PUSHED MYSELF TOO HARD.
Ooh...
NAH, YOU'VE DONE MORE THAN ENOUGH.
THANK YOU! WE'LL TAKE CARE OF THE REST.
CAN YOU DO THE SHREDDING, THEN?
It's nice and easy.
THIS...
IS FAR MORE STRESSFUL.
GRRR...

NATURAL TALENT

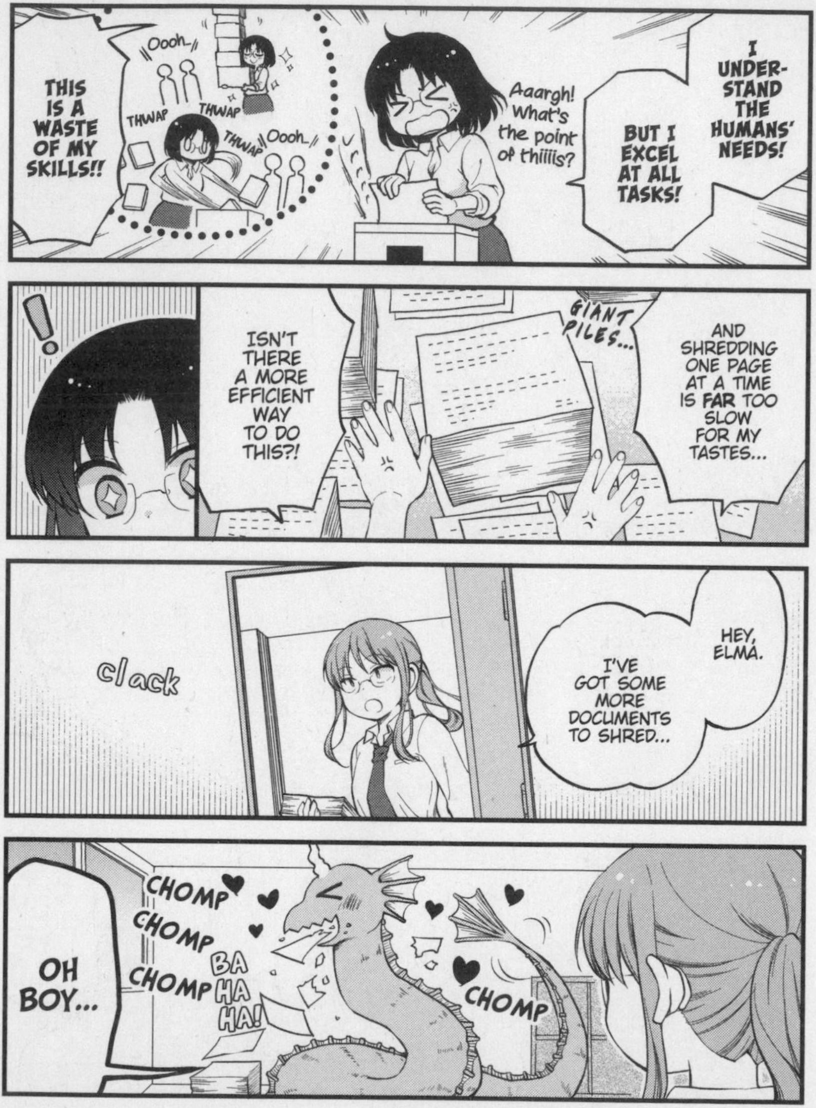
I UNDERSTAND THE HUMANS' NEEDS!
BUT I EXCEL AT ALL TASKS!
Aaargh! What's the point of thiiiis?
Oooh~
THWAP
THWAP
THWAP
Oooh~
THIS IS A WASTE OF MY SKILLS!!
AND SHREDDING ONE PAGE AT A TIME IS FAR TOO SLOW FOR MY TASTES...
GIANT PILES...
ISN'T THERE A MORE EFFICIENT WAY TO DO THIS?!
!
HEY, ELMA.
I'VE GOT SOME MORE DOCUMENTS TO SHRED...
clack
CHOMP
BA HA HA!
CHOMP
CHOMP
CHOMP
OH BOY...

MEMORIES OF THE PAST

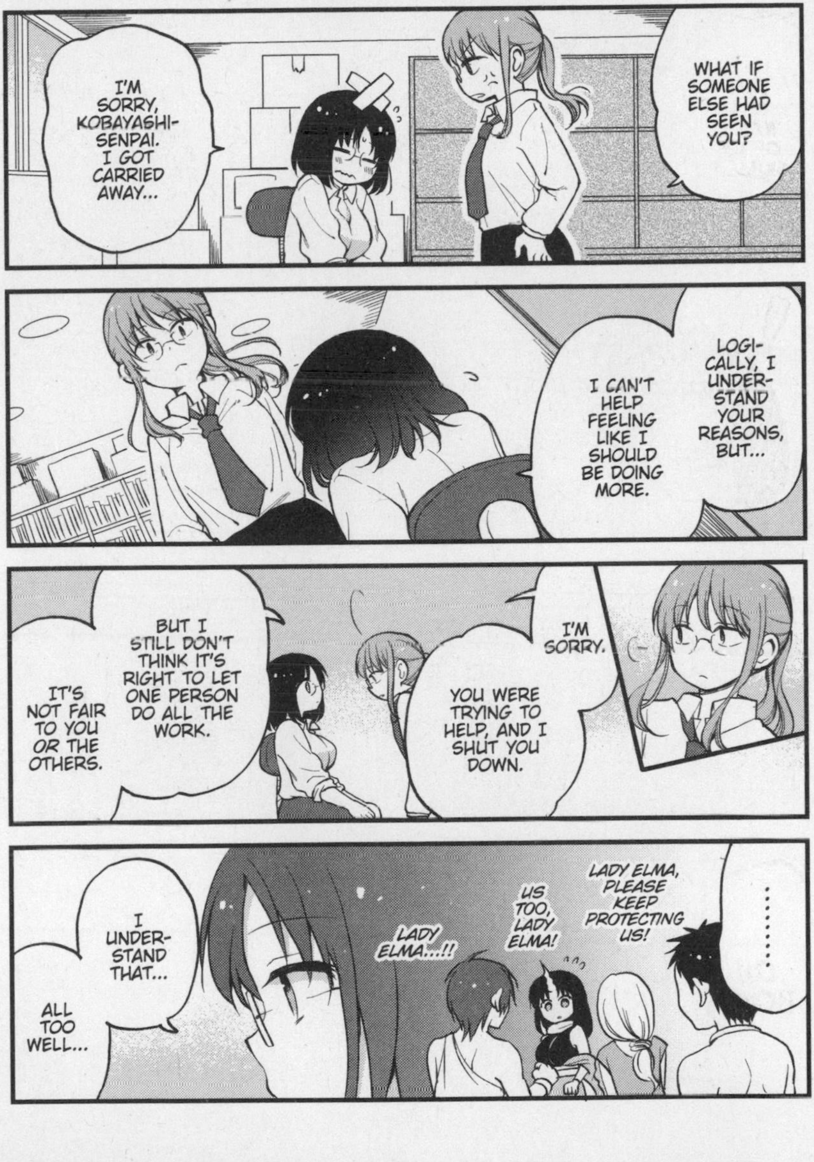
WHAT IF SOMEONE ELSE HAD SEEN YOU?
I'M SORRY, KOBAYASHI-SENPAI. I GOT CARRIED AWAY...
LOGICALLY, I UNDERSTAND YOUR REASONS, BUT...
I CAN'T HELP FEELING LIKE I SHOULD BE DOING MORE.
I'M SORRY.
YOU WERE TRYING TO HELP, AND I SHUT YOU DOWN.
BUT I STILL DON'T THINK IT'S RIGHT TO LET ONE PERSON DO ALL THE WORK.
IT'S NOT FAIR TO YOU OR THE OTHERS.
....
LADY ELMA, PLEASE KEEP PROTECTING US!
US TOO, LADY ELMA!
LADY ELMA...!!
I UNDERSTAND THAT...
ALL TOO WELL...

ENLIGHTENED EYES

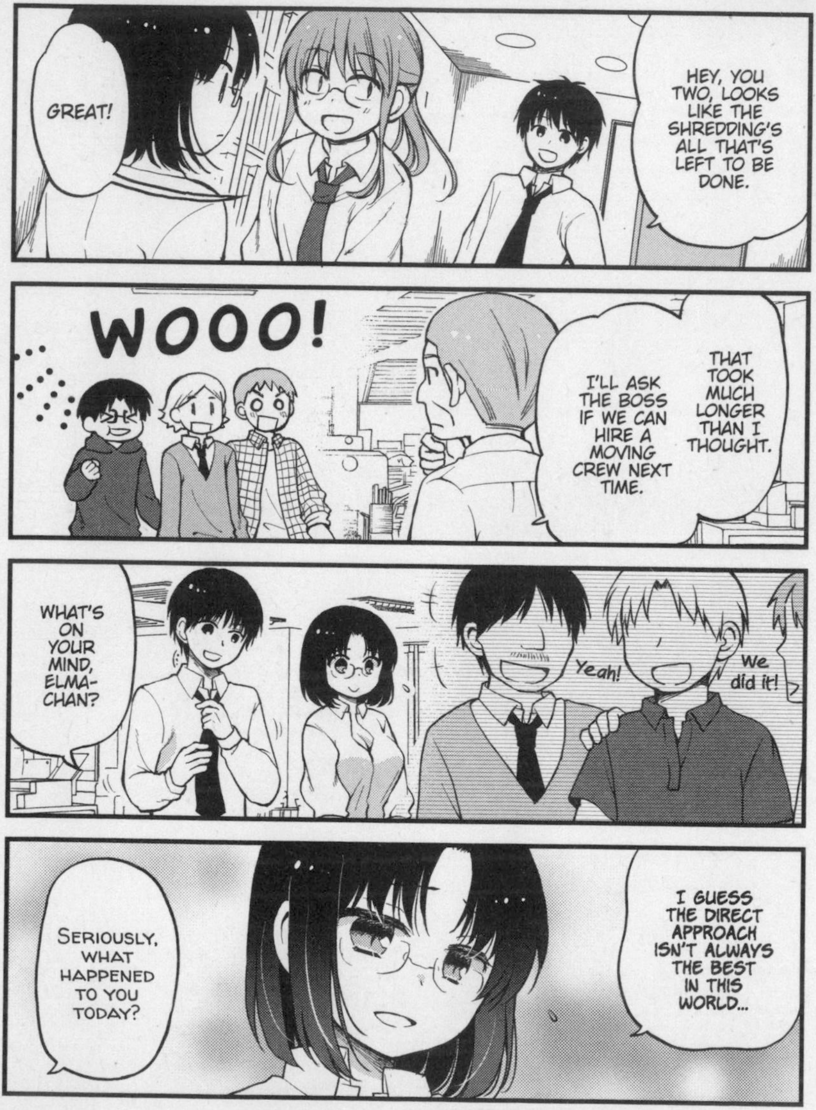
HEY, YOU TWO, LOOKS LIKE THE SHREDDING'S ALL THAT'S LEFT TO BE DONE.
GREAT!
THAT TOOK MUCH LONGER THAN I THOUGHT.
I'LL ASK THE BOSS IF WE CAN HIRE A MOVING CREW NEXT TIME.
WOOO!
We did it!
Yeah!
WHAT'S ON YOUR MIND, ELMA-CHAN?
I GUESS THE DIRECT APPROACH ISN'T ALWAYS THE BEST IN THIS WORLD...
SERIOUSLY, WHAT HAPPENED TO YOU TODAY?

CELEBRATION

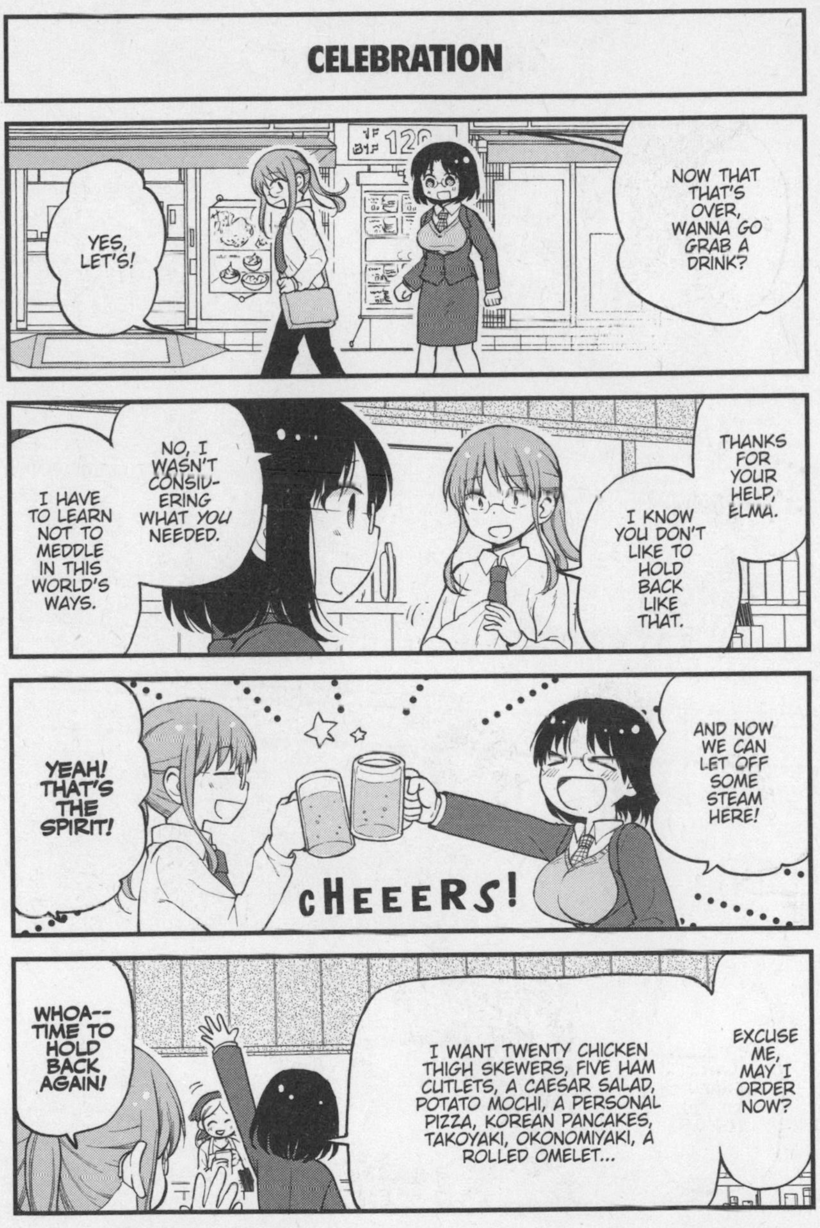
NOW THAT THAT'S OVER, WANNA GO GRAB A DRINK?
YES, LET'S!
THANKS FOR YOUR HELP, ELMA.
I KNOW YOU DON'T LIKE TO HOLD BACK LIKE THAT.
NO, I WASN'T CONSIDERING WHAT *YOU* NEEDED.
I HAVE TO LEARN NOT TO MEDDLE IN THIS WORLD'S WAYS.
AND NOW WE CAN LET OFF SOME STEAM HERE!
CHEEERS!
YEAH! THAT'S THE SPIRIT!
EXCUSE ME, MAY I ORDER NOW?
I WANT TWENTY CHICKEN THIGH SKEWERS, FIVE HAM CUTLETS, A CAESAR SALAD, POTATO MOCHI, A PERSONAL PIZZA, KOREAN PANCAKES, TAKOYAKI, OKONOMIYAKI, A ROLLED OMELET...
WHOA-- TIME TO HOLD BACK AGAIN!

BOTTOM LINE

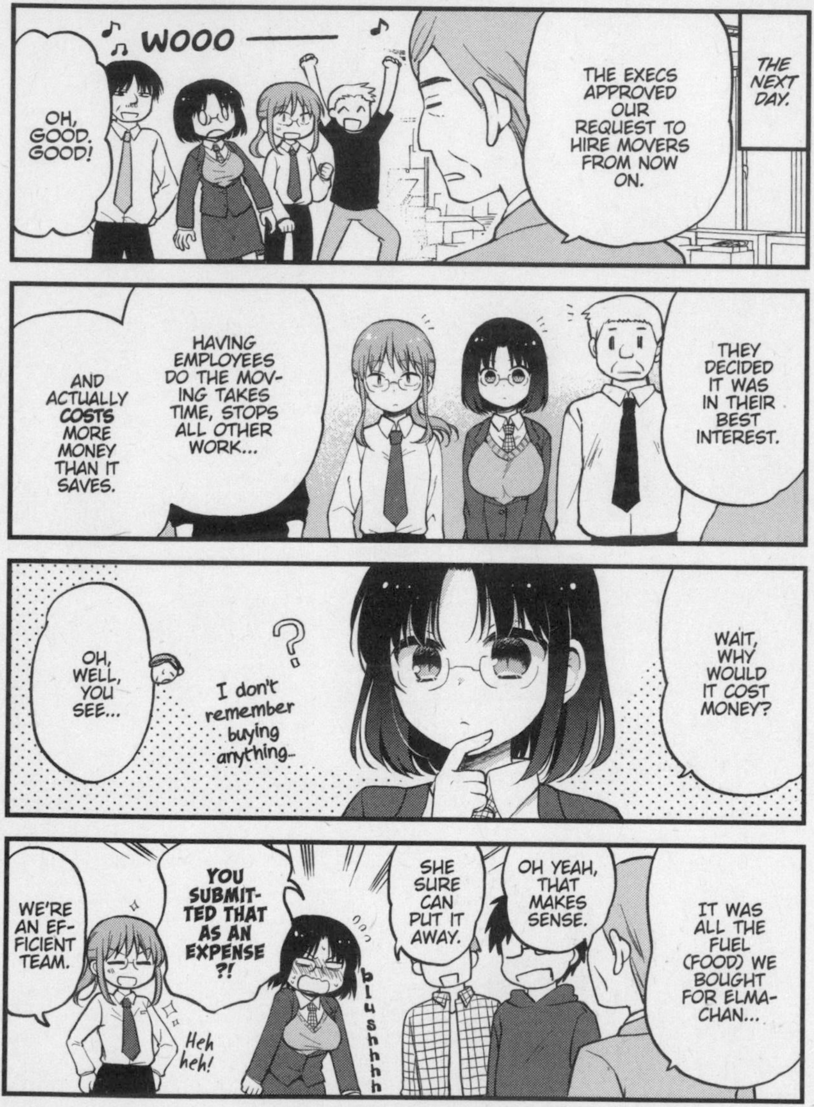
THE NEXT DAY.
THE EXECS APPROVED OUR REQUEST TO HIRE MOVERS FROM NOW ON.
WOOO ——
OH, GOOD. GOOD!
THEY DECIDED IT WAS IN THEIR BEST INTEREST.
HAVING EMPLOYEES DO THE MOV-ING TAKES TIME, STOPS ALL OTHER WORK...
AND ACTUALLY **COSTS** MORE MONEY THAN IT SAVES.
WAIT, WHY WOULD IT COST MONEY?
?
I don't remember buying anything...
OH, WELL, YOU SEE...
IT WAS ALL THE FUEL (FOOD) WE BOUGHT FOR ELMA-CHAN...
OH YEAH, THAT MAKES SENSE.
SHE SURE CAN PUT IT AWAY.
YOU SUBMIT-TED THAT AS AN EXPENSE?!
blushhhh
WE'RE AN EF-FICIENT TEAM.
Heh heh!

CHAPTER 14/END

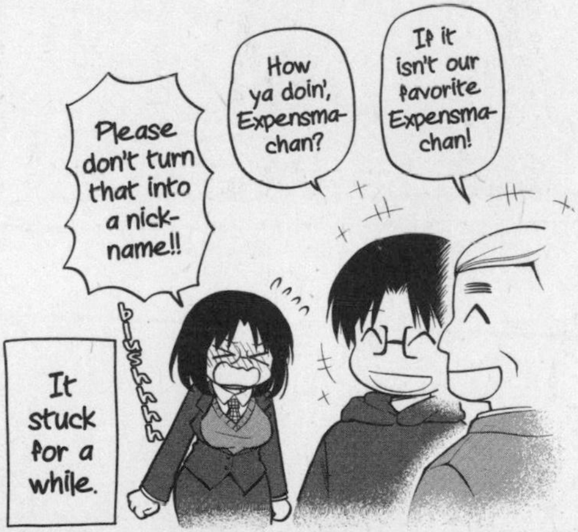
If it isn't our favorite Expensma-chan!
How ya doin', Expensma-chan?
Please don't turn that into a nick-name!!
bishhhhh
It stuck for a while.

Miss Kobayashi's Dragon Maid
Elma's Office Lady Diary

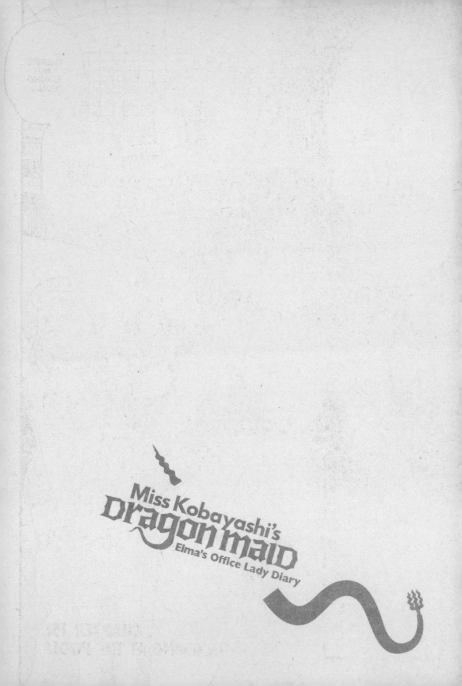

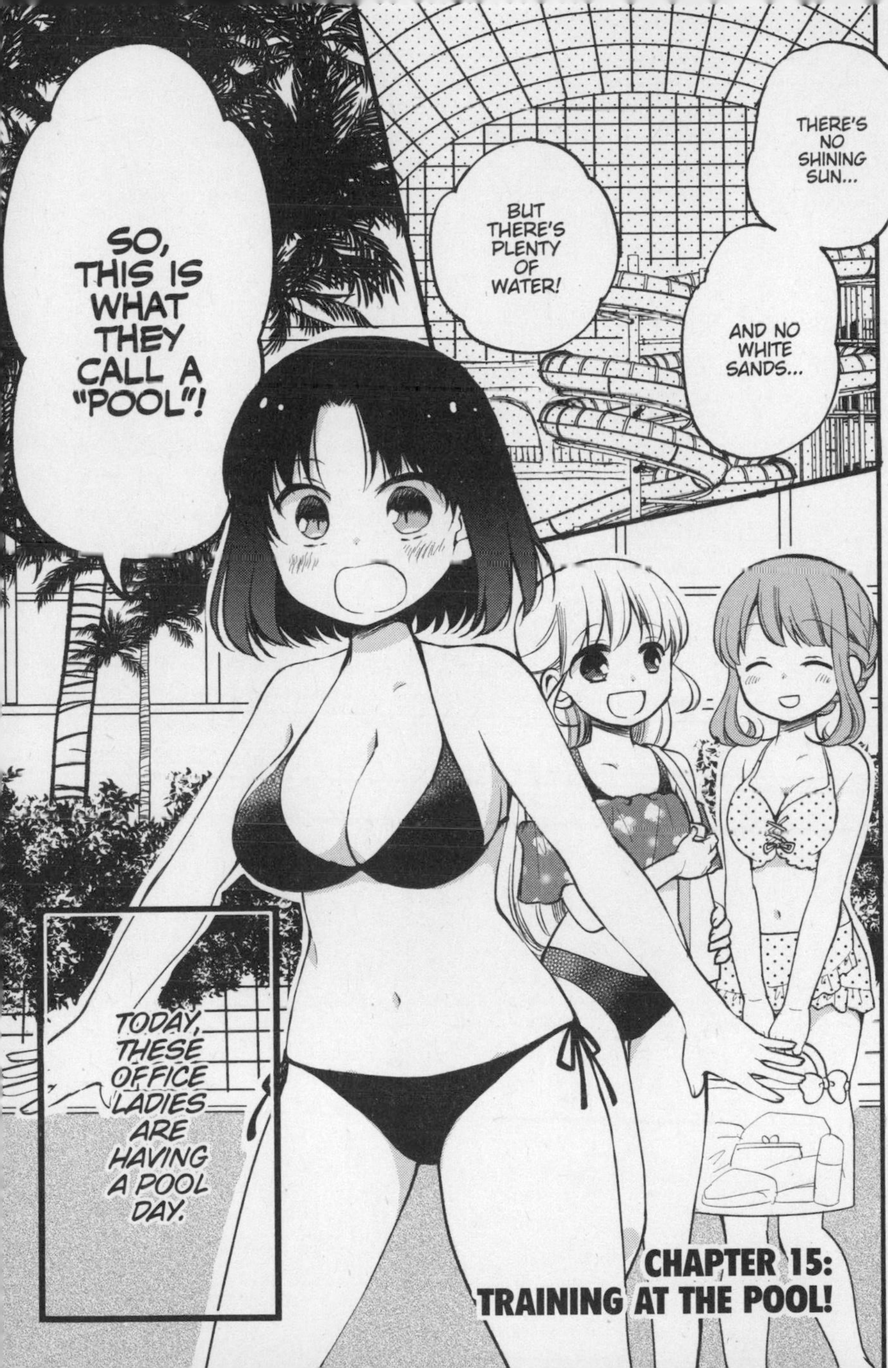
THERE'S NO SHINING SUN...
AND NO WHITE SANDS...
BUT THERE'S PLENTY OF WATER!
SO, THIS IS WHAT THEY CALL A "POOL"!
TODAY, THESE OFFICE LADIES ARE HAVING A POOL DAY.
CHAPTER 15: TRAINING AT THE POOL!

STANDARDS FROM ANOTHER WORLD

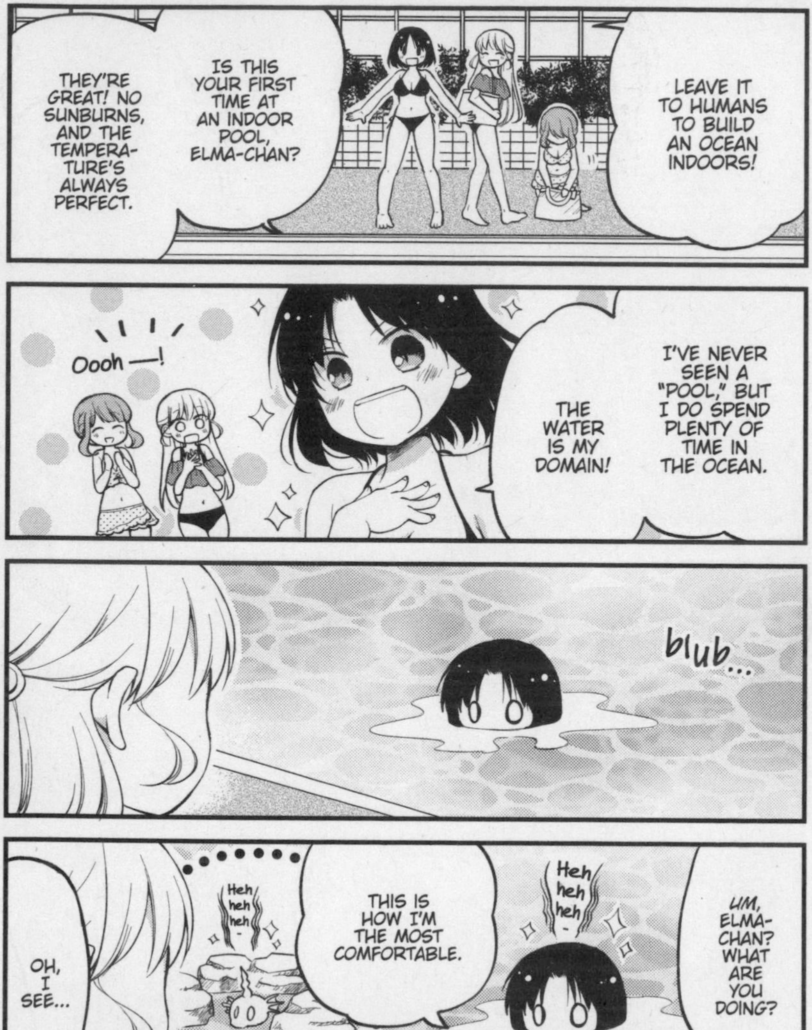
LEAVE IT TO HUMANS TO BUILD AN OCEAN INDOORS!
IS THIS YOUR FIRST TIME AT AN INDOOR POOL, ELMA-CHAN?
THEY'RE GREAT! NO SUNBURNS, AND THE TEMPERATURE'S ALWAYS PERFECT.
I'VE NEVER SEEN A "POOL," BUT I DO SPEND PLENTY OF TIME IN THE OCEAN.
THE WATER IS MY DOMAIN!
Oooh—!
blub...
UM, ELMA-CHAN? WHAT ARE YOU DOING?
Heh heh heh-
THIS IS HOW I'M THE MOST COMFORTABLE.
Heh heh heh-
OH, I SEE...

BAIT AND SWITCH

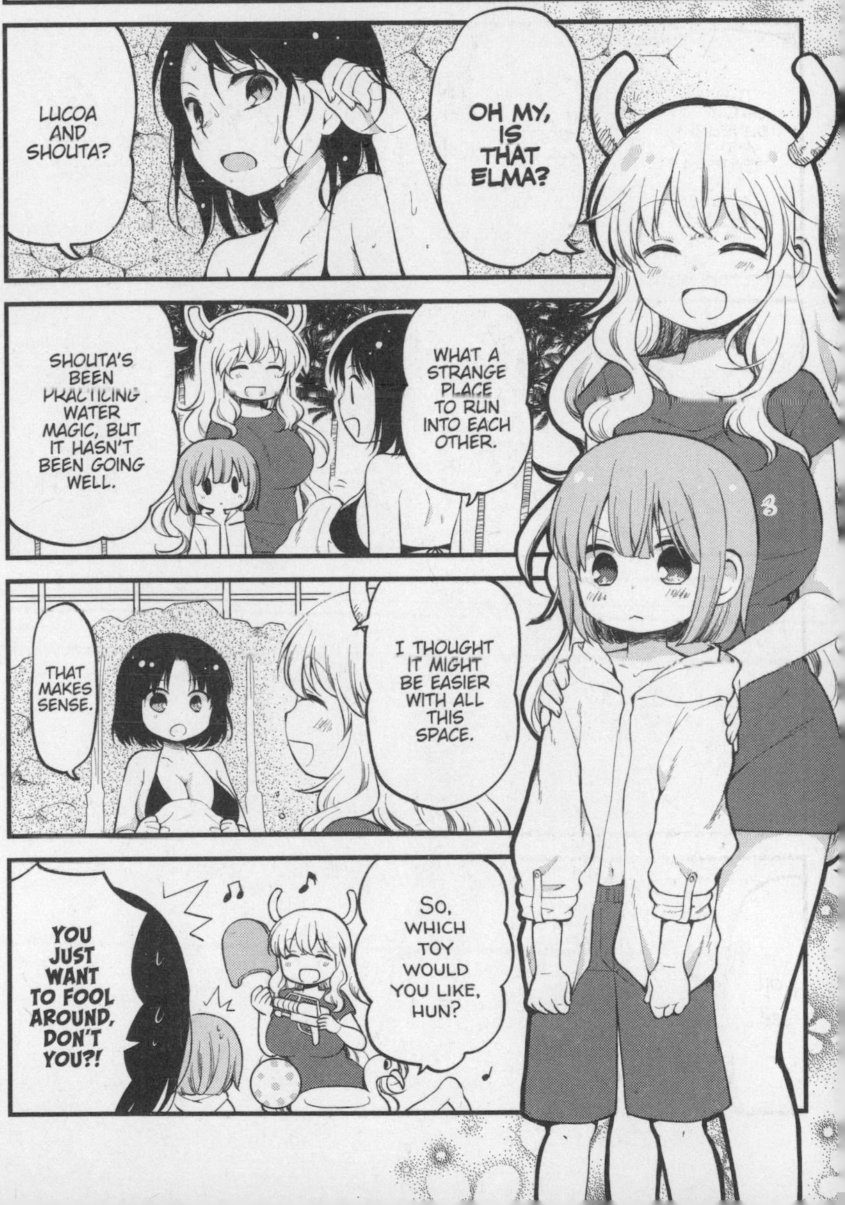
OH MY, IS THAT ELMA?
LUCOA AND SHOUTA?
WHAT A STRANGE PLACE TO RUN INTO EACH OTHER.
SHOUTA'S BEEN PRACTICING WATER MAGIC, BUT IT HASN'T BEEN GOING WELL.
I THOUGHT IT MIGHT BE EASIER WITH ALL THIS SPACE.
THAT MAKES SENSE.
SO, WHICH TOY WOULD YOU LIKE, HUN?
YOU JUST WANT TO FOOL AROUND, DON'T YOU?!

THE DARK SIDE OF SOCIETY

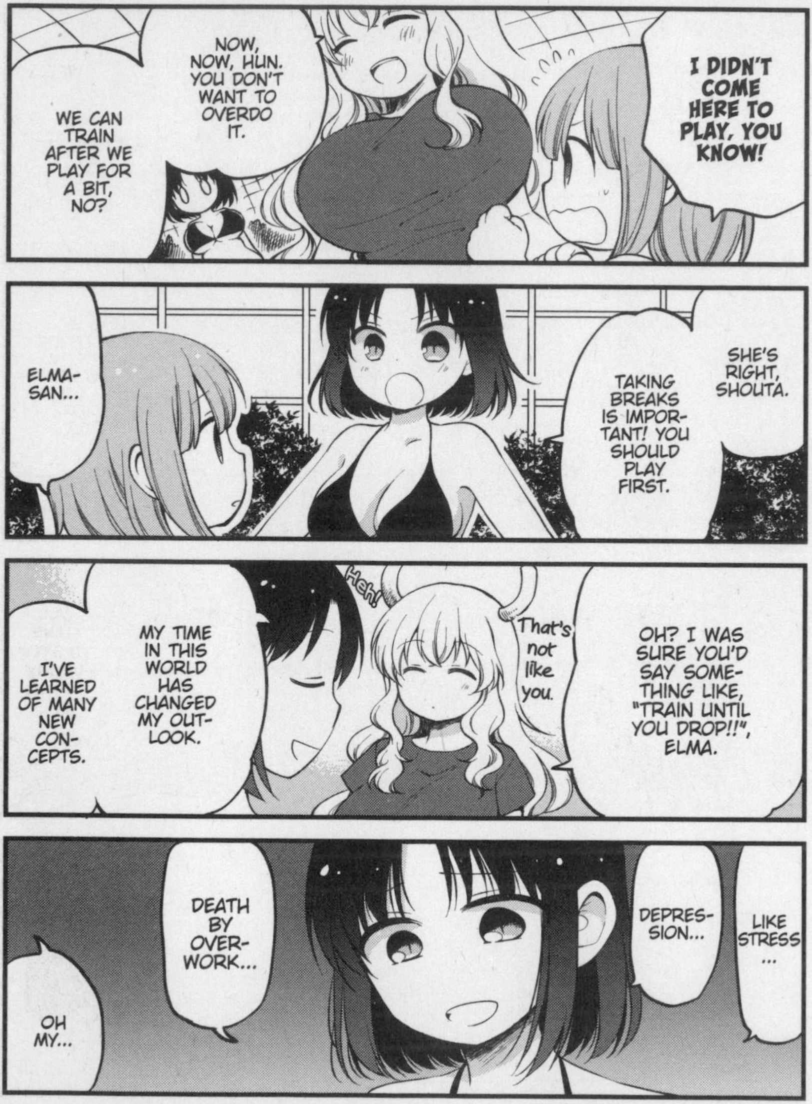
I DIDN'T COME HERE TO PLAY, YOU KNOW!
NOW, NOW, HUN. YOU DON'T WANT TO OVERDO IT.
WE CAN TRAIN AFTER WE PLAY FOR A BIT, NO?
SHE'S RIGHT, SHOUTA.
TAKING BREAKS IS IMPORTANT! YOU SHOULD PLAY FIRST.
ELMA-SAN...
OH? I WAS SURE YOU'D SAY SOMETHING LIKE, "TRAIN UNTIL YOU DROP!!", ELMA.
That's not like you.
Heh!
MY TIME IN THIS WORLD HAS CHANGED MY OUTLOOK.
I'VE LEARNED OF MANY NEW CONCEPTS.
LIKE STRESS...
DEPRESSION...
DEATH BY OVERWORK...
OH MY...

PERVERT CAPTURED

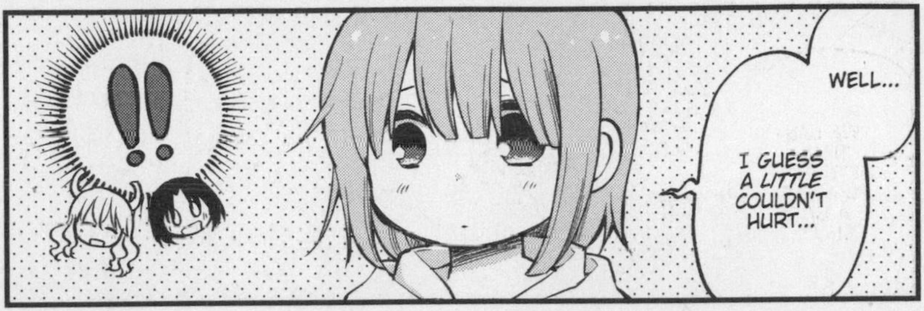
WELL...
I GUESS A *LITTLE* COULDN'T HURT...
!!

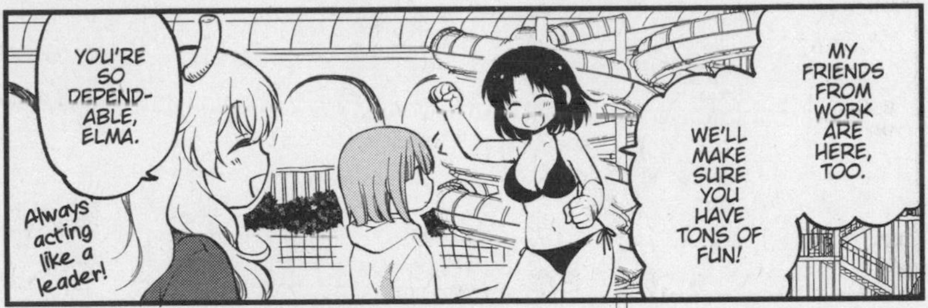
MY FRIENDS FROM WORK ARE HERE, TOO.
WE'LL MAKE SURE YOU HAVE TONS OF FUN!
YOU'RE SO DEPENDABLE, ELMA.
Always acting like a leader!

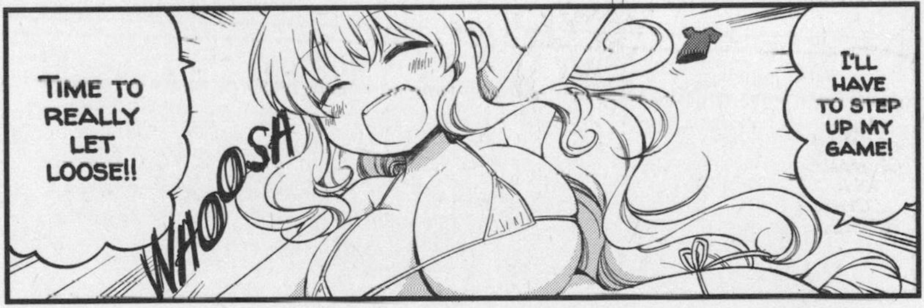
I'LL HAVE TO STEP UP MY GAME!
TIME TO REALLY LET LOOSE!!
WHOOOSH

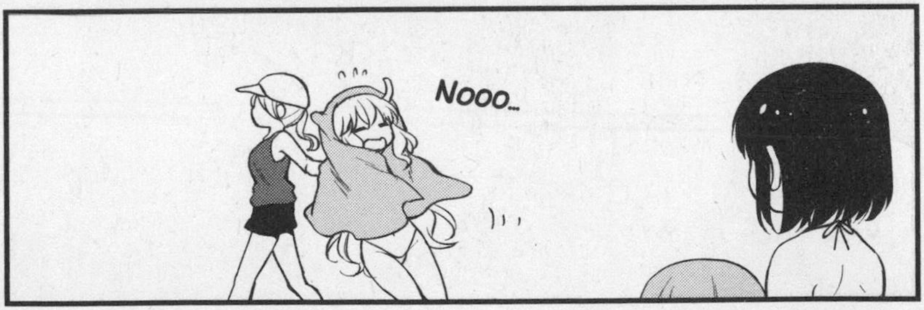
Nooo...

EXCEPTIONAL

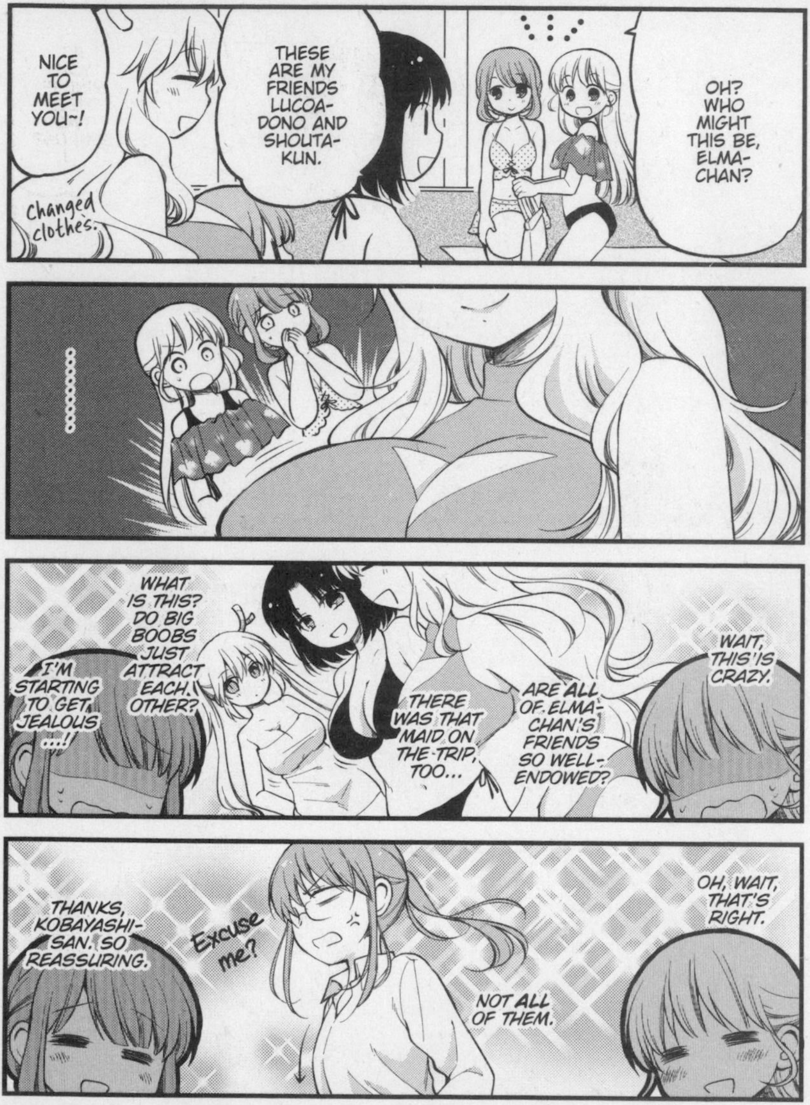
OH? WHO MIGHT THIS BE, ELMA-CHAN?
THESE ARE MY FRIENDS LUCOA-DONO AND SHOUTA-KUN.
NICE TO MEET YOU~!
Changed clothes.
WAIT, THIS IS CRAZY.
ARE ALL OF ELMA-CHAN'S FRIENDS SO WELL-ENDOWED?
THERE WAS THAT MAID ON THE TRIP, TOO...
WHAT IS THIS? DO BIG BOOBS JUST ATTRACT EACH OTHER?
I'M STARTING TO GET JEALOUS ...!
OH, WAIT, THAT'S RIGHT.
NOT ALL OF THEM.
Excuse me?
THANKS, KOBAYASHI-SAN. SO REASSURING.

NO HOLDS BARRED

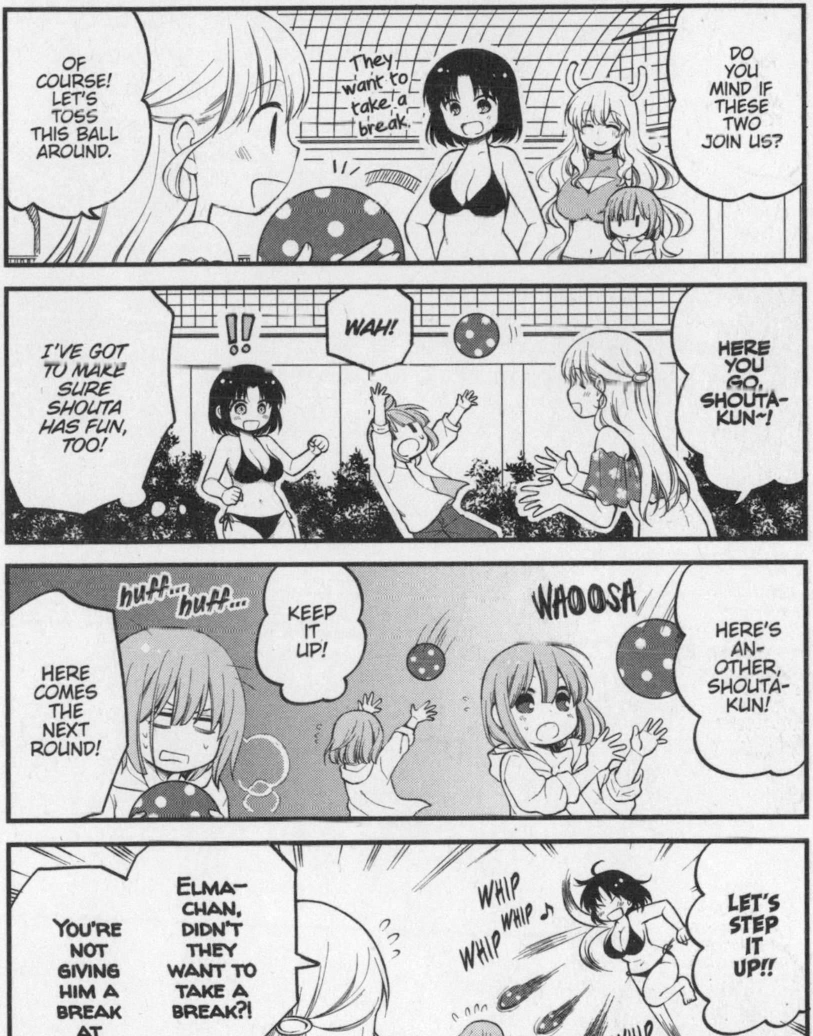
DO YOU MIND IF THESE TWO JOIN US?
They want to take a break.
OF COURSE! LET'S TOSS THIS BALL AROUND.
HERE YOU GO, SHOUTA-KUN~!
WAH!
!!
I'VE GOT TO MAKE SURE SHOUTA HAS FUN, TOO!
HERE'S AN-OTHER, SHOUTA-KUN!
WAOOSA
KEEP IT UP!
huff... huff...
HERE COMES THE NEXT ROUND!
LET'S STEP IT UP!!
WHIP WHIP ♪
WHIP
WHIP WHIP
ELMA-CHAN, DIDN'T THEY WANT TO TAKE A BREAK?!
YOU'RE NOT GIVING HIM A BREAK AT ALL!!

FORCE OF HABIT

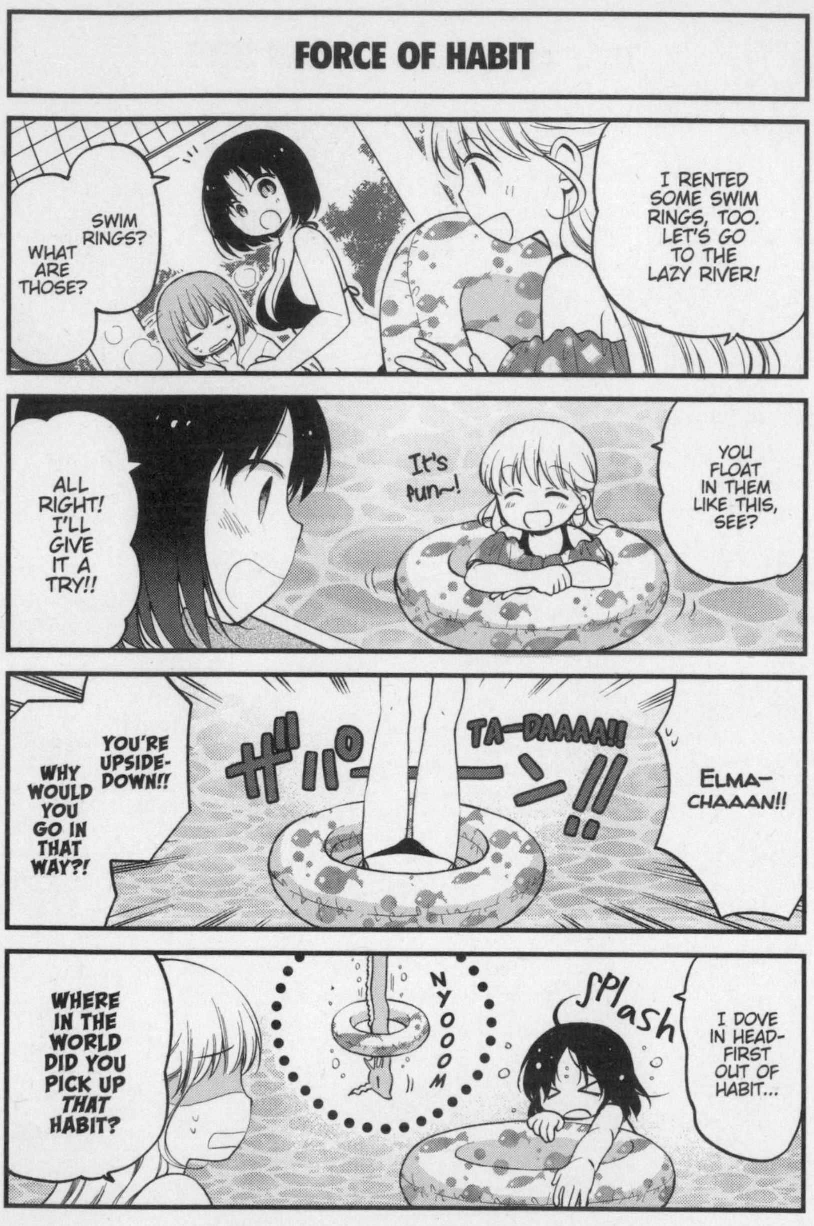
I RENTED SOME SWIM RINGS, TOO. LET'S GO TO THE LAZY RIVER!
SWIM RINGS? WHAT ARE THOSE?
YOU FLOAT IN THEM LIKE THIS, SEE?
It's fun~!
ALL RIGHT! I'LL GIVE IT A TRY!!
ELMA-CHAAAN!!
TA-DAAAA!!
ザパーーン!!
YOU'RE UPSIDE-DOWN!!
WHY WOULD YOU GO IN THAT WAY?!
I DOVE IN HEAD-FIRST OUT OF HABIT...
Splash
NYOOOOM
WHERE IN THE WORLD DID YOU PICK UP *THAT* HABIT?

THEY'RE NOT JUST DECORATIVE

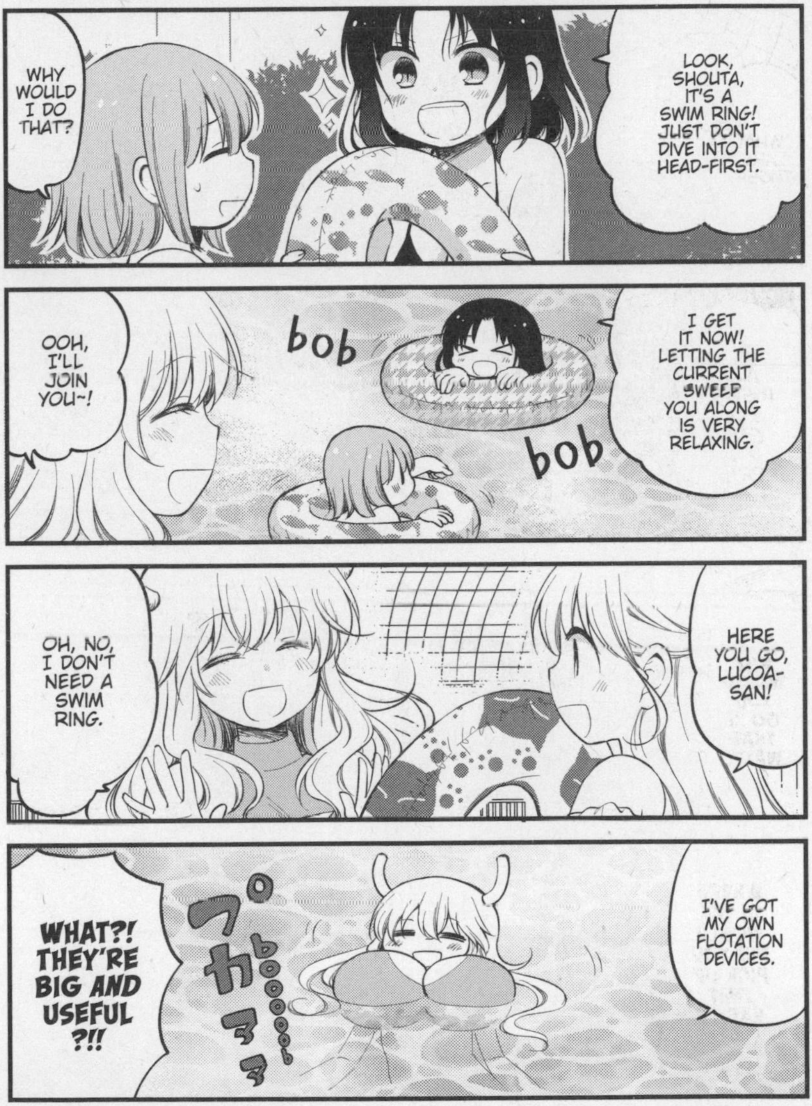
LOOK, SHOUTA, IT'S A SWIM RING! JUST DON'T DIVE INTO IT HEAD-FIRST.
WHY WOULD I DO THAT?
I GET IT NOW! LETTING THE CURRENT SWEEP YOU ALONG IS VERY RELAXING.
bob
bob
OOH, I'LL JOIN YOU~!
HERE YOU GO, LUCOA-SAN!
OH, NO, I DON'T NEED A SWIM RING.
I'VE GOT MY OWN FLOTATION DEVICES.
ぷかぁぁ
booooob
WHAT?! THEY'RE BIG AND USEFUL ?!!

ELMA'S IDEA OF A MERMAID

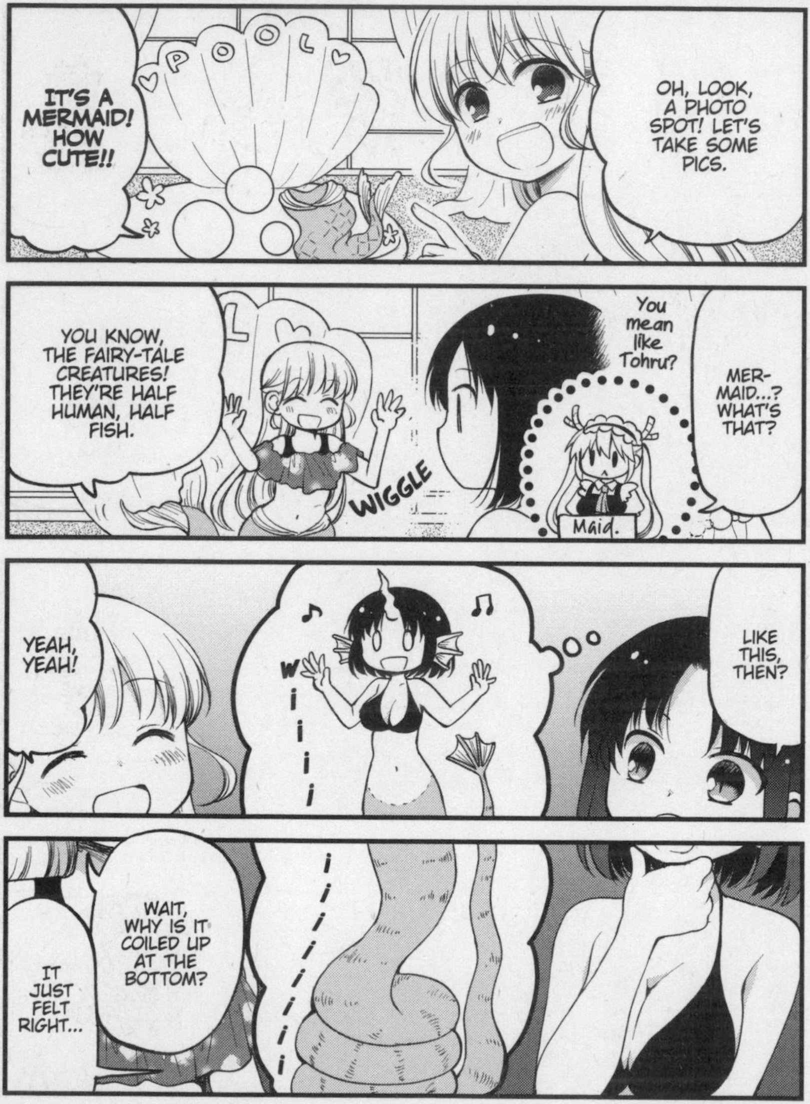
OH, LOOK, A PHOTO SPOT! LET'S TAKE SOME PICS.
POOL
IT'S A MERMAID! HOW CUTE!!
MER-MAID...? WHAT'S THAT?
You mean like Tohru?
Maid.
YOU KNOW, THE FAIRY-TALE CREATURES! THEY'RE HALF HUMAN, HALF FISH.
WIGGLE
LIKE THIS, THEN?
YEAH, YEAH!
WAIT, WHY IS IT COILED UP AT THE BOTTOM?
IT JUST FELT RIGHT...

YOU AGAIN?!

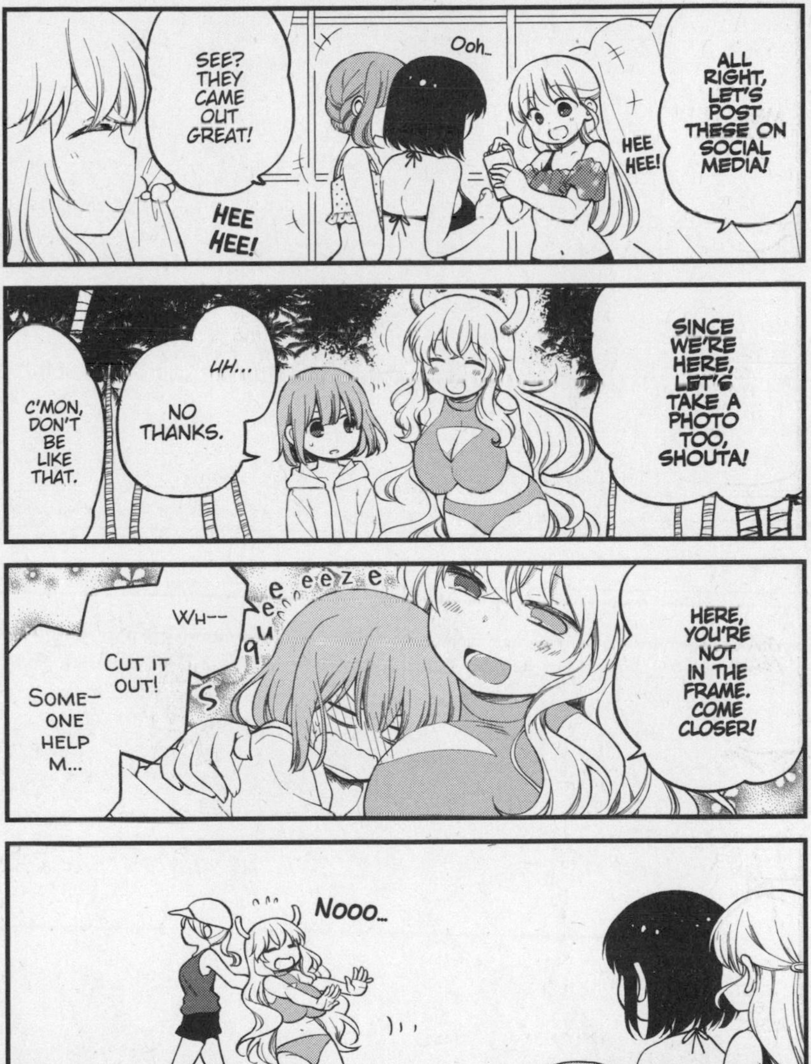
ALL RIGHT, LET'S POST THESE ON SOCIAL MEDIA!
HEE HEE!
Ooh..
SEE? THEY CAME OUT GREAT!
HEE HEE!
SINCE WE'RE HERE, LET'S TAKE A PHOTO TOO, SHOUTA!
UH...
NO THANKS.
C'MON, DON'T BE LIKE THAT.
HERE, YOU'RE NOT IN THE FRAME. COME CLOSER!
squeeeeeze
WH--
CUT IT OUT!
SOME-ONE HELP M...
Nooo...

GRR-ATITUDE

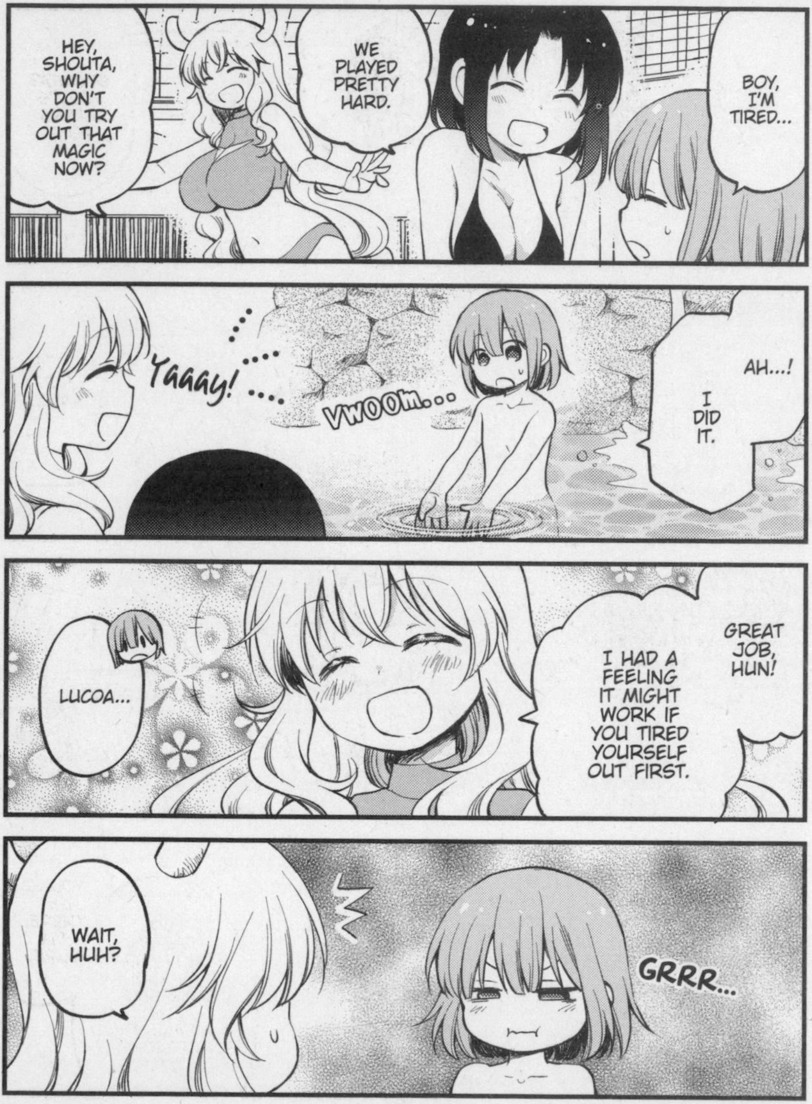
BOY, I'M TIRED...
WE PLAYED PRETTY HARD.
HEY, SHOUTA, WHY DON'T YOU TRY OUT THAT MAGIC NOW?
AH...! I DID IT.
VWOOm...
Yaaay! ....
GREAT JOB, HUN!
I HAD A FEELING IT MIGHT WORK IF YOU TIRED YOURSELF OUT FIRST.
LUCOA...
GRRR...
WAIT, HUH?

LITTLE BY LITTLE

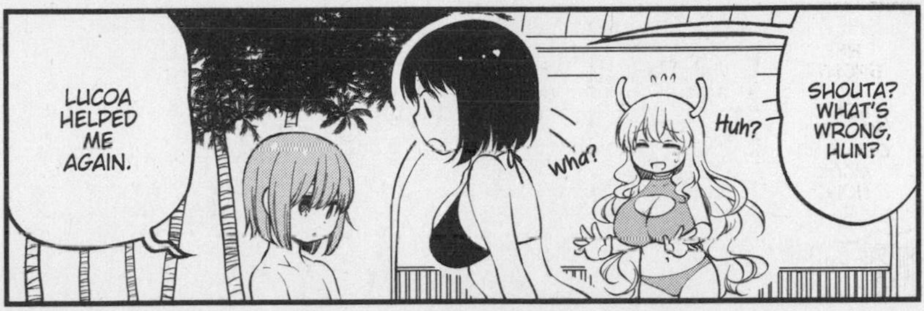
SHOUTA? WHAT'S WRONG, HUN?
Huh?
Wha?
LUCOA HELPED ME AGAIN.

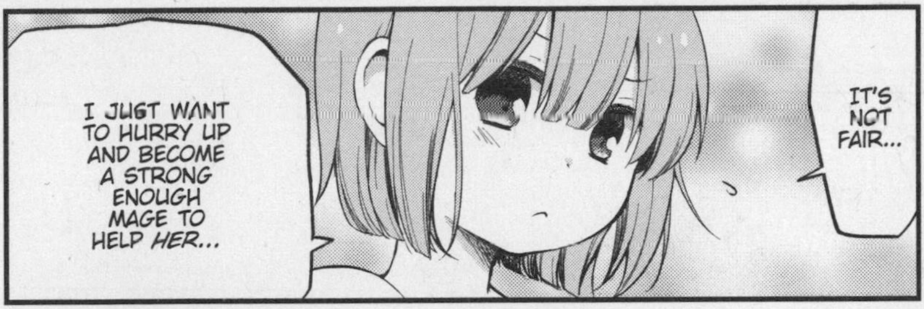
IT'S NOT FAIR...
I JUST WANT TO HURRY UP AND BECOME A STRONG ENOUGH MAGE TO HELP *HER*...

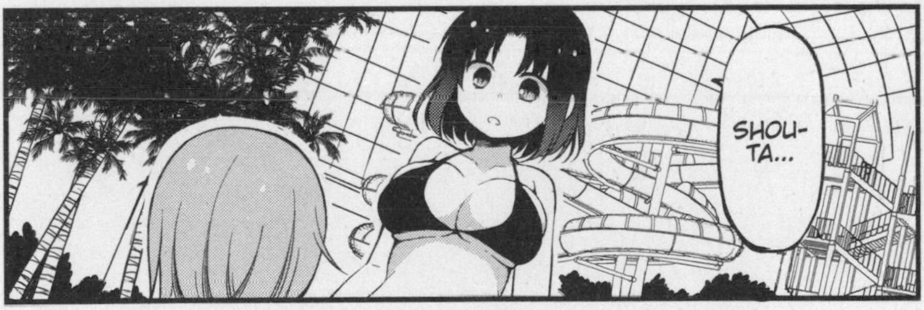
SHOU-TA...

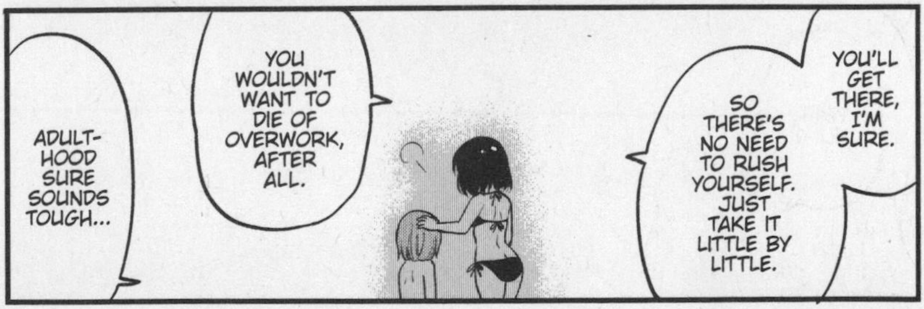
YOU'LL GET THERE, I'M SURE.
SO THERE'S NO NEED TO RUSH YOURSELF. JUST TAKE IT LITTLE BY LITTLE.
YOU WOULDN'T WANT TO DIE OF OVERWORK, AFTER ALL.
ADULT-HOOD SURE SOUNDS TOUGH...

FAMILIAR RESCUE

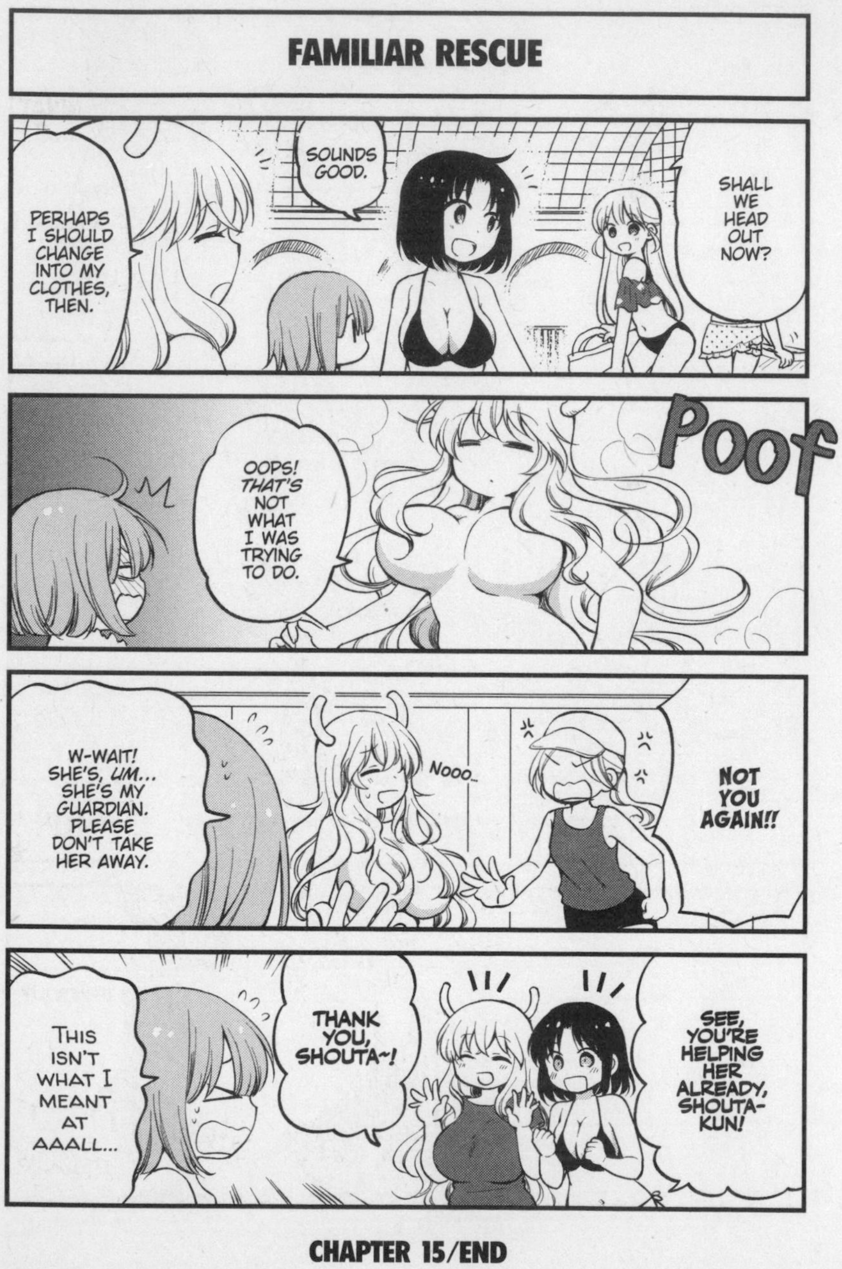
SHALL WE HEAD OUT NOW?
SOUNDS GOOD.
PERHAPS I SHOULD CHANGE INTO MY CLOTHES, THEN.
Poof
OOPS! *THAT'S* NOT WHAT I WAS TRYING TO DO.
NOT YOU AGAIN!!
Nooo..
W-WAIT! SHE'S, *UM*... SHE'S MY GUARDIAN. PLEASE DON'T TAKE HER AWAY.
SEE, YOU'RE HELPING HER ALREADY, SHOUTA-KUN!
THANK YOU, SHOUTA~!
THIS ISN'T WHAT I MEANT AT AAALL...

CHAPTER 15/END

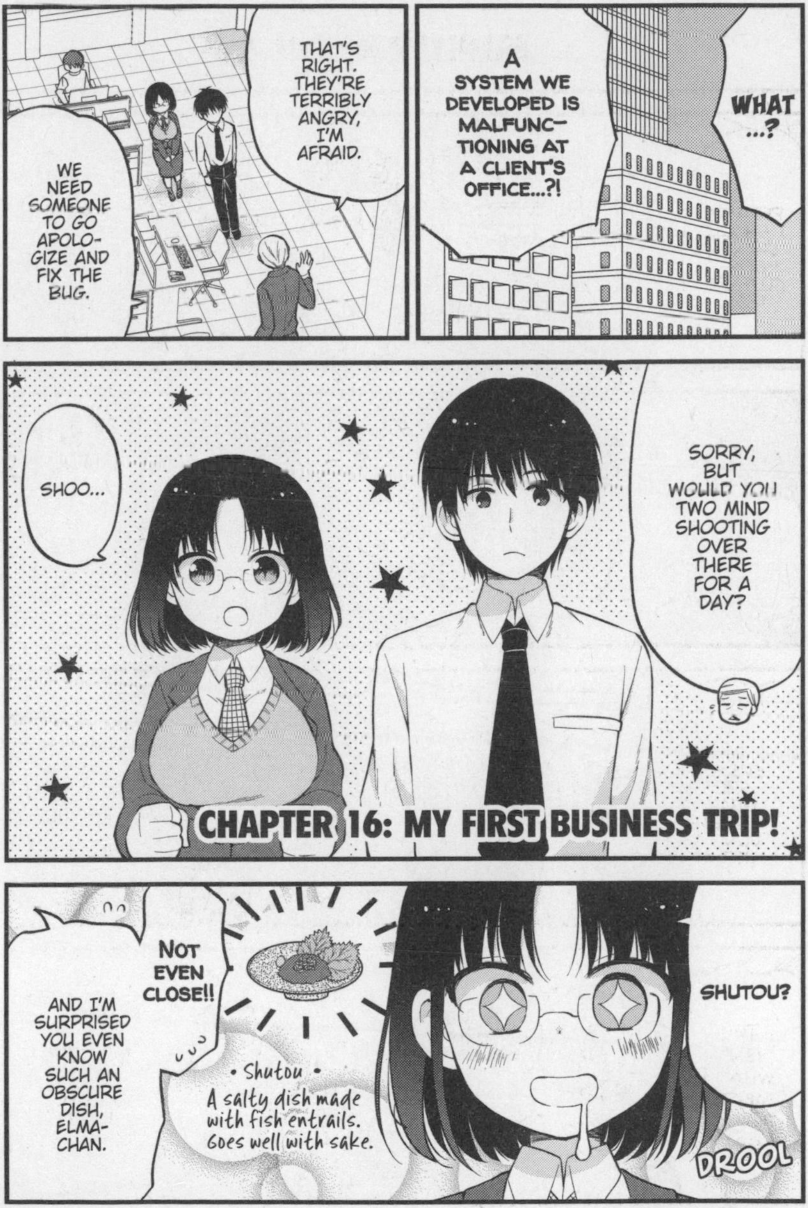
WHAT ...?
A SYSTEM WE DEVELOPED IS MALFUNCTIONING AT A CLIENT'S OFFICE...?!
THAT'S RIGHT. THEY'RE TERRIBLY ANGRY, I'M AFRAID.
WE NEED SOMEONE TO GO APOLOGIZE AND FIX THE BUG.
SORRY, BUT WOULD YOU TWO MIND SHOOTING OVER THERE FOR A DAY?
SHOO...
CHAPTER 16: MY FIRST BUSINESS TRIP!
SHUTOU?
DROOL
NOT EVEN CLOSE!!
• Shutou •
A salty dish made with fish entrails. Goes well with sake.
AND I'M SURPRISED YOU EVEN KNOW SUCH AN OBSCURE DISH, ELMA-CHAN.

CONSCIENTIOUS GLUTTON

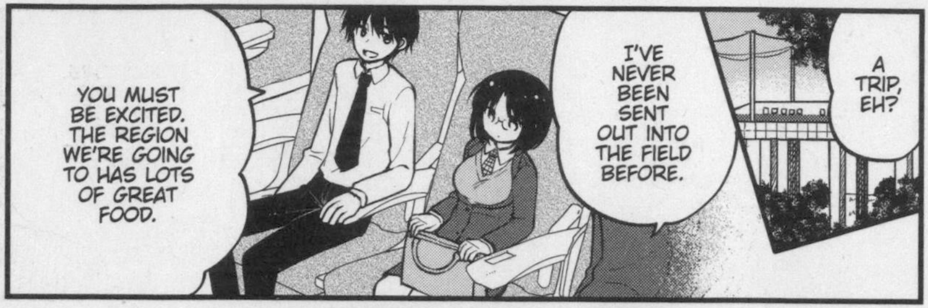
A TRIP, EH?
I'VE NEVER BEEN SENT OUT INTO THE FIELD BEFORE.
YOU MUST BE EXCITED. THE REGION WE'RE GOING TO HAS LOTS OF GREAT FOOD.

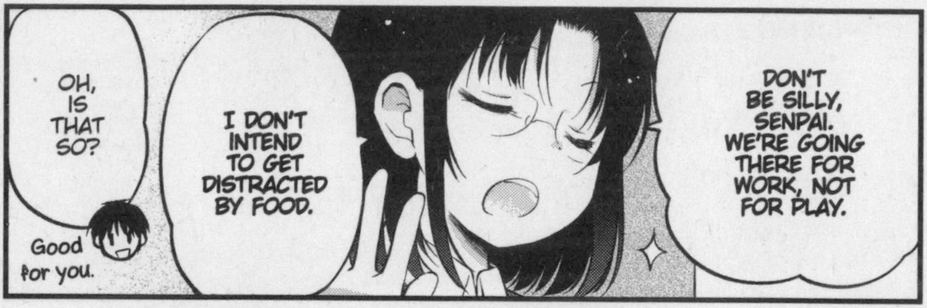
DON'T BE SILLY, SENPAI. WE'RE GOING THERE FOR WORK, NOT FOR PLAY.
I DON'T INTEND TO GET DISTRACTED BY FOOD.
OH, IS THAT SO?
Good for you.

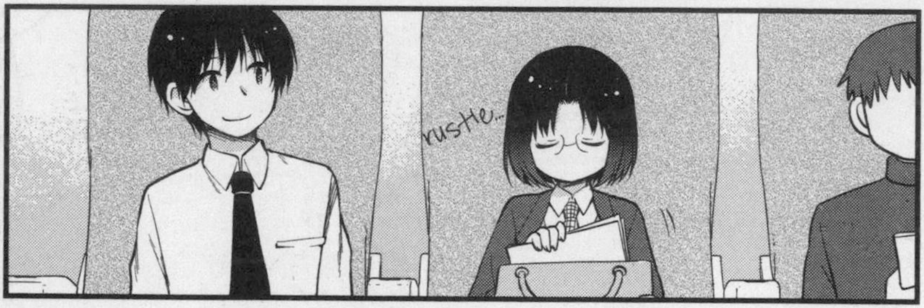
rustle...

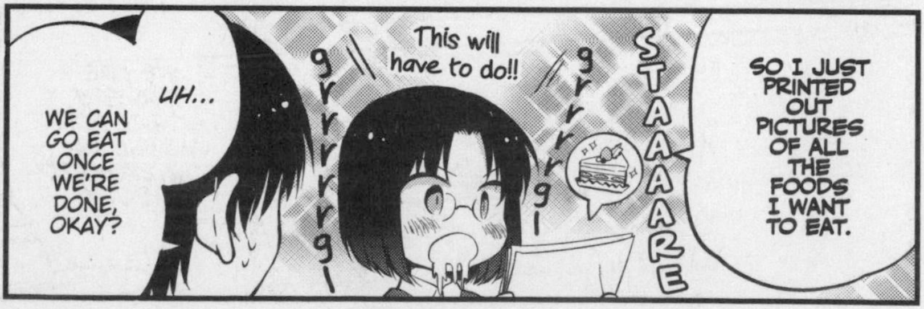
SO I JUST PRINTED OUT PICTURES OF ALL THE FOODS I WANT TO EAT.
STAAAARE
grrrrgl
This will have to do!!
grrrrrrrgl
UH...
WE CAN GO EAT ONCE WE'RE DONE, OKAY?

PERFECT POSTURE

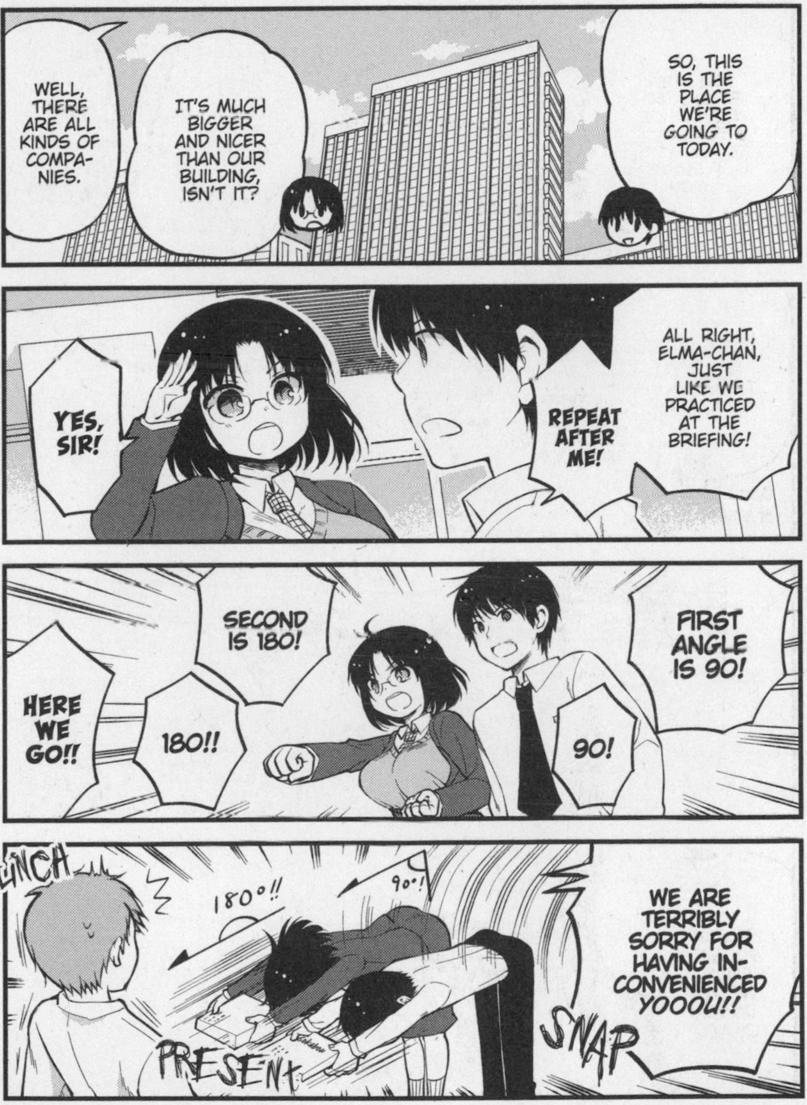
SO, THIS IS THE PLACE WE'RE GOING TO TODAY.
IT'S MUCH BIGGER AND NICER THAN OUR BUILDING, ISN'T IT?
WELL, THERE ARE ALL KINDS OF COMPA-NIES.
ALL RIGHT, ELMA-CHAN, JUST LIKE WE PRACTICED AT THE BRIEFING!
REPEAT AFTER ME!
YES, SIR!
FIRST ANGLE IS 90!
90!
SECOND IS 180!
180!!
HERE WE GO!!
WE ARE TERRIBLY SORRY FOR HAVING IN-CONVENIENCED YOOOU!!
SNAP
90°!
180°!!
PRESENT
FLINCH

SENPAI

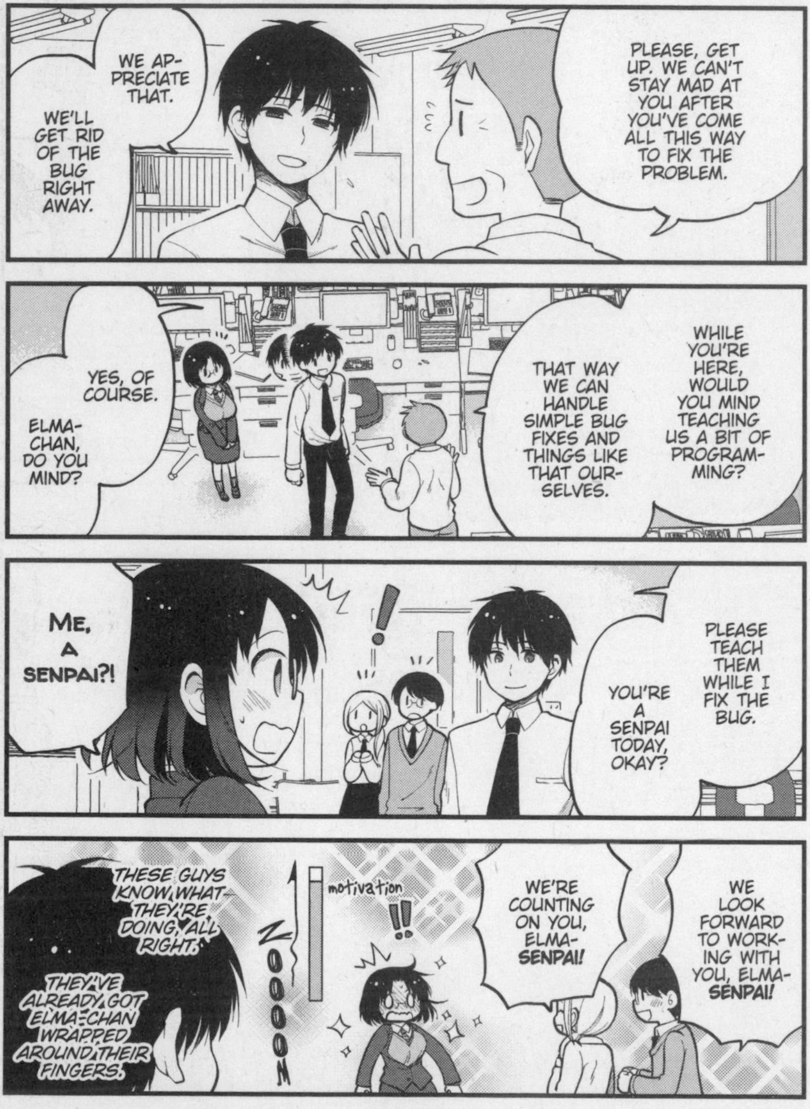
PLEASE, GET UP. WE CAN'T STAY MAD AT YOU AFTER YOU'VE COME ALL THIS WAY TO FIX THE PROBLEM.
WE APPRECIATE THAT.
WE'LL GET RID OF THE BUG RIGHT AWAY.
WHILE YOU'RE HERE, WOULD YOU MIND TEACHING US A BIT OF PROGRAMMING?
THAT WAY WE CAN HANDLE SIMPLE BUG FIXES AND THINGS LIKE THAT OURSELVES.
YES, OF COURSE.
ELMA-CHAN, DO YOU MIND?
PLEASE TEACH THEM WHILE I FIX THE BUG.
YOU'RE A SENPAI TODAY, OKAY?
!
ME, A SENPAI?!
WE LOOK FORWARD TO WORKING WITH YOU, ELMA-SENPAI!
WE'RE COUNTING ON YOU, ELMA-SENPAI!
!!
motivation
ZOOOOOM
THESE GUYS KNOW WHAT THEY'RE DOING, ALL RIGHT.
THEY'VE ALREADY GOT ELMA-CHAN WRAPPED AROUND THEIR FINGERS.

HIGH LEVEL

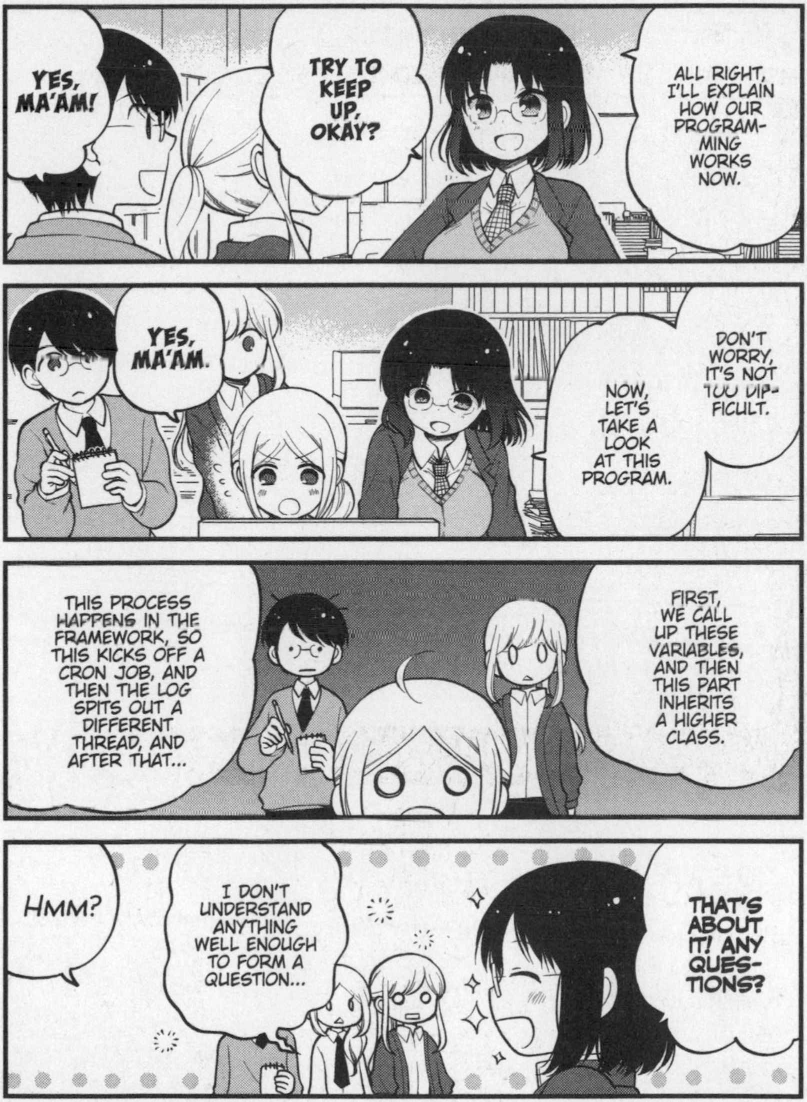
ALL RIGHT, I'LL EXPLAIN HOW OUR PROGRAMMING WORKS NOW.
TRY TO KEEP UP, OKAY?
YES, MA'AM!
DON'T WORRY, IT'S NOT TOO DIFFICULT.
NOW, LET'S TAKE A LOOK AT THIS PROGRAM.
YES, MA'AM.
FIRST, WE CALL UP THESE VARIABLES, AND THEN THIS PART INHERITS A HIGHER CLASS.
THIS PROCESS HAPPENS IN THE FRAMEWORK, SO THIS KICKS OFF A CRON JOB, AND THEN THE LOG SPITS OUT A DIFFERENT THREAD, AND AFTER THAT...
THAT'S ABOUT IT! ANY QUESTIONS?
I DON'T UNDERSTAND ANYTHING WELL ENOUGH TO FORM A QUESTION...
HMM?

A PERFECT RECREATION

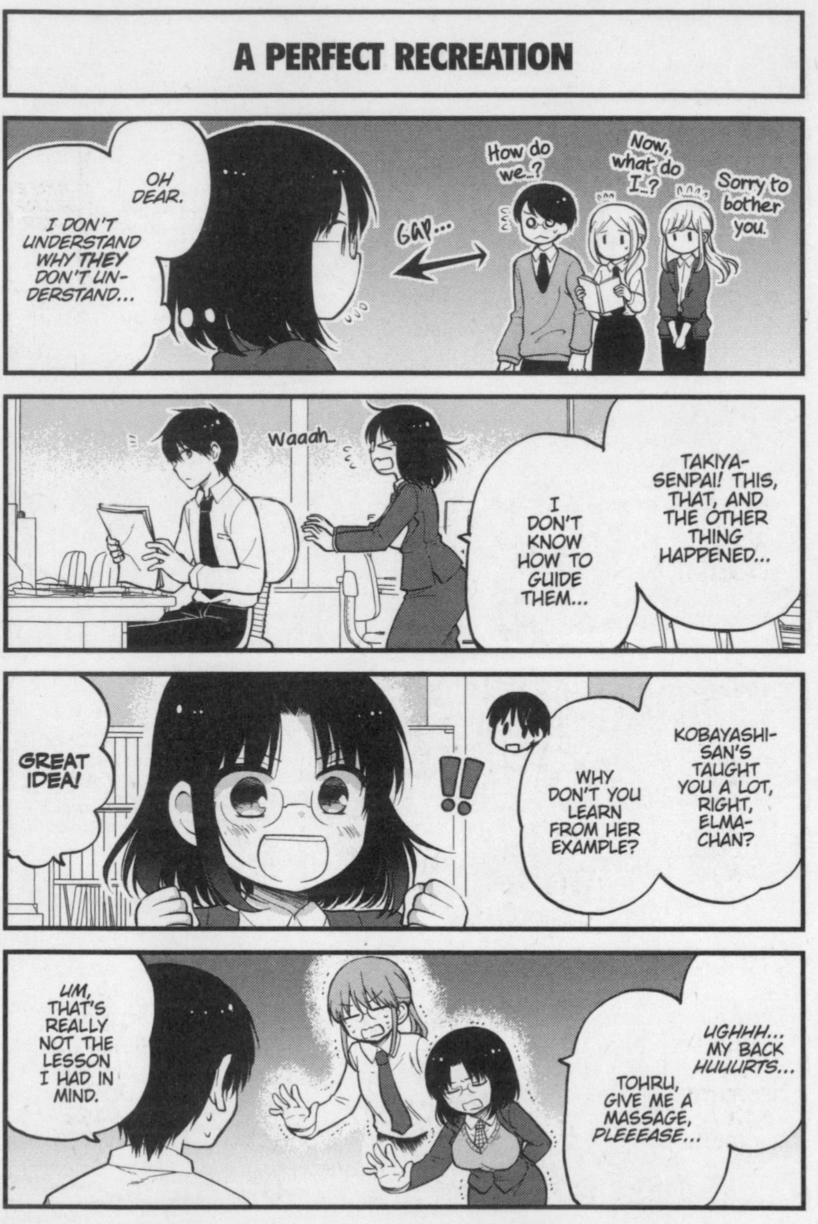
Sorry to bother you.
Now, what do I..?
How do we..?
Gap...
OH DEAR. I DON'T UNDERSTAND WHY THEY DON'T UNDERSTAND...
TAKIYA-SENPAI! THIS, THAT, AND THE OTHER THING HAPPENED...
I DON'T KNOW HOW TO GUIDE THEM...
Waaah
KOBAYASHI-SAN'S TAUGHT YOU A LOT, RIGHT, ELMA-CHAN?
WHY DON'T YOU LEARN FROM HER EXAMPLE?
!!
GREAT IDEA!
UGHHH... MY BACK HUUURTS...
TOHRU, GIVE ME A MASSAGE, PLEEEASE...
UM, THAT'S REALLY NOT THE LESSON I HAD IN MIND.

IMPULSE SPEED

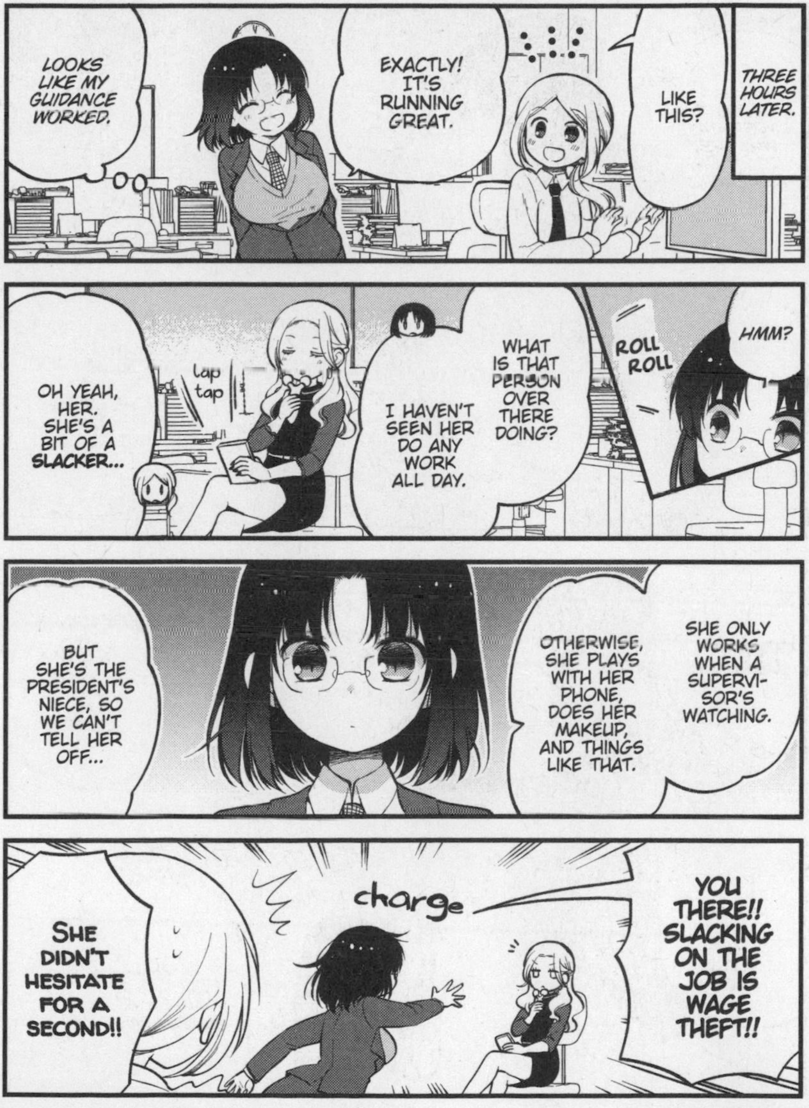
THREE HOURS LATER.
LIKE THIS?
EXACTLY! IT'S RUNNING GREAT.
LOOKS LIKE MY GUIDANCE WORKED.
HMM?
ROLL ROLL
WHAT IS THAT PERSON OVER THERE DOING?
I HAVEN'T SEEN HER DO ANY WORK ALL DAY.
tap tap
OH YEAH, HER. SHE'S A BIT OF A SLACKER...
SHE ONLY WORKS WHEN A SUPERVISOR'S WATCHING.
OTHERWISE, SHE PLAYS WITH HER PHONE, DOES HER MAKEUP, AND THINGS LIKE THAT.
BUT SHE'S THE PRESIDENT'S NIECE, SO WE CAN'T TELL HER OFF...
YOU THERE!! SLACKING ON THE JOB IS WAGE THEFT!!
charge
SHE DIDN'T HESITATE FOR A SECOND!!

BIG ATTITUDE

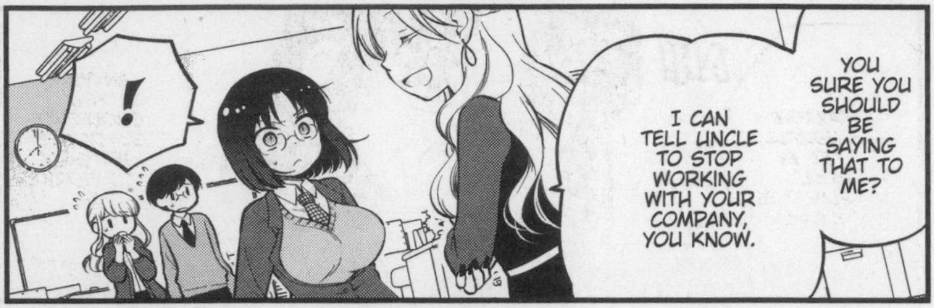

YOU SURE YOU SHOULD BE SAYING THAT TO ME?
I CAN TELL UNCLE TO STOP WORKING WITH YOUR COMPANY, YOU KNOW.
!

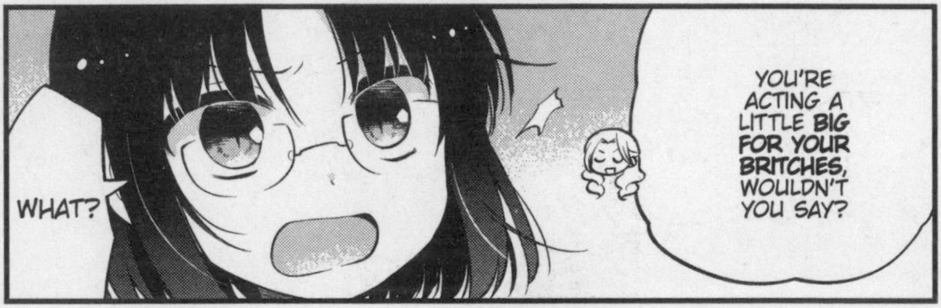

YOU'RE ACTING A LITTLE **BIG FOR YOUR BRITCHES,** WOULDN'T YOU SAY?
WHAT?

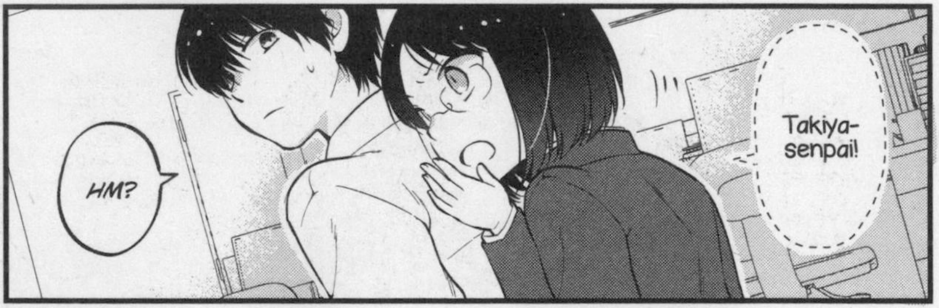

Takiya-senpai!
HM?

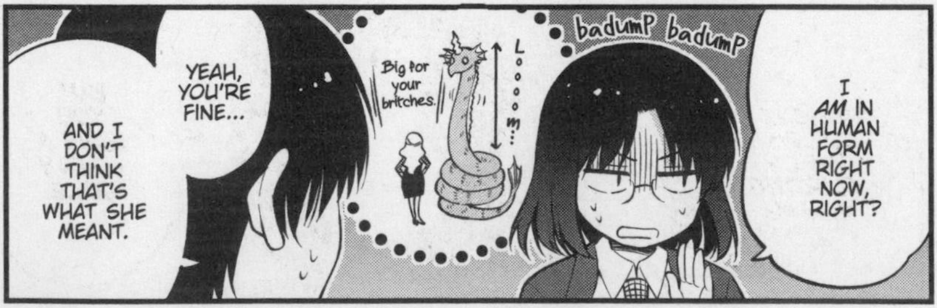

I *AM* IN HUMAN FORM RIGHT NOW, RIGHT?
badump badump
Looooom...
Big for your britches.
YEAH, YOU'RE FINE...
AND I DON'T THINK THAT'S WHAT SHE MEANT.

COMPLIMENT SANDWICH

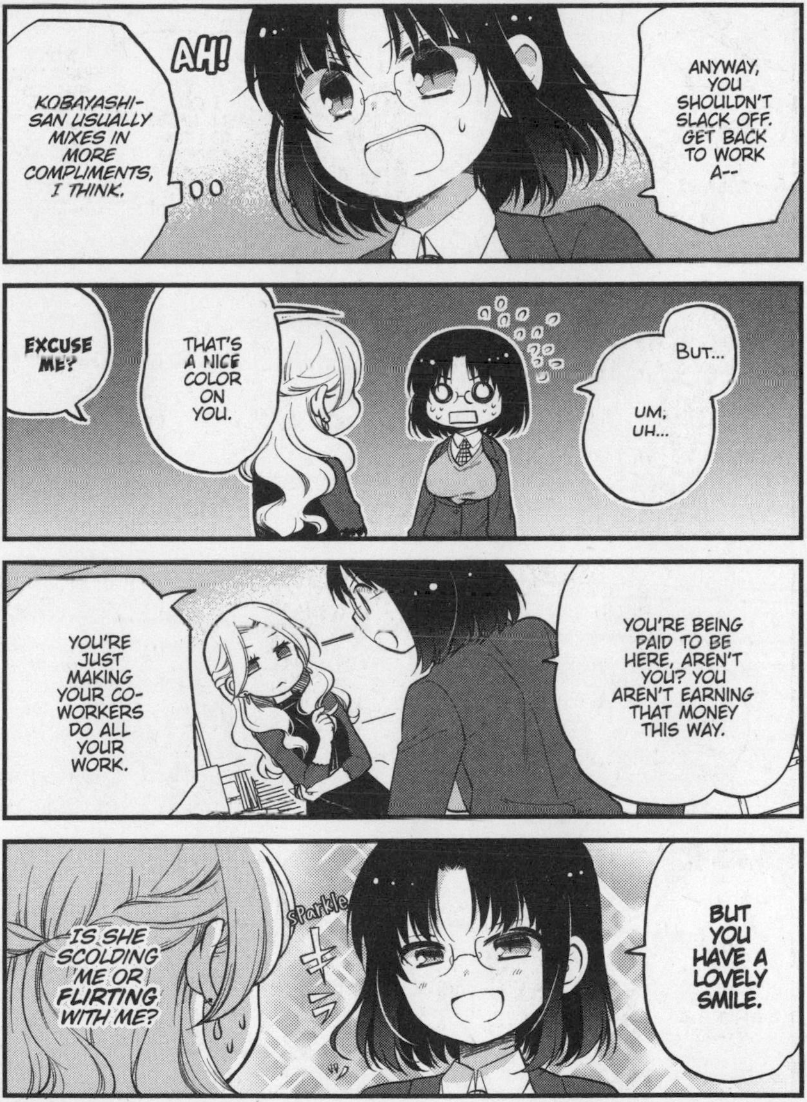
ANYWAY, YOU SHOULDN'T SLACK OFF. GET BACK TO WORK A--
AH!
KOBAYASHI-SAN USUALLY MIXES IN MORE COMPLIMENTS, I THINK.
BUT...
UM, UH...
THAT'S A NICE COLOR ON YOU.
EXCUSE ME?
YOU'RE BEING PAID TO BE HERE, AREN'T YOU? YOU AREN'T EARNING THAT MONEY THIS WAY.
YOU'RE JUST MAKING YOUR CO-WORKERS DO ALL YOUR WORK.
BUT YOU HAVE A LOVELY SMILE.
sparkle
IS SHE SCOLDING ME OR FLIRTING WITH ME?

DISTANCE IS MEANINGLESS

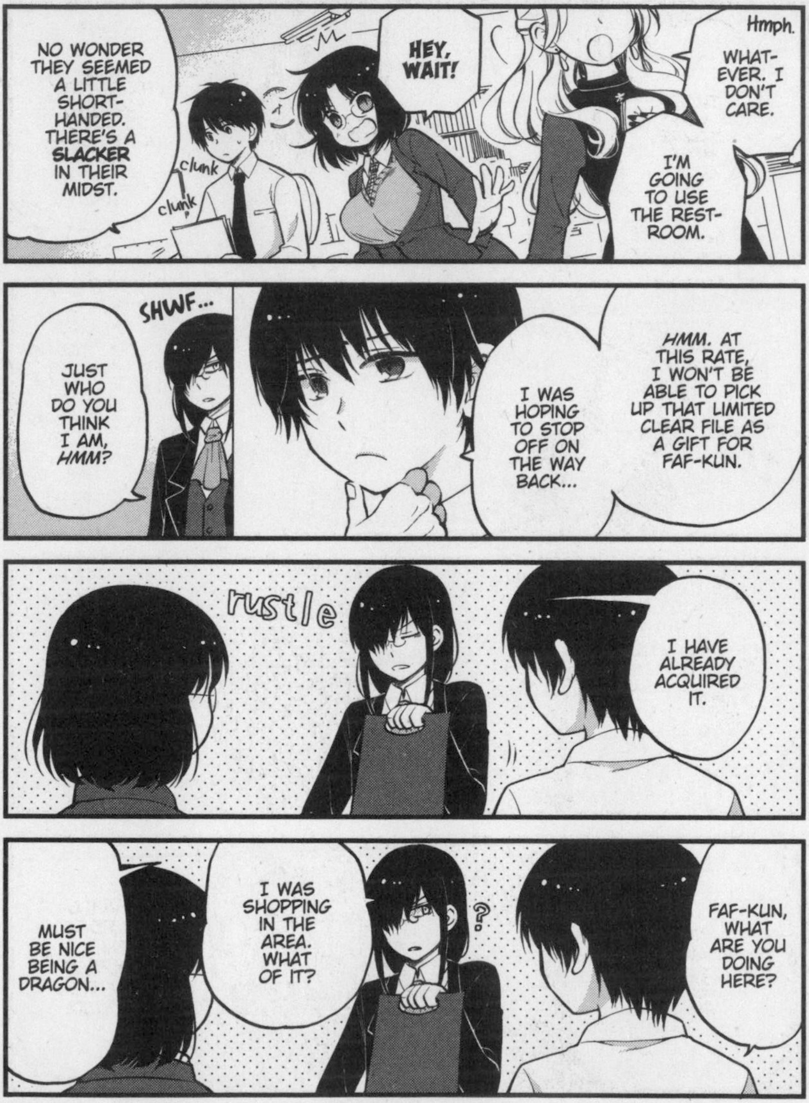
Hmph.
WHAT-EVER. I DON'T CARE.
I'M GOING TO USE THE REST-ROOM.
HEY, WAIT!
clunk
clunk
NO WONDER THEY SEEMED A LITTLE SHORT-HANDED. THERE'S A **SLACKER** IN THEIR MIDST.
HMM. AT THIS RATE, I WON'T BE ABLE TO PICK UP THAT LIMITED CLEAR FILE AS A GIFT FOR FAF-KUN.
I WAS HOPING TO STOP OFF ON THE WAY BACK...
SHWF...
JUST WHO DO YOU THINK I AM, *HMM?*
I HAVE ALREADY ACQUIRED IT.
rustle
FAF-KUN, WHAT ARE YOU DOING HERE?
?
I WAS SHOPPING IN THE AREA. WHAT OF IT?
MUST BE NICE BEING A DRAGON...

FAF-KUN'S HELP

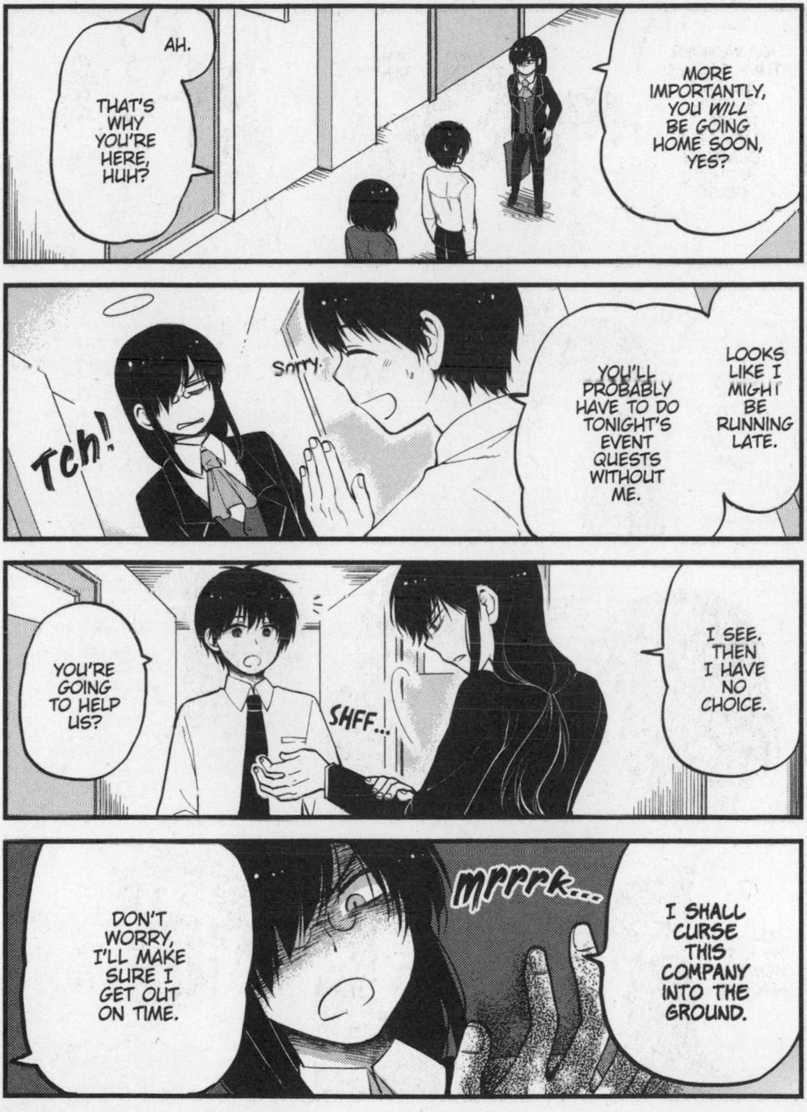
MORE IMPORTANTLY, YOU *WILL* BE GOING HOME SOON, YES?
AH. THAT'S WHY YOU'RE HERE, HUH?
LOOKS LIKE I MIGHT BE RUNNING LATE.
YOU'LL PROBABLY HAVE TO DO TONIGHT'S EVENT QUESTS WITHOUT ME.
Sorry.
Tch!
I SEE. THEN I HAVE NO CHOICE.
SHFF...
YOU'RE GOING TO HELP US?
I SHALL CURSE THIS COMPANY INTO THE GROUND.
mrrrk...
DON'T WORRY, I'LL MAKE SURE I GET OUT ON TIME.

TEAMING UP

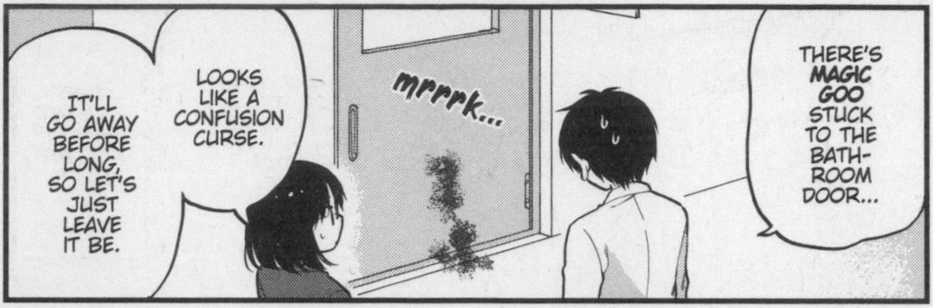
THERE'S MAGIC GOO STUCK TO THE BATH-ROOM DOOR...
mrrrk...
LOOKS LIKE A CONFUSION CURSE.
IT'LL GO AWAY BEFORE LONG, SO LET'S JUST LEAVE IT BE.

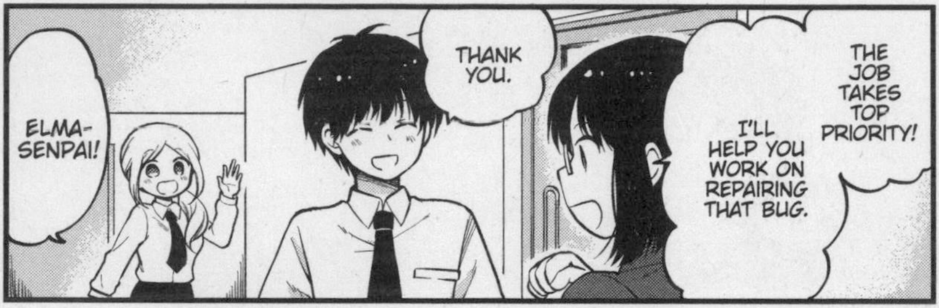
THE JOB TAKES TOP PRIORITY!
I'LL HELP YOU WORK ON REPAIRING THAT BUG.
THANK YOU.
ELMA-SENPAI!

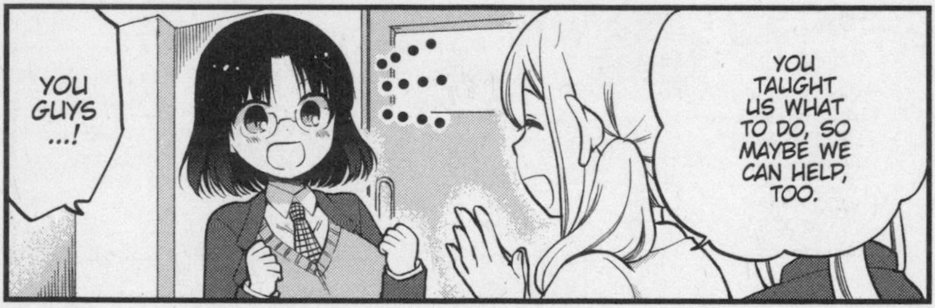
YOU TAUGHT US WHAT TO DO, SO MAYBE WE CAN HELP, TOO.
YOU GUYS ...!

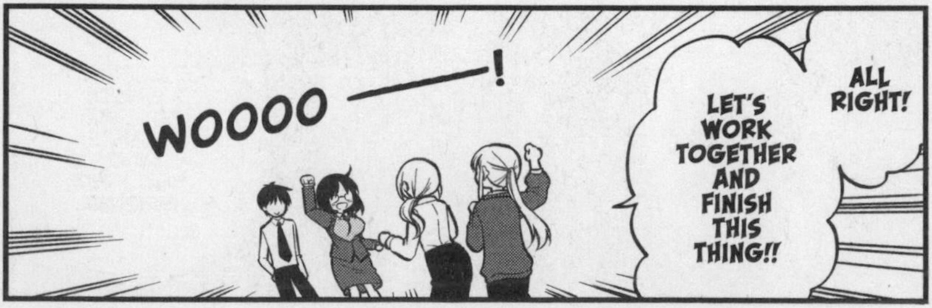
ALL RIGHT!
LET'S WORK TOGETHER AND FINISH THIS THING!!
WOOOO——!

NIPPED IT IN THE BUD...

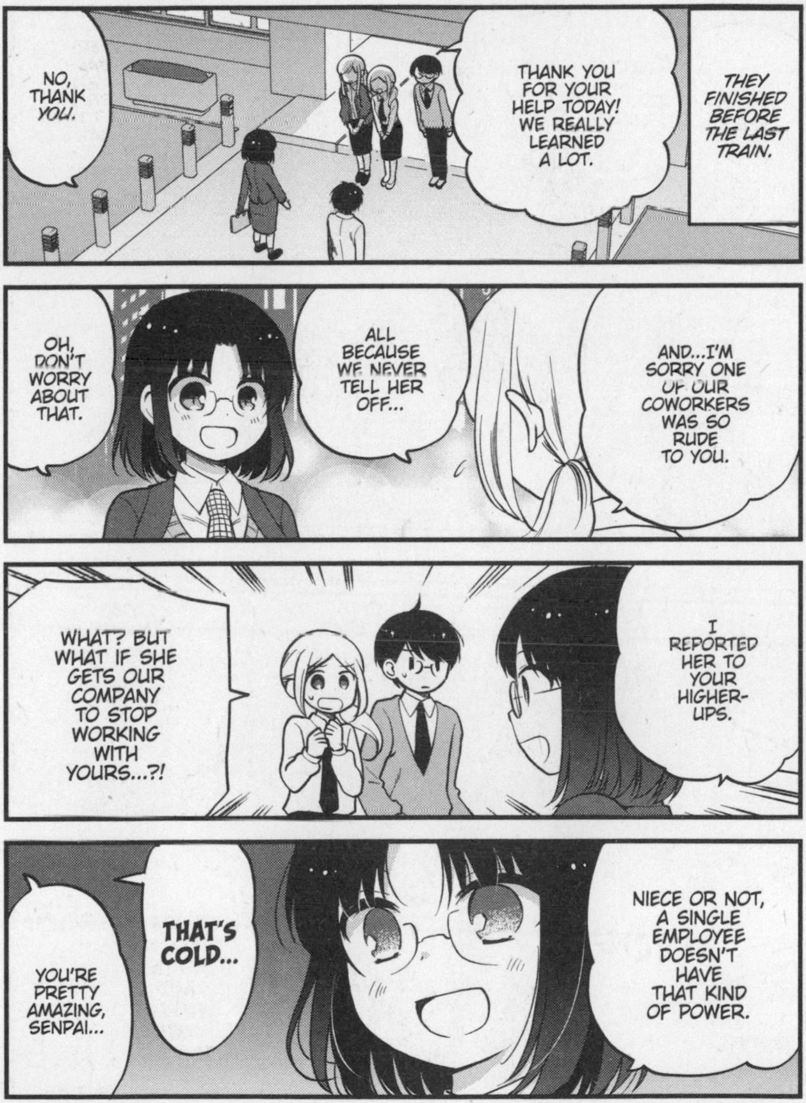
THEY FINISHED BEFORE THE LAST TRAIN.
THANK YOU FOR YOUR HELP TODAY! WE REALLY LEARNED A LOT.
NO, THANK YOU.
AND...I'M SORRY ONE OF OUR COWORKERS WAS SO RUDE TO YOU.
ALL BECAUSE WE NEVER TELL HER OFF...
OH, DON'T WORRY ABOUT THAT.
I REPORTED HER TO YOUR HIGHER-UPS.
WHAT? BUT WHAT IF SHE GETS OUR COMPANY TO STOP WORKING WITH YOURS...?!
NIECE OR NOT, A SINGLE EMPLOYEE DOESN'T HAVE THAT KIND OF POWER.
THAT'S COLD...
YOU'RE PRETTY AMAZING, SENPAI...

IT'S SUPER EFFECTIVE!

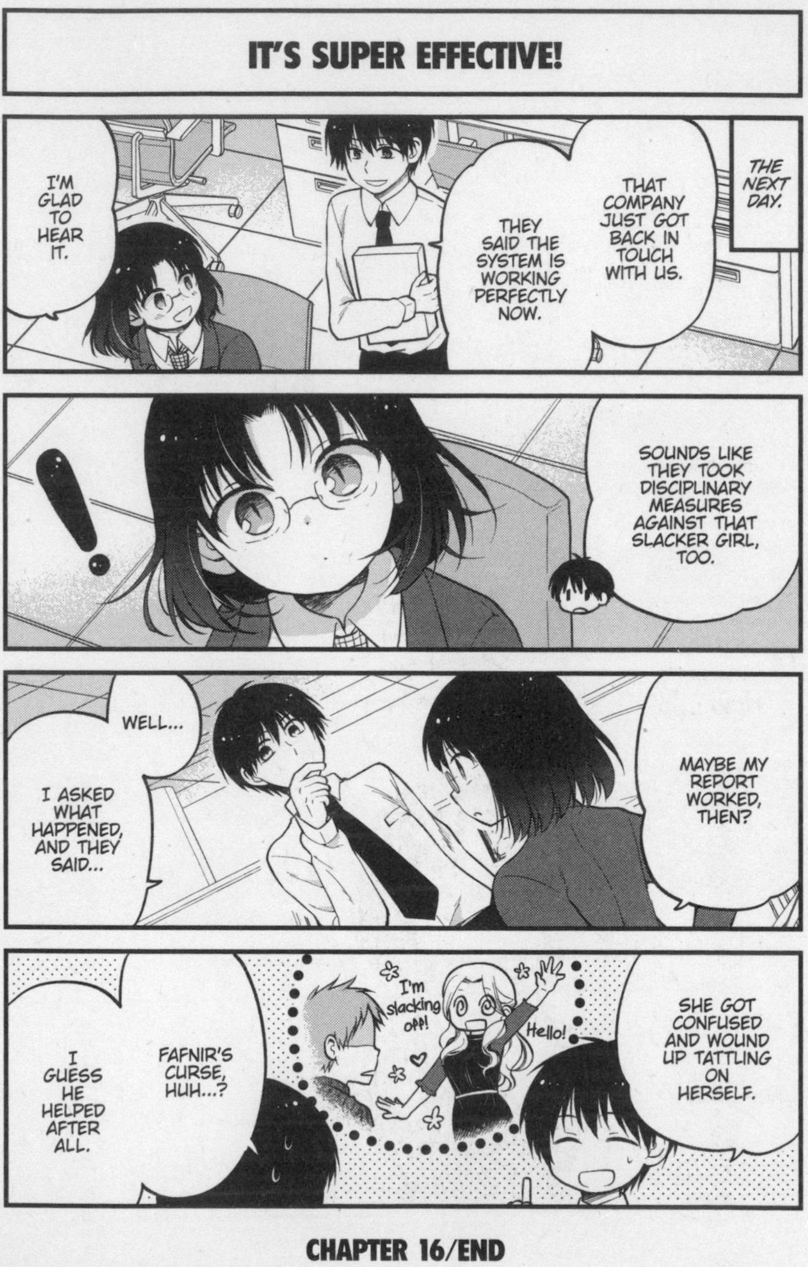
THE NEXT DAY.
THAT COMPANY JUST GOT BACK IN TOUCH WITH US.
THEY SAID THE SYSTEM IS WORKING PERFECTLY NOW.
I'M GLAD TO HEAR IT.
SOUNDS LIKE THEY TOOK DISCIPLINARY MEASURES AGAINST THAT SLACKER GIRL, TOO.
!
MAYBE MY REPORT WORKED, THEN?
WELL...
I ASKED WHAT HAPPENED, AND THEY SAID...
SHE GOT CONFUSED AND WOUND UP TATTLING ON HERSELF.
Hello!
I'm slacking off!
FAFNIR'S CURSE, HUH...?
I GUESS HE HELPED AFTER ALL.

CHAPTER 16/END

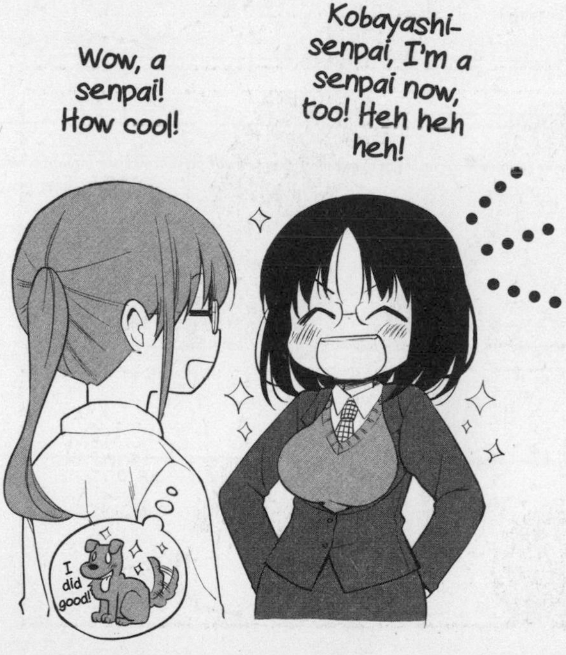
Kobayashi-senpai, I'm a senpai now, too! Heh heh heh!
Wow, a senpai! How cool!
I did good!

Miss Kobayashi's Dragon Maid
Elma's Office Lady Diary

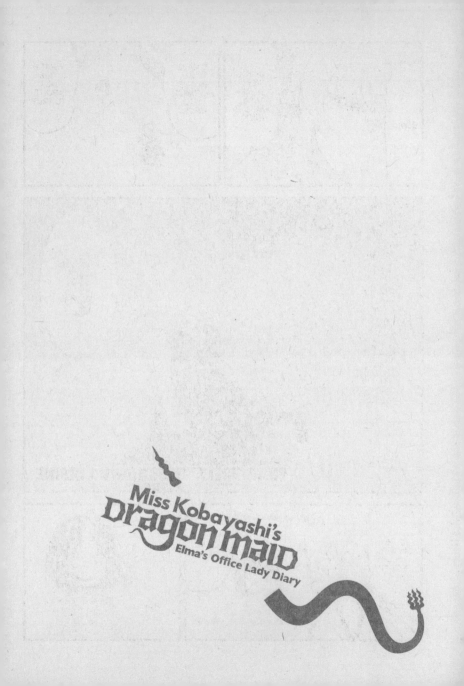

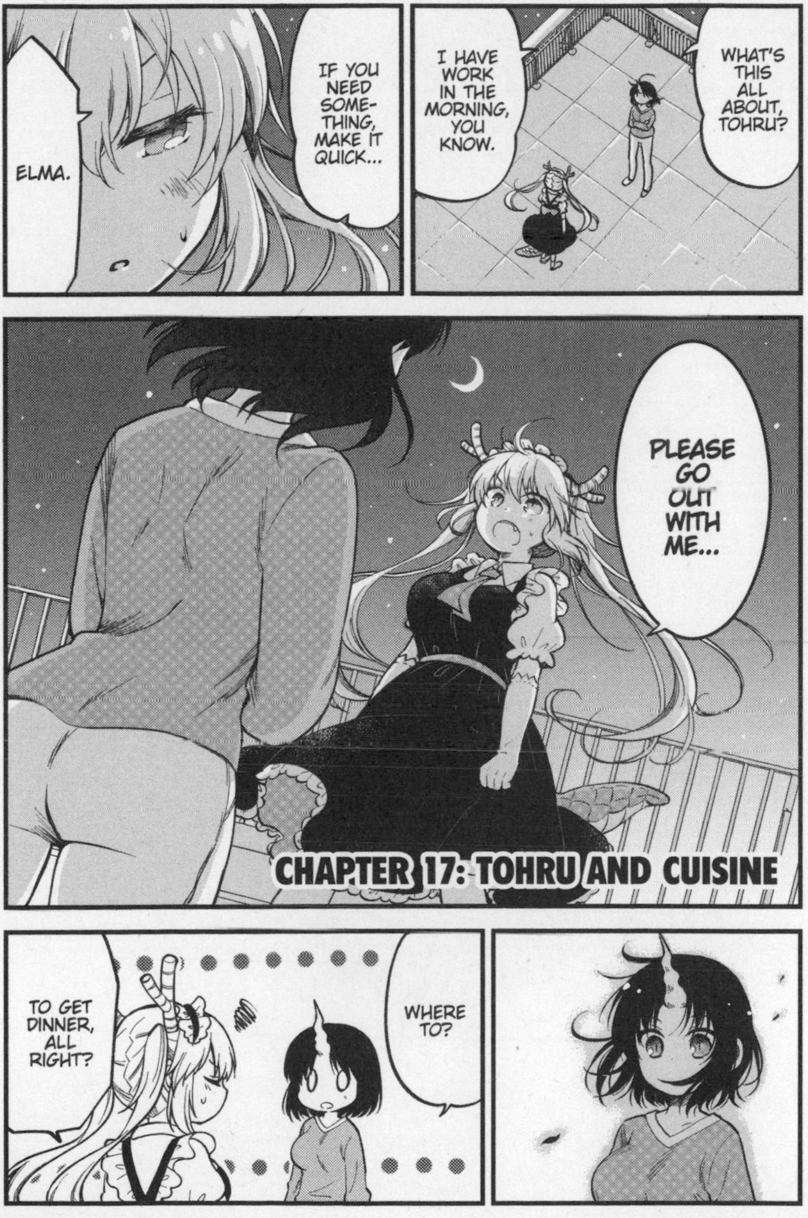
WHAT'S THIS ALL ABOUT, TOHRU?
I HAVE WORK IN THE MORNING, YOU KNOW.
IF YOU NEED SOME-THING, MAKE IT QUICK...
ELMA.
PLEASE GO OUT WITH ME...
CHAPTER 17: TOHRU AND CUISINE
WHERE TO?
TO GET DINNER, ALL RIGHT?

EXCITED

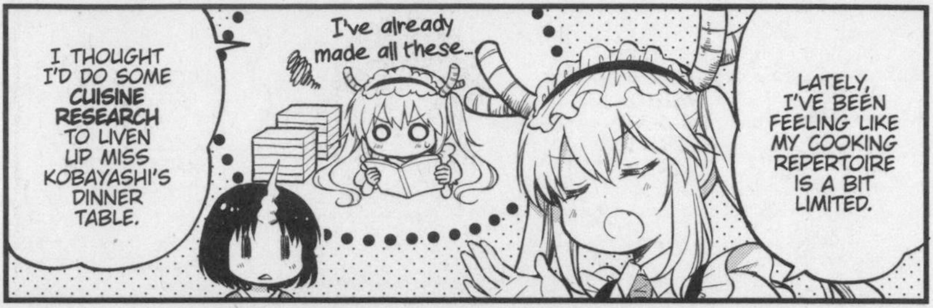
LATELY, I'VE BEEN FEELING LIKE MY COOKING REPERTOIRE IS A BIT LIMITED.
I've already made all these...
I THOUGHT I'D DO SOME CUISINE RESEARCH TO LIVEN UP MISS KOBAYASHI'S DINNER TABLE.

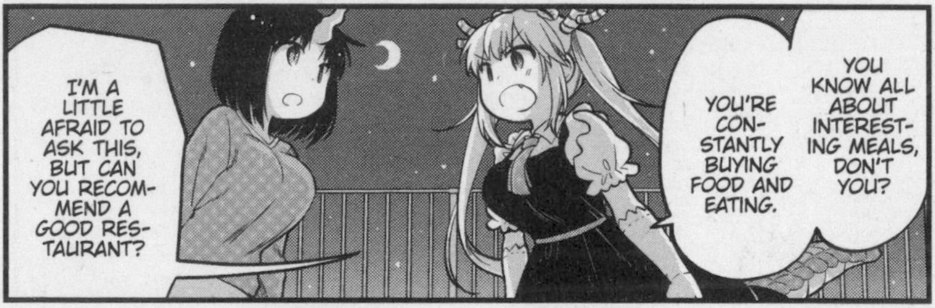
YOU KNOW ALL ABOUT INTEREST-ING MEALS, DON'T YOU?
YOU'RE CON-STANTLY BUYING FOOD AND EATING.
I'M A LITTLE AFRAID TO ASK THIS, BUT CAN YOU RECOM-MEND A GOOD RES-TAURANT?

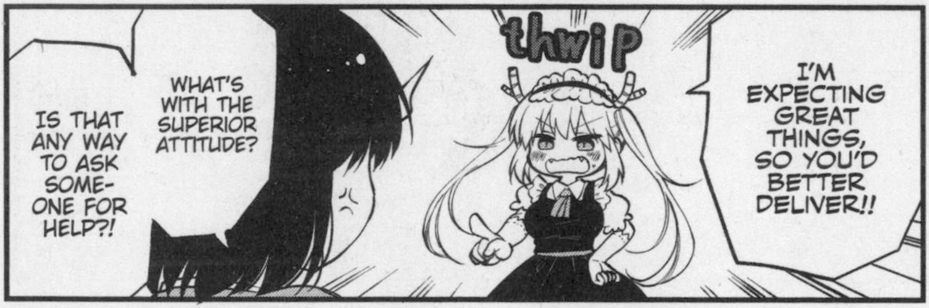
thwip
I'M EXPECTING GREAT THINGS, SO YOU'D BETTER DELIVER!!
WHAT'S WITH THE SUPERIOR ATTITUDE?
IS THAT ANY WAY TO ASK SOME-ONE FOR HELP?!

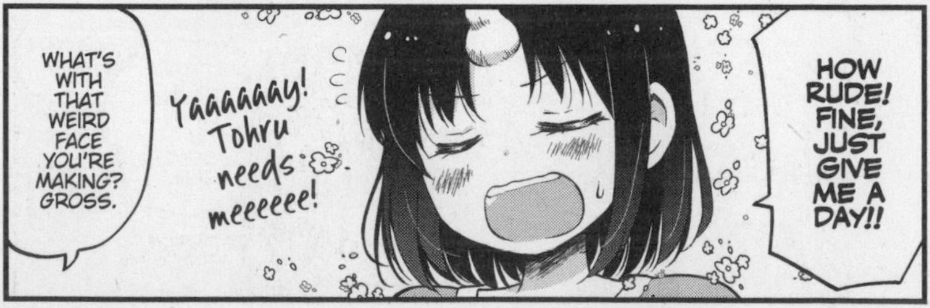
HOW RUDE! FINE, JUST GIVE ME A DAY!!
Yaaaaaay! Tohru needs meeeeee!
WHAT'S WITH THAT WEIRD FACE YOU'RE MAKING? GROSS.

OO LA LA?

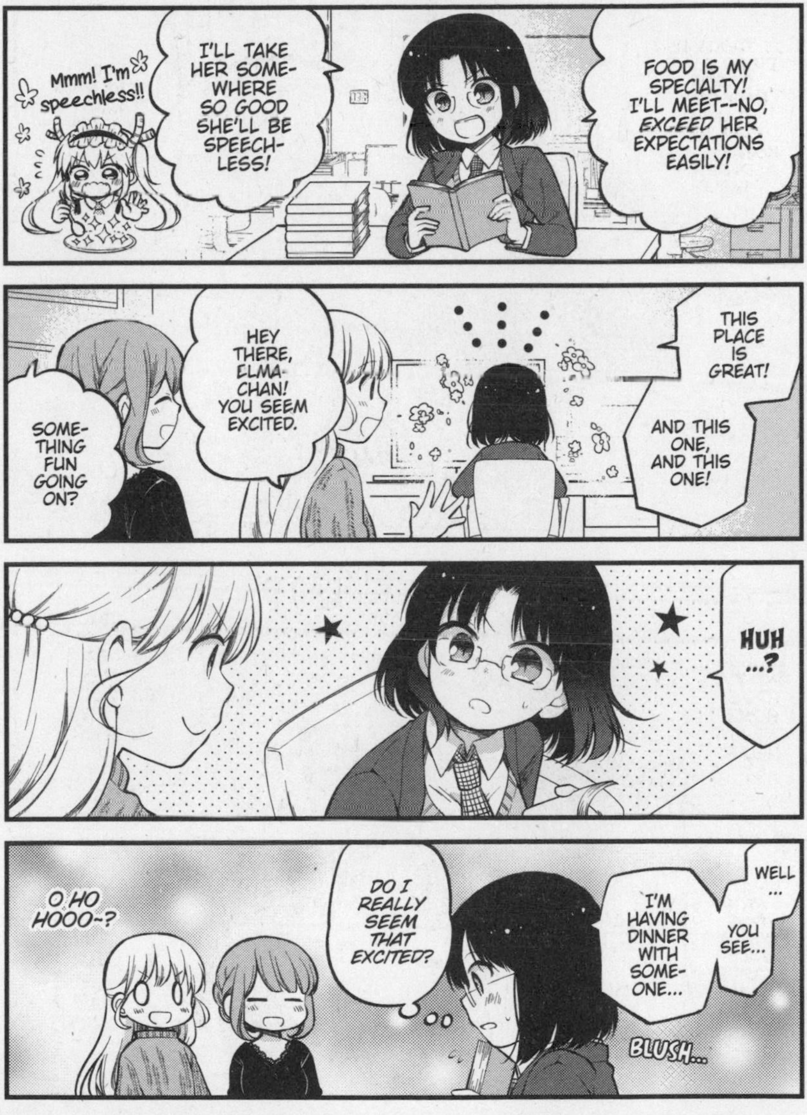
FOOD IS MY SPECIALTY! I'LL MEET--NO, *EXCEED* HER EXPECTATIONS EASILY!
I'LL TAKE HER SOME-WHERE SO GOOD SHE'LL BE SPEECH-LESS!
Mmm! I'm speechless!!
THIS PLACE IS GREAT!
AND THIS ONE, AND THIS ONE!
HEY THERE, ELMA-CHAN! YOU SEEM EXCITED.
SOME-THING FUN GOING ON?
HUH ...?
WELL ...
YOU SEE...
I'M HAVING DINNER WITH SOME-ONE...
DO I REALLY SEEM THAT EXCITED?
BLUSH...
O HO HOOO~?

THEY LOVE A LOVE STORY

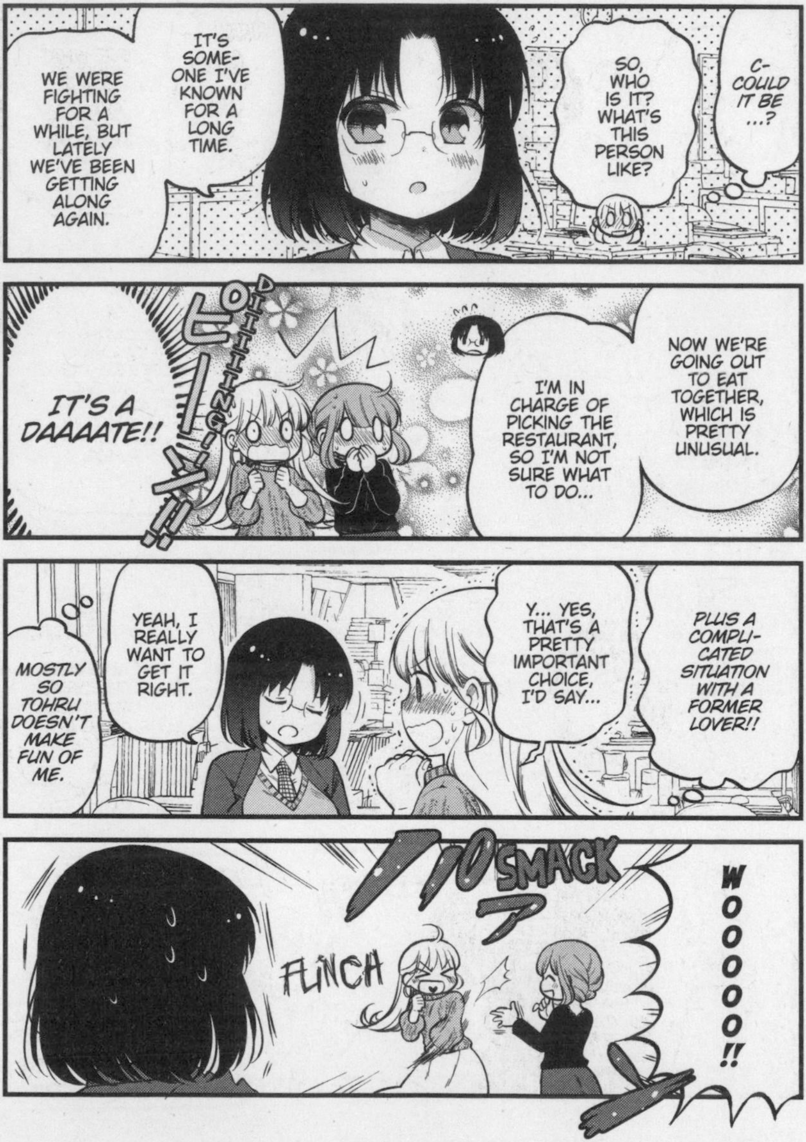
C-COULD IT BE ...?
SO, WHO IS IT? WHAT'S THIS PERSON LIKE?
IT'S SOMEONE I'VE KNOWN FOR A LONG TIME.
WE WERE FIGHTING FOR A WHILE, BUT LATELY WE'VE BEEN GETTING ALONG AGAIN.
NOW WE'RE GOING OUT TO EAT TOGETHER, WHICH IS PRETTY UNUSUAL.
I'M IN CHARGE OF PICKING THE RESTAURANT, SO I'M NOT SURE WHAT TO DO...
DIIIIIING-!
IT'S A DAAAATE!!
PLUS A COMPLICATED SITUATION WITH A FORMER LOVER!!
Y... YES, THAT'S A PRETTY IMPORTANT CHOICE, I'D SAY...
YEAH, I REALLY WANT TO GET IT RIGHT.
MOSTLY SO TOHRU DOESN'T MAKE FUN OF ME.
WOOOOOO!!
SMACK
FLINCH

SORT OF SCARY

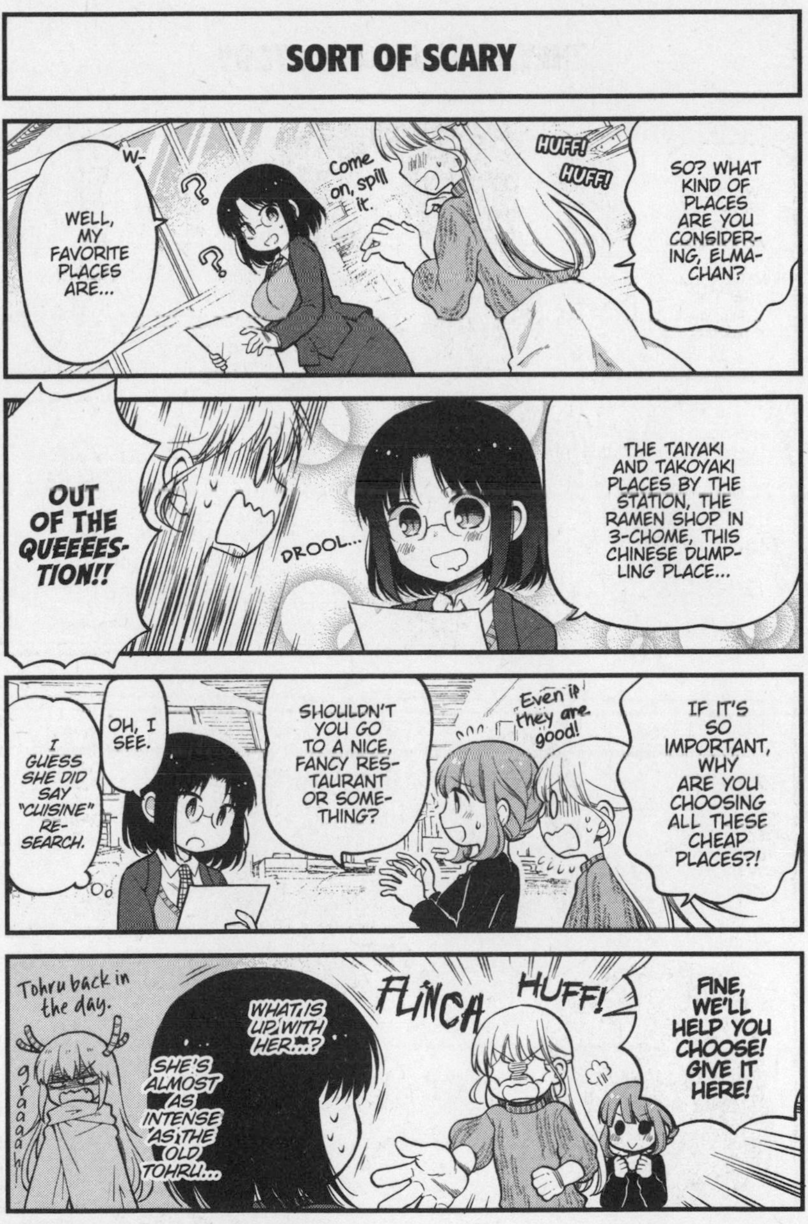
SO? WHAT KIND OF PLACES ARE YOU CONSIDERING, ELMA-CHAN?
HUFF!
HUFF!
Come on, spill it.
W-
WELL, MY FAVORITE PLACES ARE...
THE TAIYAKI AND TAKOYAKI PLACES BY THE STATION, THE RAMEN SHOP IN 3-CHOME, THIS CHINESE DUMPLING PLACE...
DROOL...
OUT OF THE QUEEEEESTION!!
IF IT'S SO IMPORTANT, WHY ARE YOU CHOOSING ALL THESE CHEAP PLACES?!
Even if they are good!
SHOULDN'T YOU GO TO A NICE, FANCY RESTAURANT OR SOMETHING?
OH, I SEE.
I GUESS SHE DID SAY "CUISINE" RESEARCH.
FINE, WE'LL HELP YOU CHOOSE! GIVE IT HERE!
HUFF!
FLINCH
WHAT IS UP WITH HER...?
SHE'S ALMOST AS INTENSE AS THE OLD TOHRU...
Tohru back in the day.
graaaah

TECHNICALLY CORRECT

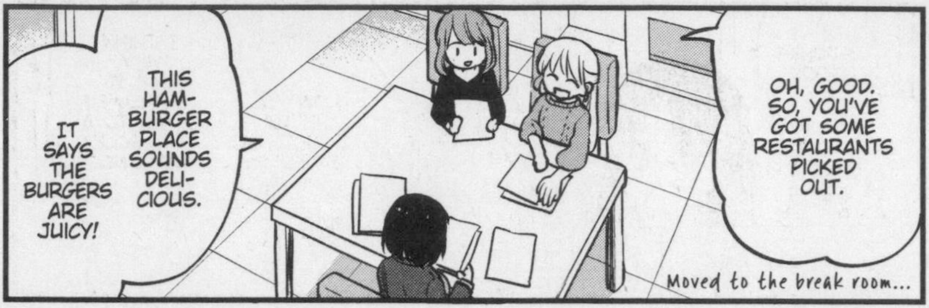
OH, GOOD. SO, YOU'VE GOT SOME RESTAURANTS PICKED OUT.
Moved to the break room...
THIS HAMBURGER PLACE SOUNDS DELICIOUS.
IT SAYS THE BURGERS ARE JUICY!

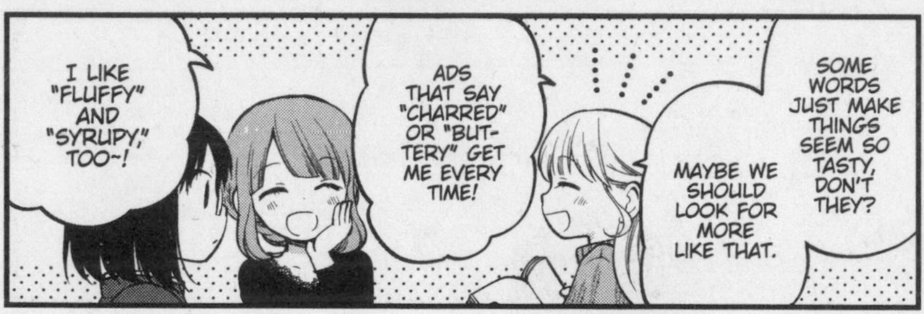
SOME WORDS JUST MAKE THINGS SEEM SO TASTY, DON'T THEY?
MAYBE WE SHOULD LOOK FOR MORE LIKE THAT.
ADS THAT SAY "CHARRED" OR "BUTTERY" GET ME EVERY TIME!
I LIKE "FLUFFY" AND "SYRUPY," TOO~!

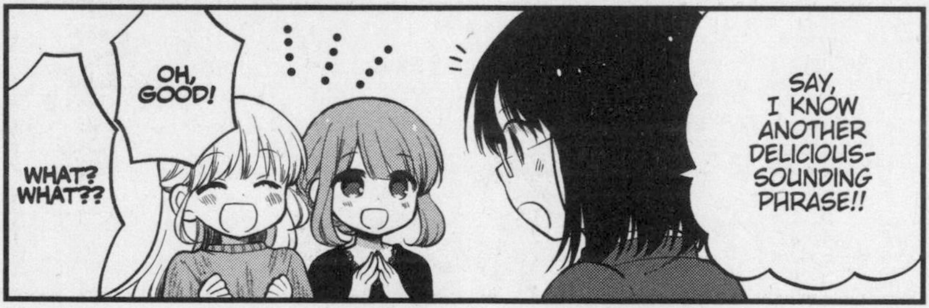
SAY, I KNOW ANOTHER DELICIOUS-SOUNDING PHRASE!!
OH, GOOD!
WHAT? WHAT??

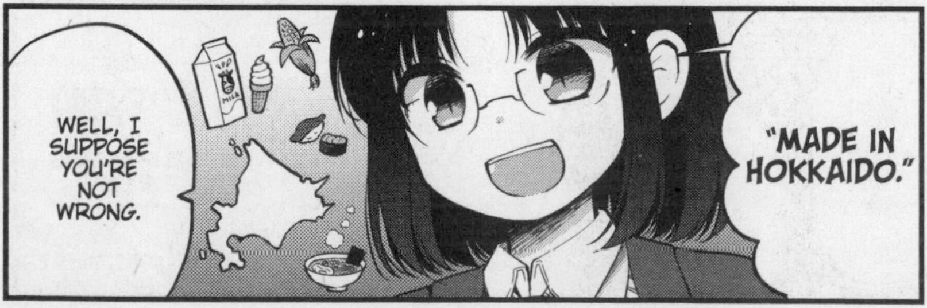
"MADE IN HOKKAIDO."
WELL, I SUPPOSE YOU'RE NOT WRONG.

SEXY TECHNIQUE ①

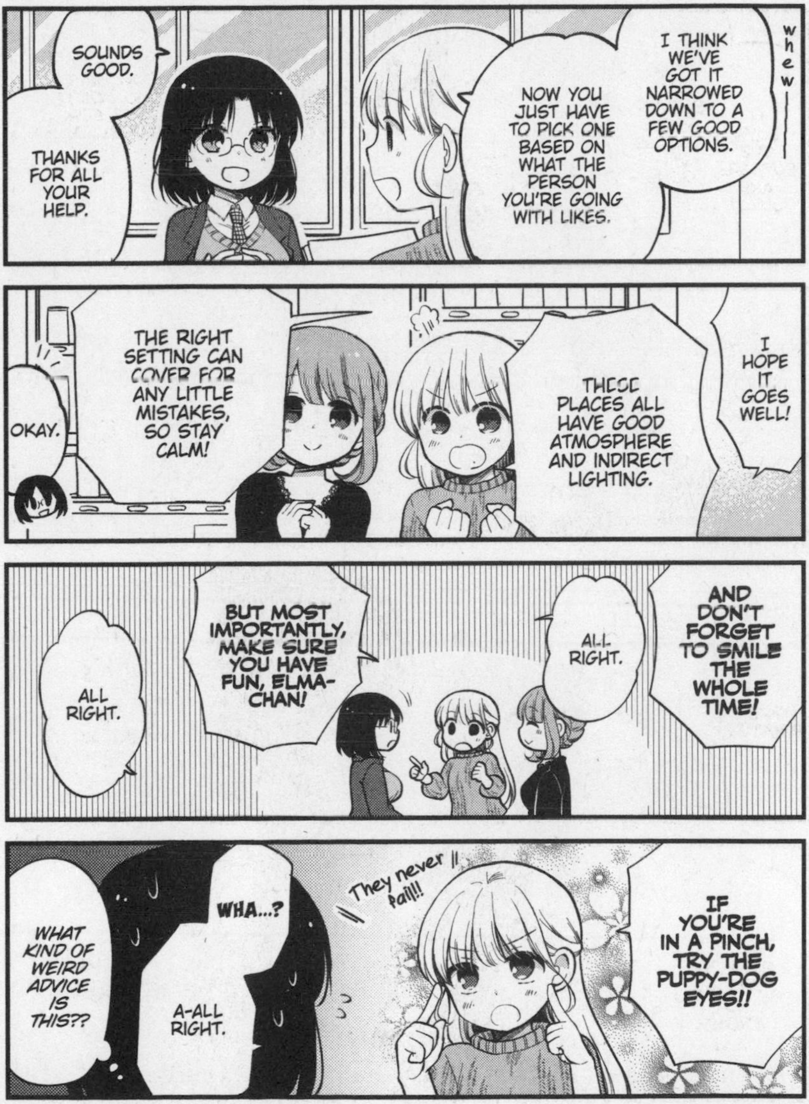
whew
I THINK WE'VE GOT IT NARROWED DOWN TO A FEW GOOD OPTIONS.
NOW YOU JUST HAVE TO PICK ONE BASED ON WHAT THE PERSON YOU'RE GOING WITH LIKES.
SOUNDS GOOD.
THANKS FOR ALL YOUR HELP.
I HOPE IT GOES WELL!
THESE PLACES ALL HAVE GOOD ATMOSPHERE AND INDIRECT LIGHTING.
THE RIGHT SETTING CAN COVER FOR ANY LITTLE MISTAKES, SO STAY CALM!
OKAY.
AND DON'T FORGET TO SMILE THE WHOLE TIME!
ALL RIGHT.
BUT MOST IMPORTANTLY, MAKE SURE YOU HAVE FUN, ELMA-CHAN!
ALL RIGHT.
IF YOU'RE IN A PINCH, TRY THE PUPPY-DOG EYES!!
They never fail!!
WHA...?
A-ALL RIGHT.
WHAT KIND OF WEIRD ADVICE IS THIS??

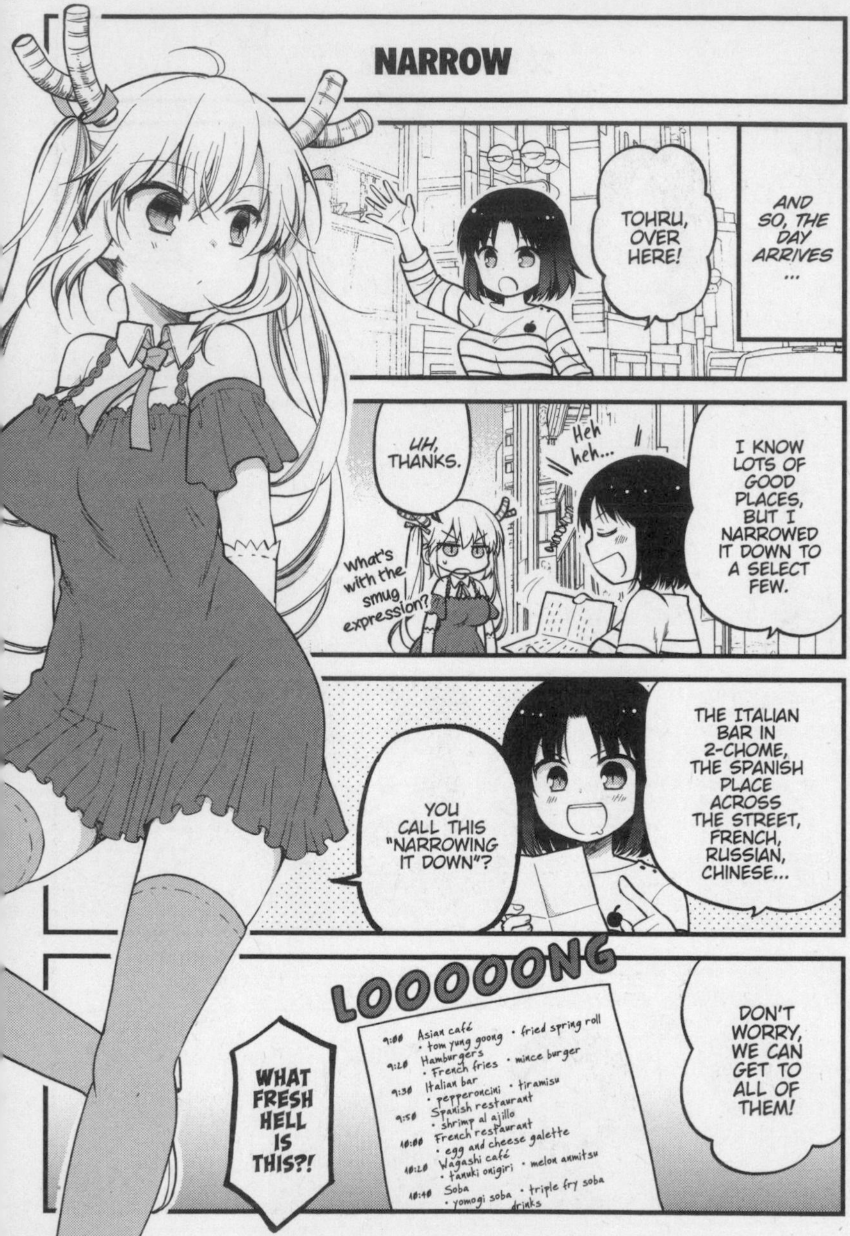
NARROW
AND SO, THE DAY ARRIVES...
TOHRU, OVER HERE!
I KNOW LOTS OF GOOD PLACES, BUT I NARROWED IT DOWN TO A SELECT FEW.
Heh heh...
UH, THANKS.
What's with the smug expression?
THE ITALIAN BAR IN 2-CHOME, THE SPANISH PLACE ACROSS THE STREET, FRENCH, RUSSIAN, CHINESE...
YOU CALL THIS "NARROWING IT DOWN"?
DON'T WORRY, WE CAN GET TO ALL OF THEM!
LOOOOONG
9:00 Asian café
• tom yung goong • fried spring roll
9:20 Hamburgers
• French fries • mince burger
9:30 Italian bar
• pepperoncini • tiramisu
9:50 Spanish restaurant
• shrimp al ajillo
10:00 French restaurant
• egg and cheese galette
10:20 Wagashi café
• tanuki onigiri • melon anmitsu
10:40 Soba
• yomogi soba • triple fry soba
drinks
WHAT FRESH HELL IS THIS?!

SPICE OF LIFE

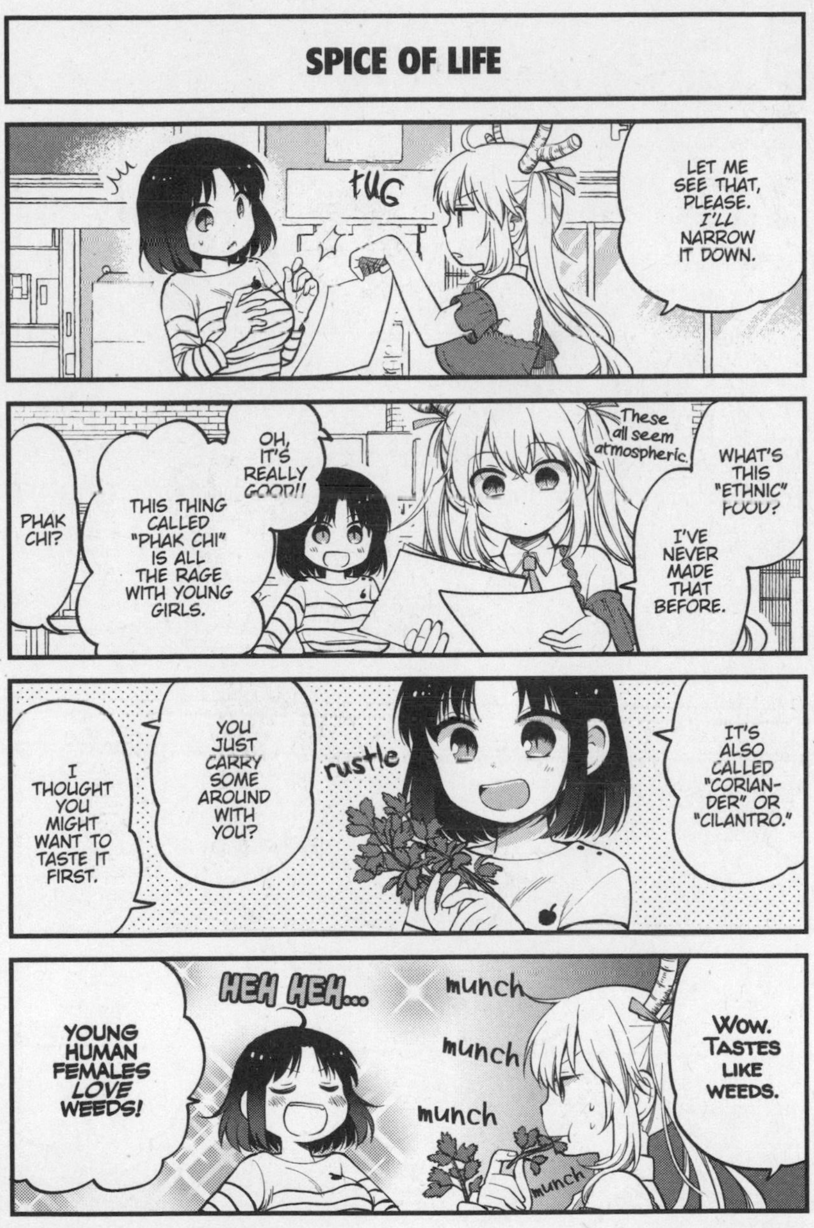
LET ME SEE THAT, PLEASE. I'LL NARROW IT DOWN.
TUG
WHAT'S THIS "ETHNIC" FOOD?
I'VE NEVER MADE THAT BEFORE.
These all seem atmospheric.
OH, IT'S REALLY GOOD!!
THIS THING CALLED "PHAK CHI" IS ALL THE RAGE WITH YOUNG GIRLS.
PHAK CHI?
IT'S ALSO CALLED "CORIANDER" OR "CILANTRO."
rustle
YOU JUST CARRY SOME AROUND WITH YOU?
I THOUGHT YOU MIGHT WANT TO TASTE IT FIRST.
WOW. TASTES LIKE WEEDS.
munch
munch
munch
munch
HEH HEH...
YOUNG HUMAN FEMALES LOVE WEEDS!

REALITY CHECK-UP

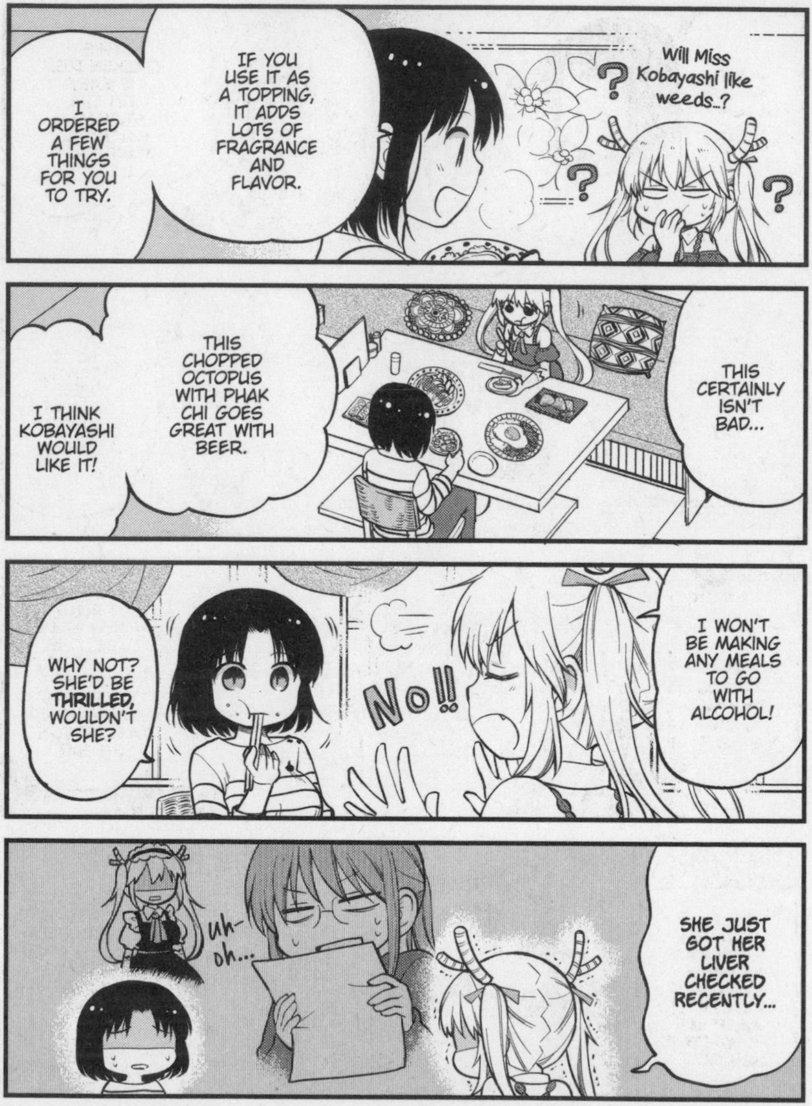
Will Miss Kobayashi like weeds..?
IF YOU USE IT AS A TOPPING, IT ADDS LOTS OF FRAGRANCE AND FLAVOR.
I ORDERED A FEW THINGS FOR YOU TO TRY.
THIS CERTAINLY ISN'T BAD...
THIS CHOPPED OCTOPUS WITH PHAK CHI GOES GREAT WITH BEER.
I THINK KOBAYASHI WOULD LIKE IT!
I WON'T BE MAKING ANY MEALS TO GO WITH ALCOHOL!
No!!
WHY NOT? SHE'D BE **THRILLED**, WOULDN'T SHE?
SHE JUST GOT HER LIVER CHECKED RECENTLY...
uh-oh...

TOHRU'S POWER

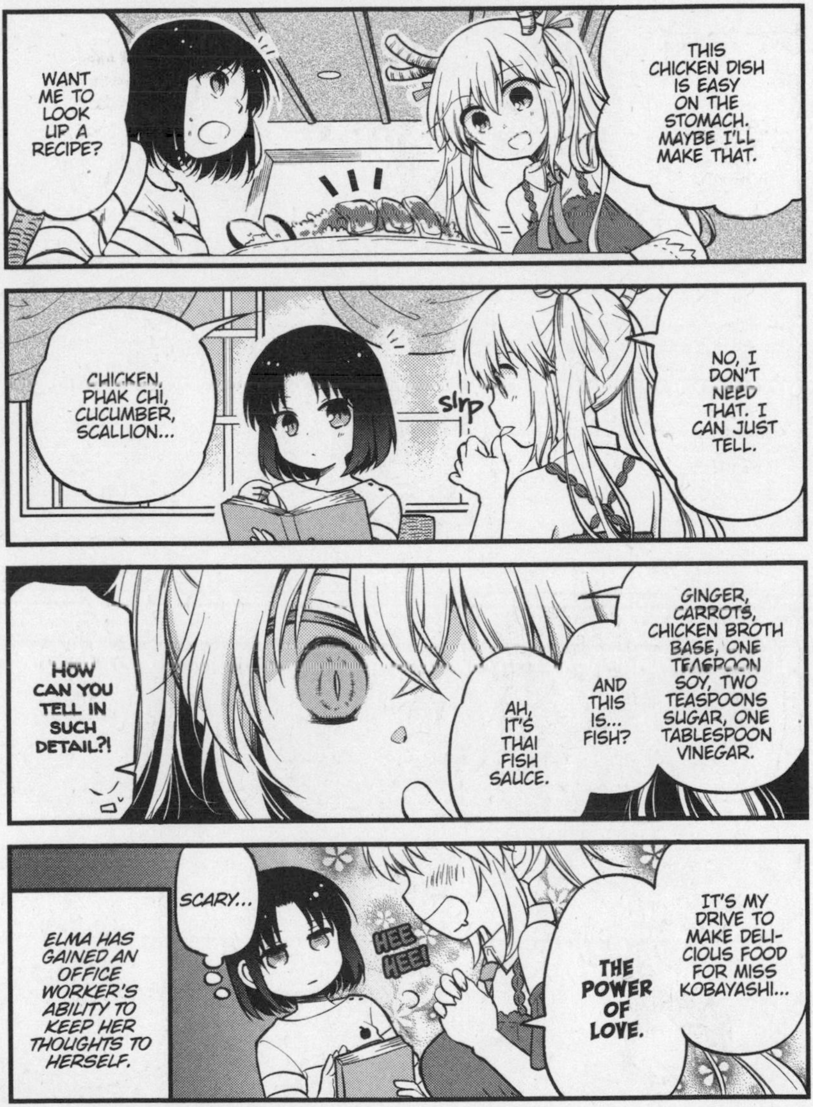
THIS CHICKEN DISH IS EASY ON THE STOMACH. MAYBE I'LL MAKE THAT.
WANT ME TO LOOK UP A RECIPE?
NO, I DON'T NEED THAT. I CAN JUST TELL.
SLRP
CHICKEN, PHAK CHI, CUCUMBER, SCALLION...
GINGER, CARROTS, CHICKEN BROTH BASE, ONE TEASPOON SOY, TWO TEASPOONS SUGAR, ONE TABLESPOON VINEGAR.
AND THIS IS... FISH?
AH, IT'S THAI FISH SAUCE.
HOW CAN YOU TELL IN SUCH DETAIL?!
IT'S MY DRIVE TO MAKE DELI-CIOUS FOOD FOR MISS KOBAYASHI...
THE POWER OF LOVE.
HEE HEE!
SCARY...
ELMA HAS GAINED AN OFFICE WORKER'S ABILITY TO KEEP HER THOUGHTS TO HERSELF.

HAPPY PLACE

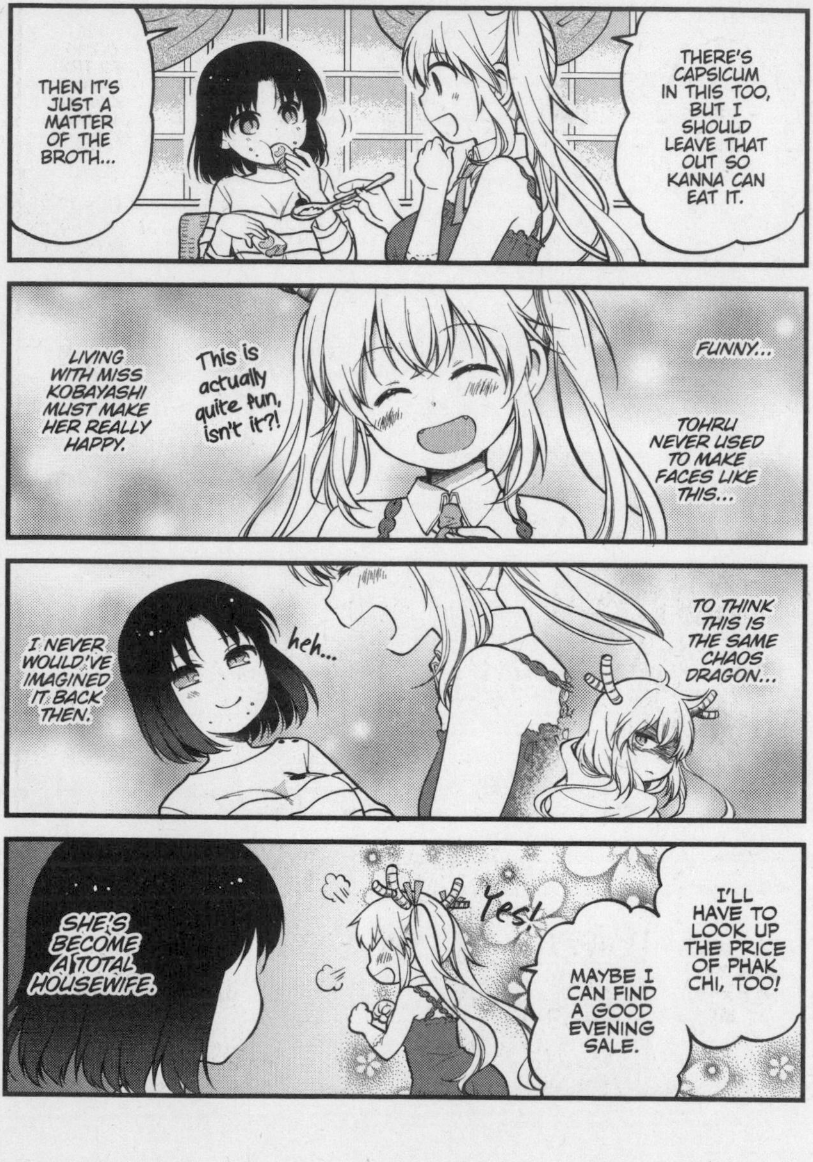
THERE'S CAPSICUM IN THIS TOO, BUT I SHOULD LEAVE THAT OUT SO KANNA CAN EAT IT.
THEN IT'S JUST A MATTER OF THE BROTH...
FUNNY...
TOHRU NEVER USED TO MAKE FACES LIKE THIS...
This is actually quite fun, isn't it?!
LIVING WITH MISS KOBAYASHI MUST MAKE HER REALLY HAPPY.
TO THINK THIS IS THE SAME CHAOS DRAGON...
heh...
I NEVER WOULD'VE IMAGINED IT BACK THEN.
I'LL HAVE TO LOOK UP THE PRICE OF PHAK CHI, TOO!
MAYBE I CAN FIND A GOOD EVENING SALE.
Yes!
SHE'S BECOME A TOTAL HOUSEWIFE.

SEXY TECHNIQUE ②

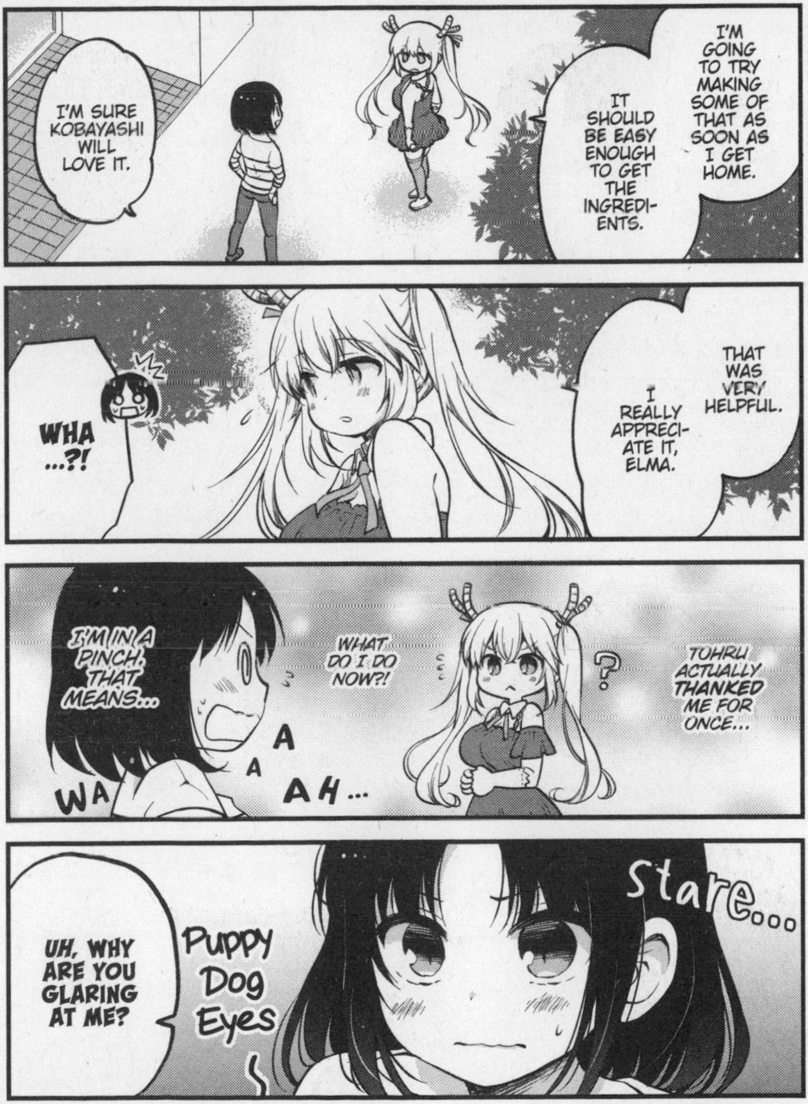
I'M GOING TO TRY MAKING SOME OF THAT AS SOON AS I GET HOME.
IT SHOULD BE EASY ENOUGH TO GET THE INGREDI-ENTS.
I'M SURE KOBAYASHI WILL LOVE IT.
THAT WAS VERY HELPFUL.
I REALLY APPRECI-ATE IT, ELMA.
WHA ...?!
TOHRU ACTUALLY THANKED ME FOR ONCE...
WHAT DO I DO NOW?!
I'M IN A PINCH. THAT MEANS...
WA A A AH...
Stare...
Puppy Dog Eyes
UH, WHY ARE YOU GLARING AT ME?

TOHRU CAN'T HELP HERSELF

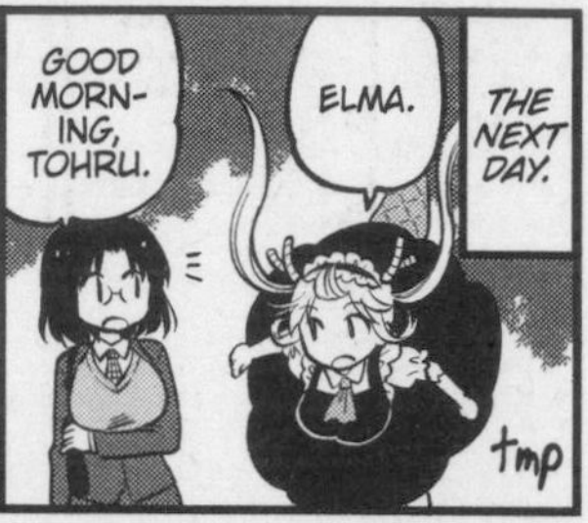
THE NEXT DAY.
ELMA.
GOOD MORNING, TOHRU.
tmp

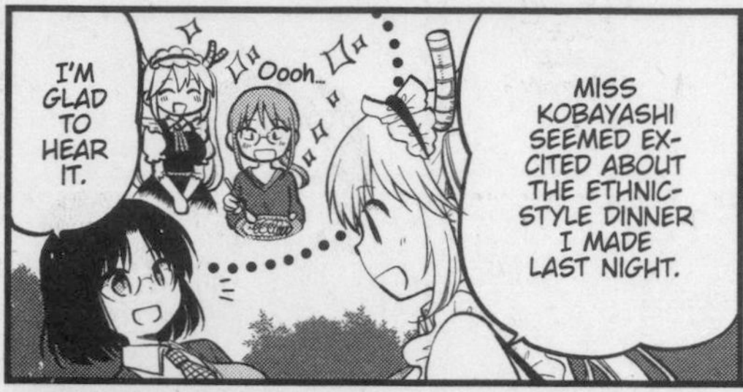
MISS KOBAYASHI SEEMED EXCITED ABOUT THE ETHNIC-STYLE DINNER I MADE LAST NIGHT.
Oooh...
I'M GLAD TO HEAR IT.

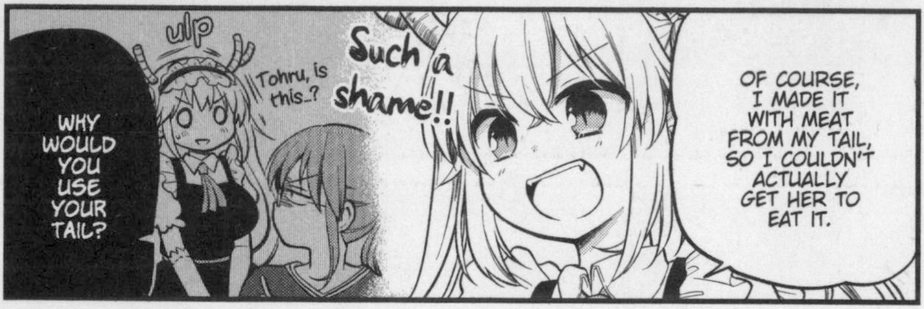
OF COURSE, I MADE IT WITH MEAT FROM MY TAIL, SO I COULDN'T ACTUALLY GET HER TO EAT IT.
Such a shame!!
Tohru, is this...?
ulp
WHY WOULD YOU USE YOUR TAIL?

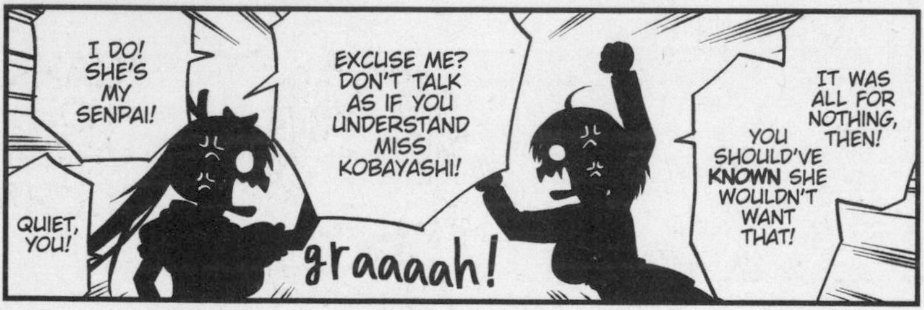
IT WAS ALL FOR NOTHING, THEN!
YOU SHOULD'VE **KNOWN** SHE WOULDN'T WANT THAT!
EXCUSE ME? DON'T TALK AS IF YOU UNDERSTAND MISS KOBAYASHI!
graaaah!
I DO! SHE'S MY SENPAI!
QUIET, YOU!

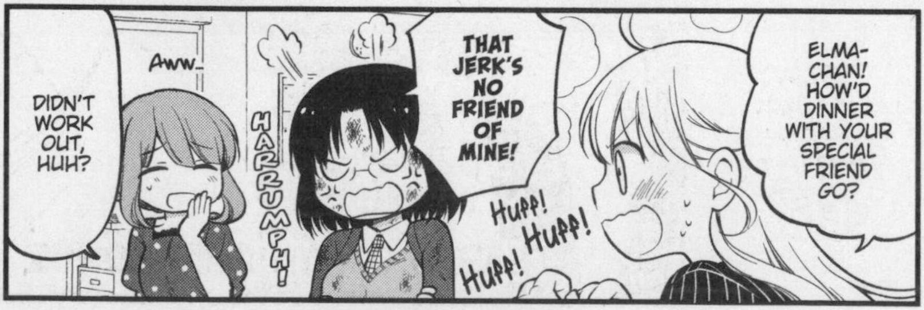
ELMA-CHAN! HOW'D DINNER WITH YOUR SPECIAL FRIEND GO?
Huff! Huff! Huff!
THAT JERK'S NO FRIEND OF MINE!
HARRUMPH!
Aww...
DIDN'T WORK OUT, HUH?

CHAPTER 17/END

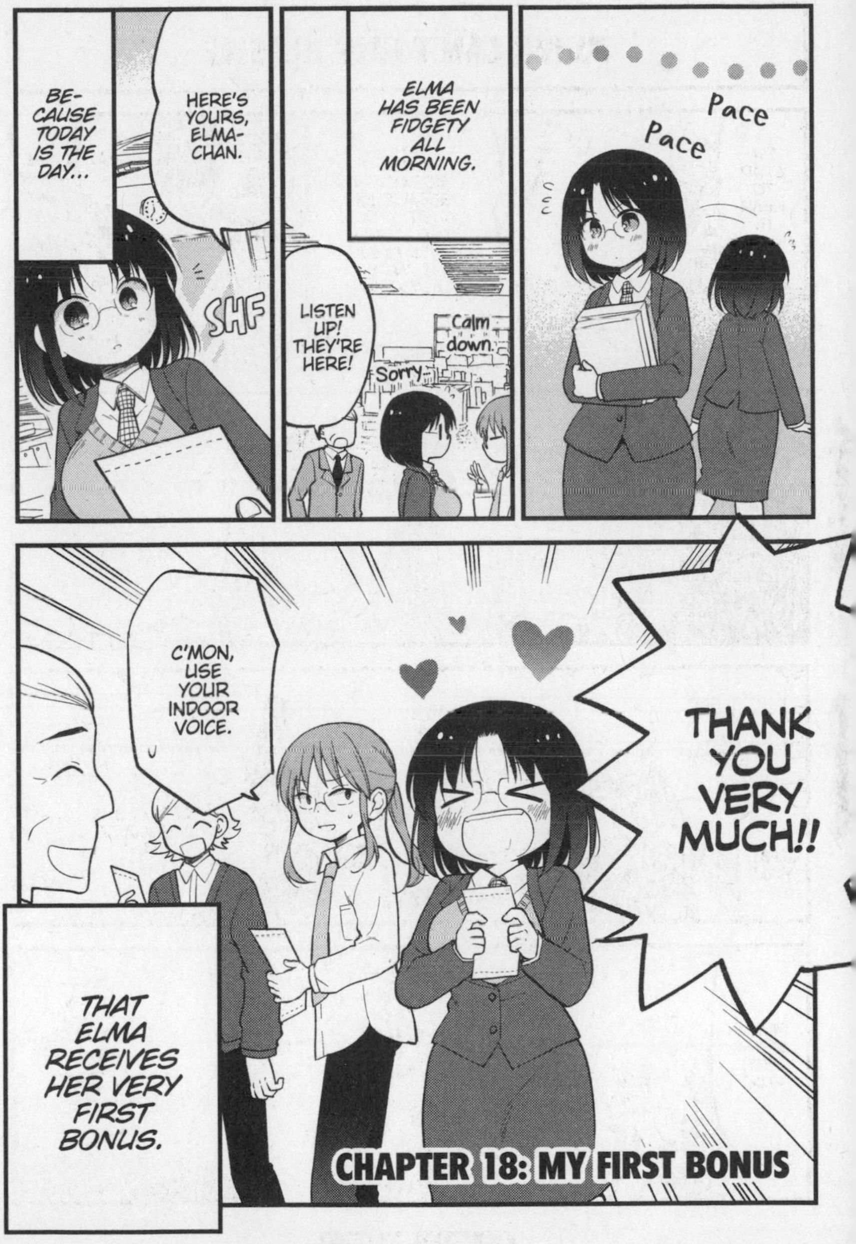
Pace
Pace
ELMA HAS BEEN FIDGETY ALL MORNING.
LISTEN UP! THEY'RE HERE!
Calm down.
Sorry...
HERE'S YOURS, ELMA-CHAN.
SHF
BE-CAUSE TODAY IS THE DAY...
THANK YOU VERY MUCH!!
C'MON, USE YOUR INDOOR VOICE.
THAT ELMA RECEIVES HER VERY FIRST BONUS.

CHAPTER 18: MY FIRST BONUS

TOO HAPPY

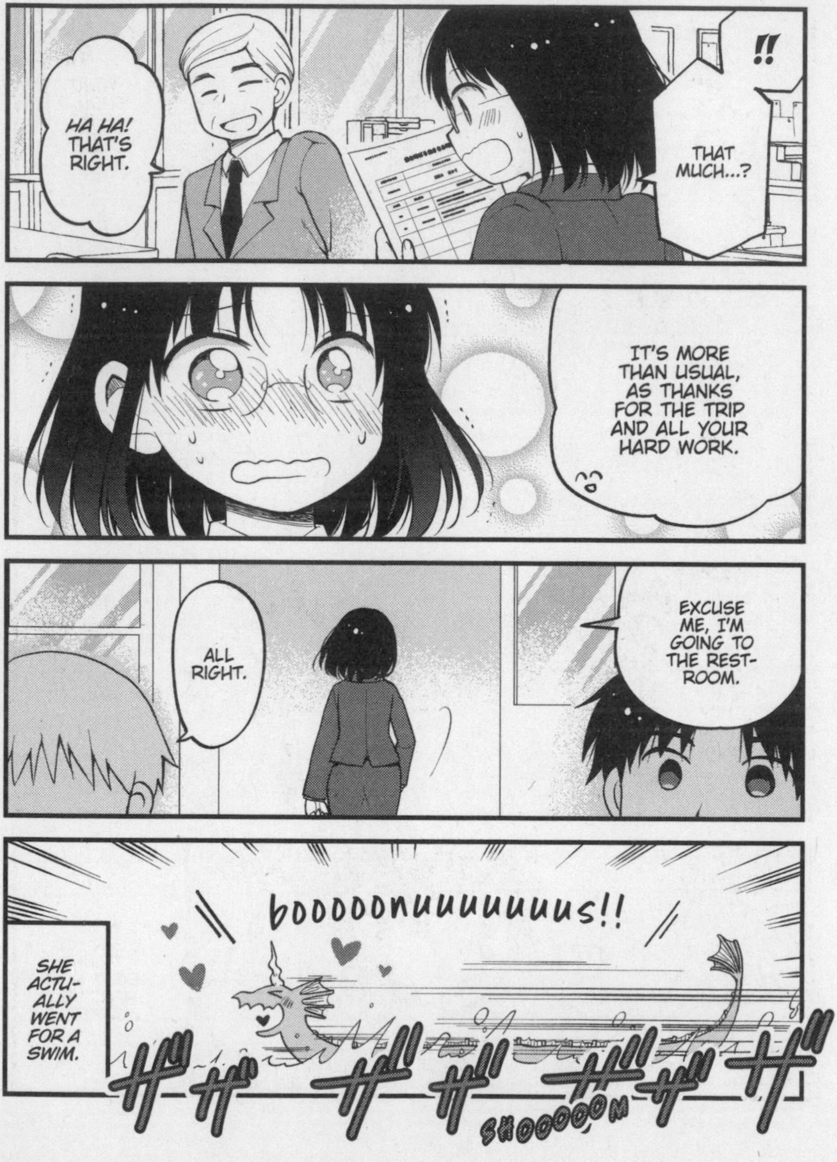
!!
THAT MUCH...?
HA HA! THAT'S RIGHT.
IT'S MORE THAN USUAL, AS THANKS FOR THE TRIP AND ALL YOUR HARD WORK.
EXCUSE ME, I'M GOING TO THE REST-ROOM.
ALL RIGHT.
booooonuuuuuuuus!!
SHE ACTU-ALLY WENT FOR A SWIM.
SHOOOOOOM

BOGUS BONUS

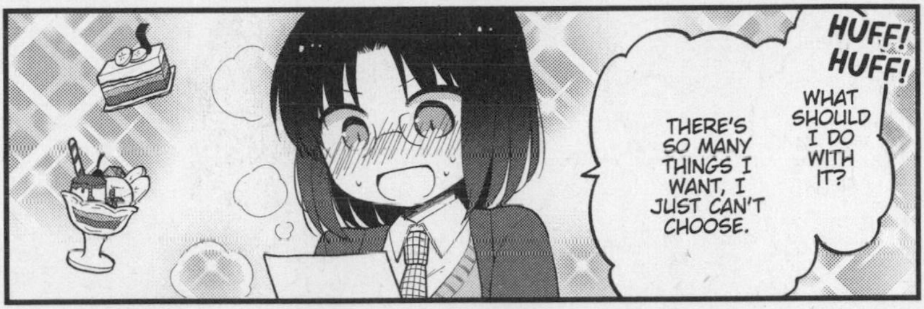
HUFF! HUFF!
WHAT SHOULD I DO WITH IT?
THERE'S SO MANY THINGS I WANT, I JUST CAN'T CHOOSE.

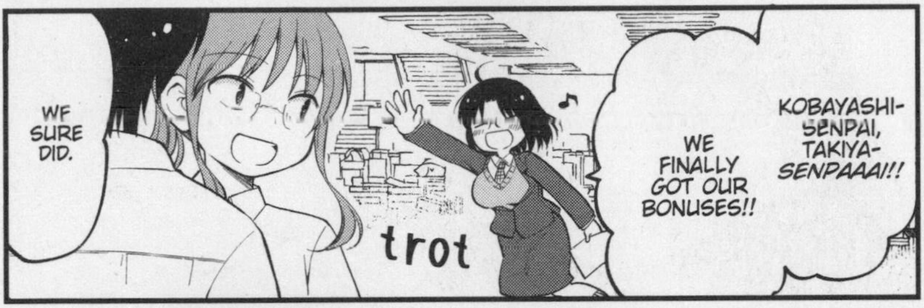
KOBAYASHI-SENPAI, TAKIYA-SENPAAAI!!
WE FINALLY GOT OUR BONUSES!!
trot
WF SURE DID.

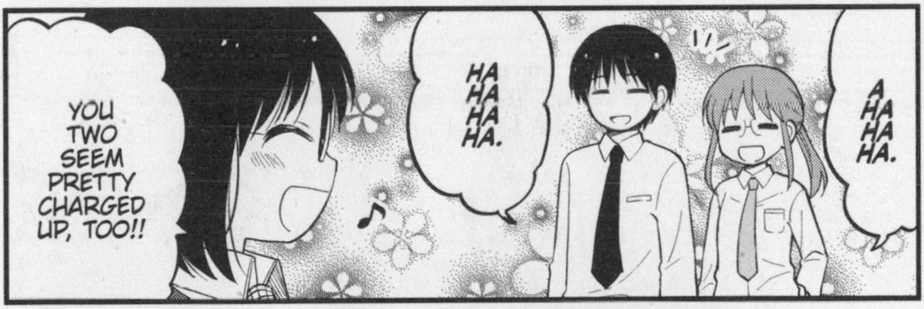
A HA HA HA.
HA HA HA HA.
YOU TWO SEEM PRETTY CHARGED UP, TOO!!

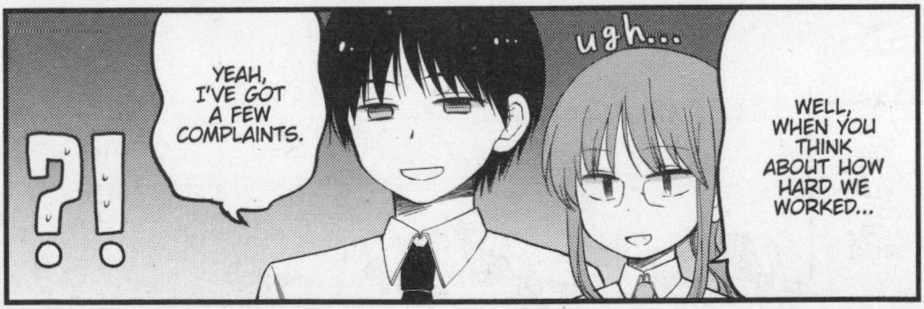
WELL, WHEN YOU THINK ABOUT HOW HARD WE WORKED...
ugh...
YEAH, I'VE GOT A FEW COMPLAINTS.
?!

BORING BONUS

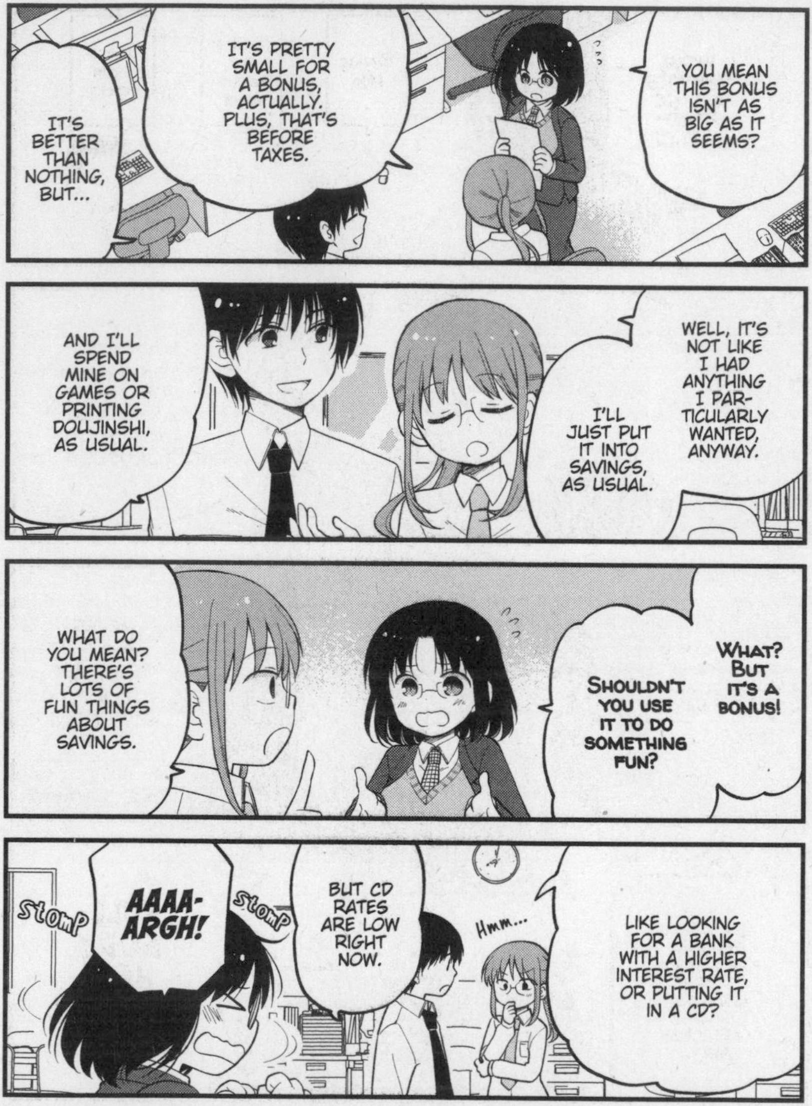
YOU MEAN THIS BONUS ISN'T AS BIG AS IT SEEMS?
IT'S PRETTY SMALL FOR A BONUS, ACTUALLY. PLUS, THAT'S BEFORE TAXES.
IT'S BETTER THAN NOTHING, BUT...
WELL, IT'S NOT LIKE I HAD ANYTHING I PARTICULARLY WANTED, ANYWAY.
I'LL JUST PUT IT INTO SAVINGS, AS USUAL.
AND I'LL SPEND MINE ON GAMES OR PRINTING DOUJINSHI, AS USUAL.
WHAT? BUT IT'S A BONUS!
SHOULDN'T YOU USE IT TO DO SOMETHING FUN?
WHAT DO YOU MEAN? THERE'S LOTS OF FUN THINGS ABOUT SAVINGS.
LIKE LOOKING FOR A BANK WITH A HIGHER INTEREST RATE, OR PUTTING IT IN A CD?
Hmm...
BUT CD RATES ARE LOW RIGHT NOW.
STOMP
AAAA-ARGH!
STOMP

MODERN LADY

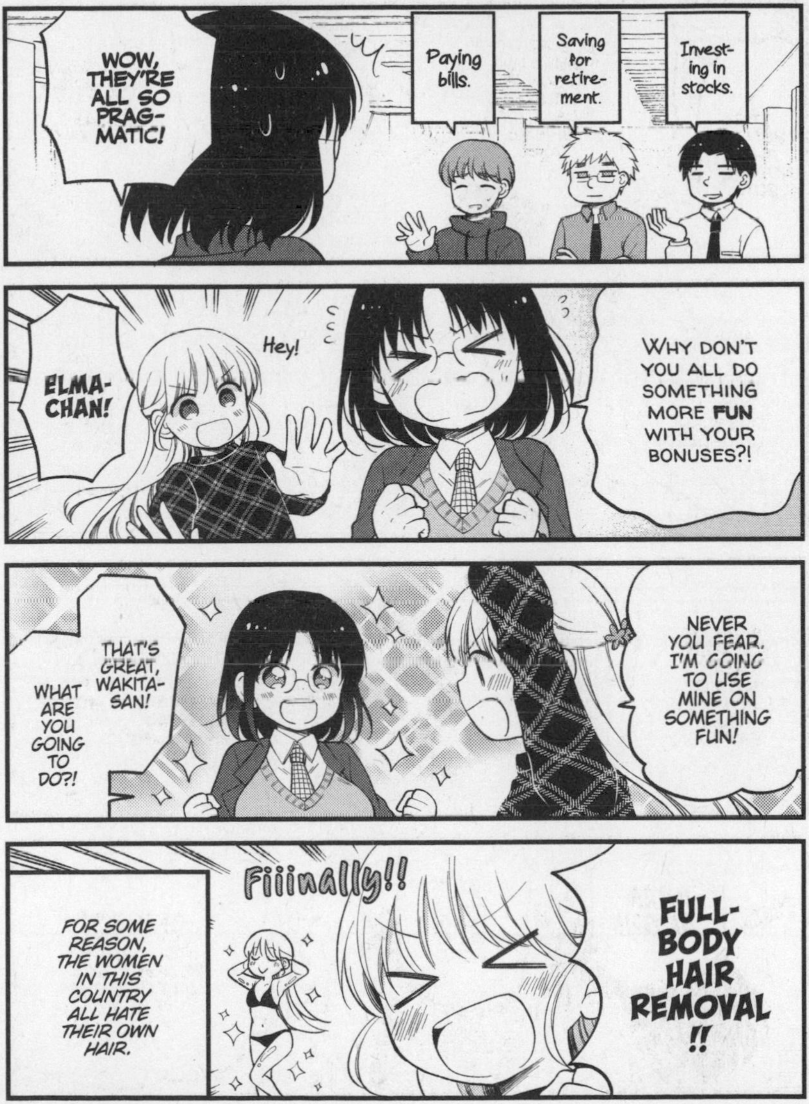
Invest-ing in stocks.
Saving for retire-ment.
Paying bills.
WOW, THEY'RE ALL SO PRAG-MATIC!
WHY DON'T YOU ALL DO SOMETHING MORE FUN WITH YOUR BONUSES?!
Hey!
ELMA-CHAN!
NEVER YOU FEAR. I'M GOING TO USE MINE ON SOMETHING FUN!
THAT'S GREAT, WAKITA-SAN!
WHAT ARE YOU GOING TO DO?!
FULL-BODY HAIR REMOVAL!!
Fiiinally!!
FOR SOME REASON, THE WOMEN IN THIS COUNTRY ALL HATE THEIR OWN HAIR.

THE WAY HOME

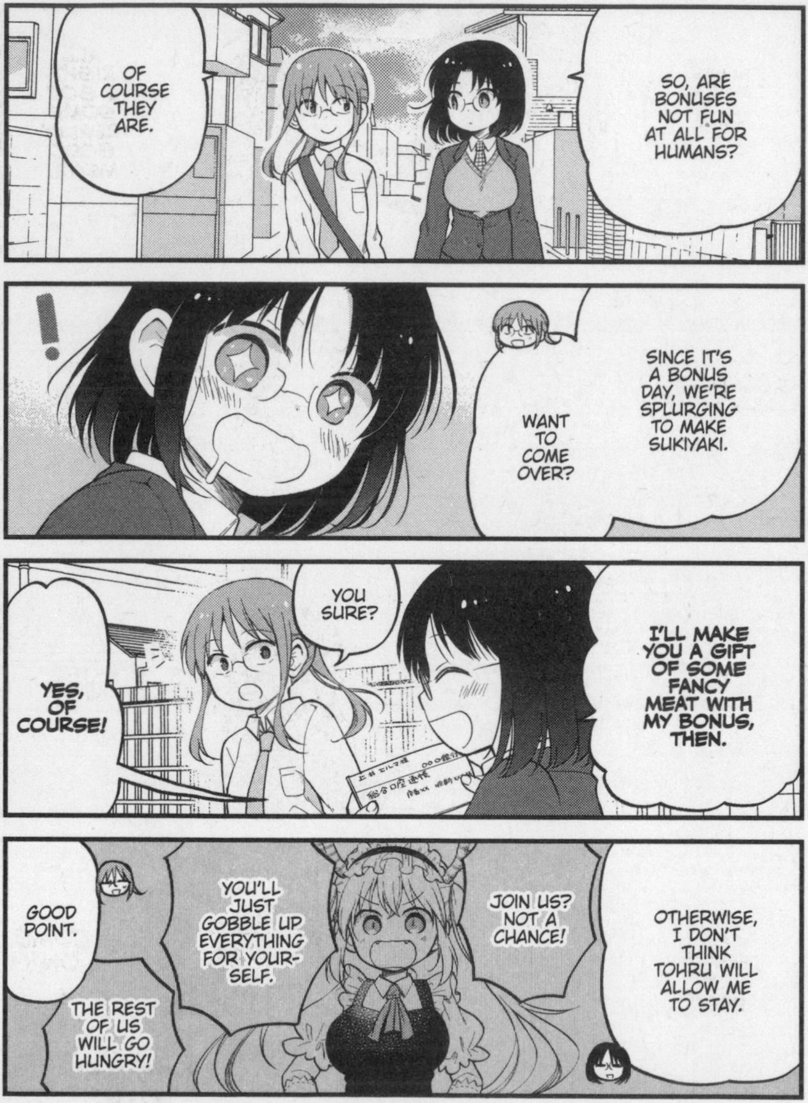
SO, ARE BONUSES NOT FUN AT ALL FOR HUMANS?
OF COURSE THEY ARE.
!
SINCE IT'S A BONUS DAY, WE'RE SPLURGING TO MAKE SUKIYAKI.
WANT TO COME OVER?
I'LL MAKE YOU A GIFT OF SOME FANCY MEAT WITH MY BONUS, THEN.
YOU SURE?
YES, OF COURSE!
OTHERWISE, I DON'T THINK TOHRU WILL ALLOW ME TO STAY.
JOIN US? NOT A CHANCE!
YOU'LL JUST GOBBLE UP EVERYTHING FOR YOUR-SELF.
THE REST OF US WILL GO HUNGRY!
GOOD POINT.

OLD HABITS DIE HARD

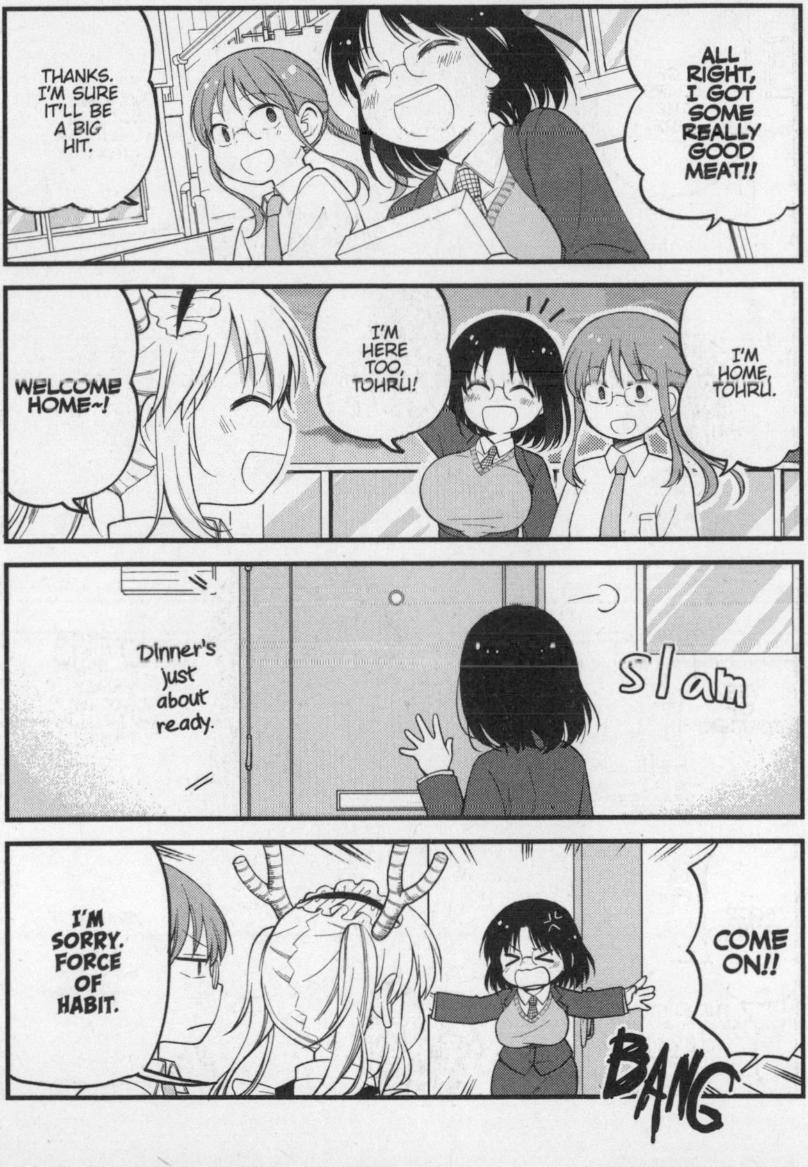
ALL RIGHT, I GOT SOME REALLY GOOD MEAT!!
THANKS. I'M SURE IT'LL BE A BIG HIT.
I'M HOME, TOHRU.
I'M HERE TOO, TOHRU!
WELCOME HOME~!
slam
Dinner's just about ready.
COME ON!!
BANG
I'M SORRY. FORCE OF HABIT.

SHE REALLY SAID IT

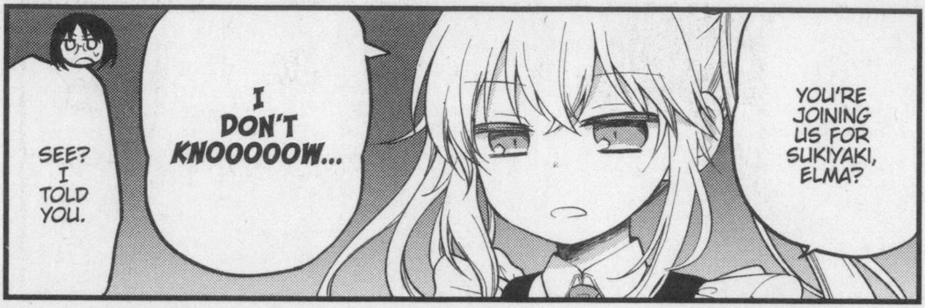
YOU'RE JOINING US FOR SUKIYAKI, ELMA?
I DON'T KNOOOOOW...
SEE? I TOLD YOU.

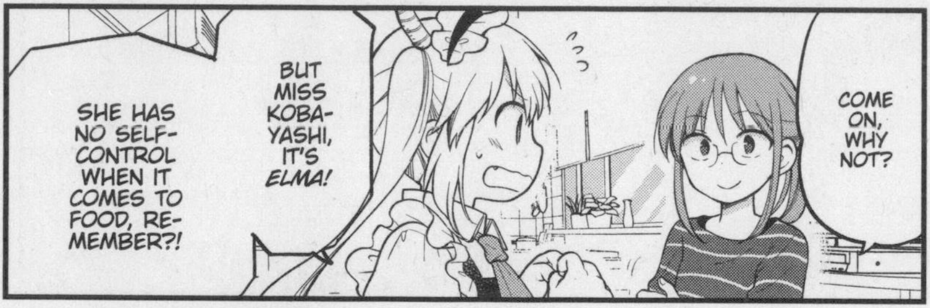
COME ON, WHY NOT?
BUT MISS KOBAYASHI, IT'S *ELMA!*
SHE HAS NO SELF-CONTROL WHEN IT COMES TO FOOD, REMEMBER?!

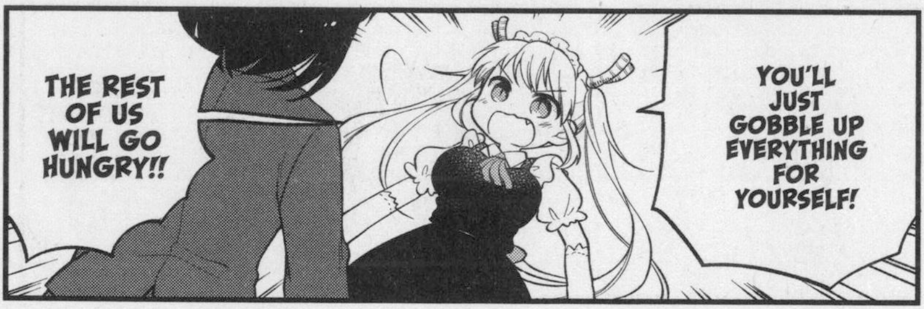
YOU'LL JUST GOBBLE UP EVERYTHING FOR YOURSELF!
THE REST OF US WILL GO HUNGRY!!

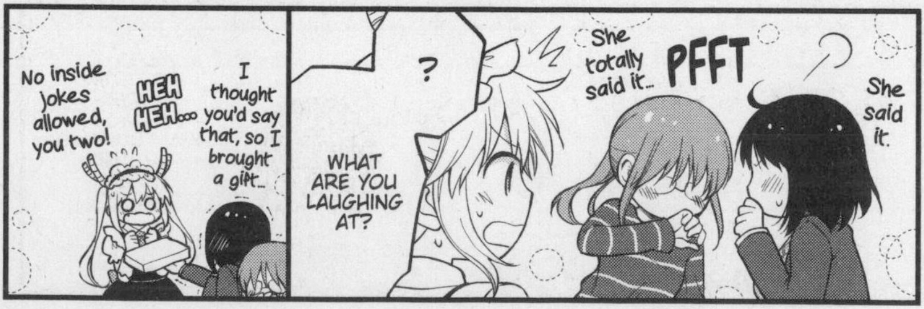
She said it.
PFFT
She totally said it...
?
WHAT ARE YOU LAUGHING AT?
I thought you'd say that, so I brought a gift...
HEH HEH...
No inside jokes allowed, you two!

THE WAY TO A KID'S HEART

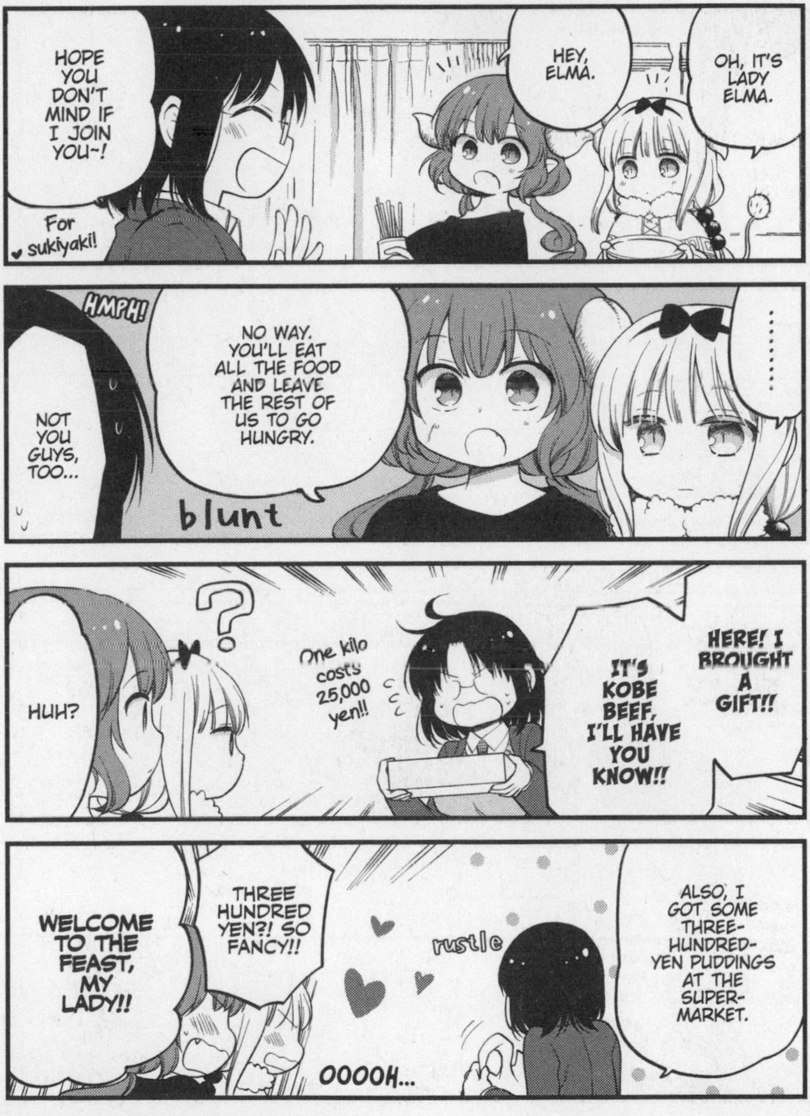
OH, IT'S LADY ELMA.
HEY, ELMA.
HOPE YOU DON'T MIND IF I JOIN YOU~!
For sukiyaki!
......
NO WAY. YOU'LL EAT ALL THE FOOD AND LEAVE THE REST OF US TO GO HUNGRY.
HMPH!
blunt
NOT YOU GUYS, TOO...
HERE! I BROUGHT A GIFT!!
IT'S KOBE BEEF, I'LL HAVE YOU KNOW!!
One kilo costs 25,000 yen!!
HUH?
ALSO, I GOT SOME THREE-HUNDRED-YEN PUDDINGS AT THE SUPER-MARKET.
rustle
OOOOH...
THREE HUNDRED YEN?! SO FANCY!!
WELCOME TO THE FEAST, MY LADY!!

HOUSEWIFE KNOW-HOW

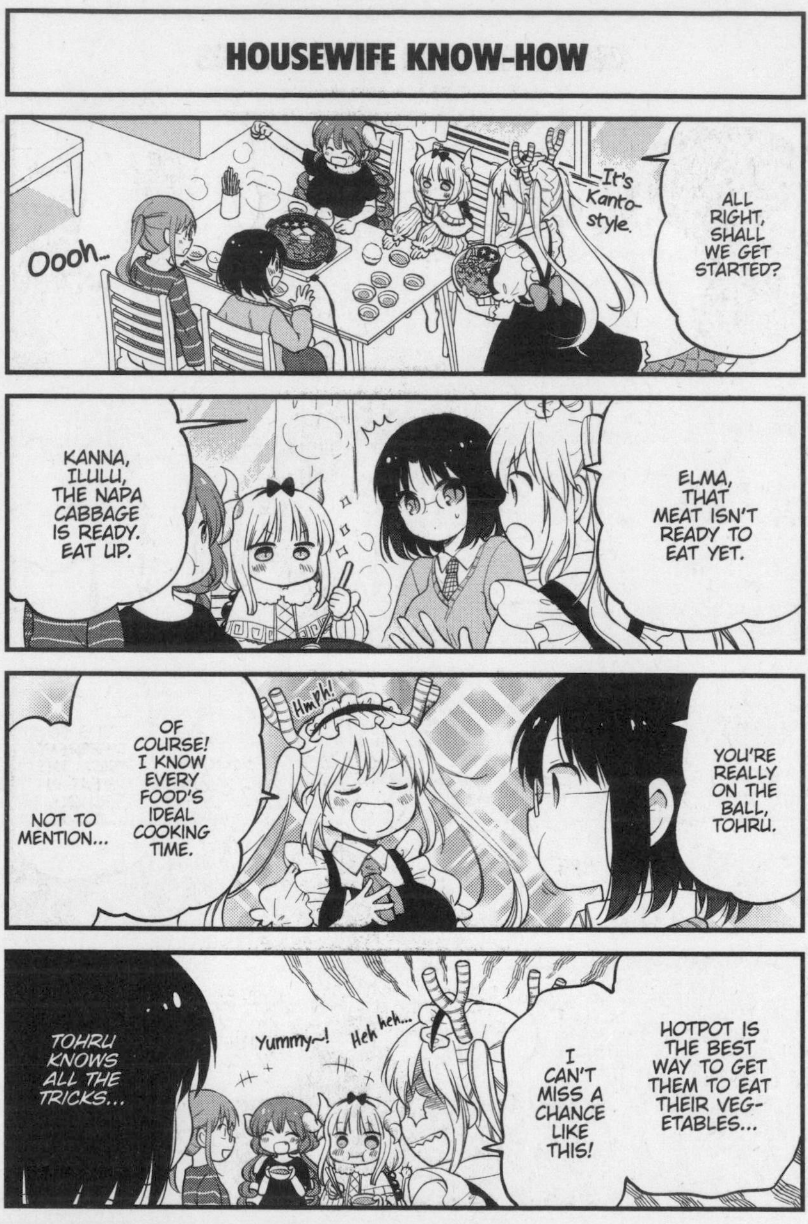
ALL RIGHT, SHALL WE GET STARTED?
It's Kanto-style.
Oooh...
ELMA, THAT MEAT ISN'T READY TO EAT YET.
KANNA, ILULU, THE NAPA CABBAGE IS READY. EAT UP.
YOU'RE REALLY ON THE BALL, TOHRU.
Hmph!
OF COURSE! I KNOW EVERY FOOD'S IDEAL COOKING TIME.
NOT TO MENTION...
HOTPOT IS THE BEST WAY TO GET THEM TO EAT THEIR VEG-ETABLES...
I CAN'T MISS A CHANCE LIKE THIS!
Heh heh...
Yummy~!
TOHRU KNOWS ALL THE TRICKS...

DRAGONS WILL BE DRAGONS

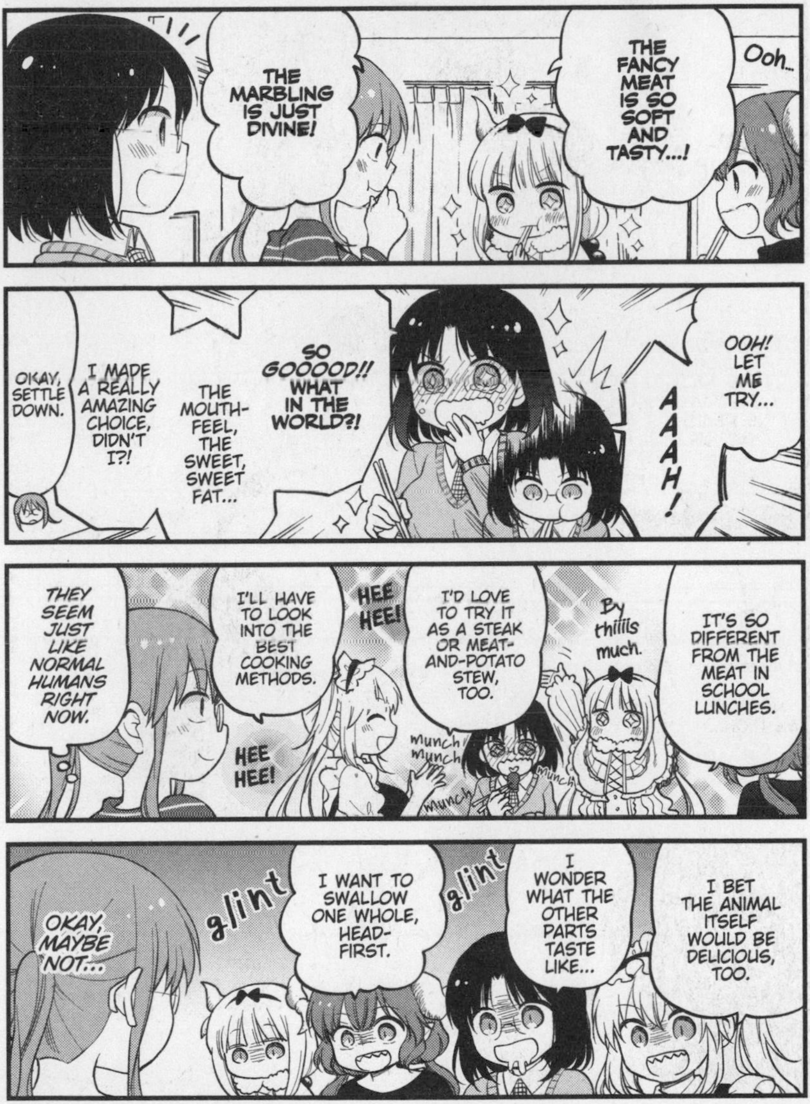
Ooh..
THE FANCY MEAT IS SO SOFT AND TASTY...!
THE MARBLING IS JUST DIVINE!
OOH! LET ME TRY...
AAAAH!
SO GOOOOD!! WHAT IN THE WORLD?!
THE MOUTH-FEEL, THE SWEET, SWEET FAT...
I MADE A REALLY AMAZING CHOICE, DIDN'T I?!
OKAY, SETTLE DOWN.
IT'S SO DIFFERENT FROM THE MEAT IN SCHOOL LUNCHES.
By thiiiis much.
I'D LOVE TO TRY IT AS A STEAK OR MEAT-AND-POTATO STEW, TOO.
munch munch
munch
munch
HEE HEE!
I'LL HAVE TO LOOK INTO THE BEST COOKING METHODS.
HEE HEE!
THEY SEEM JUST LIKE NORMAL HUMANS RIGHT NOW.
I BET THE ANIMAL ITSELF WOULD BE DELICIOUS, TOO.
I WONDER WHAT THE OTHER PARTS TASTE LIKE...
glint
I WANT TO SWALLOW ONE WHOLE, HEAD-FIRST.
glint
OKAY, MAYBE NOT...

SHARED HAPPINESS

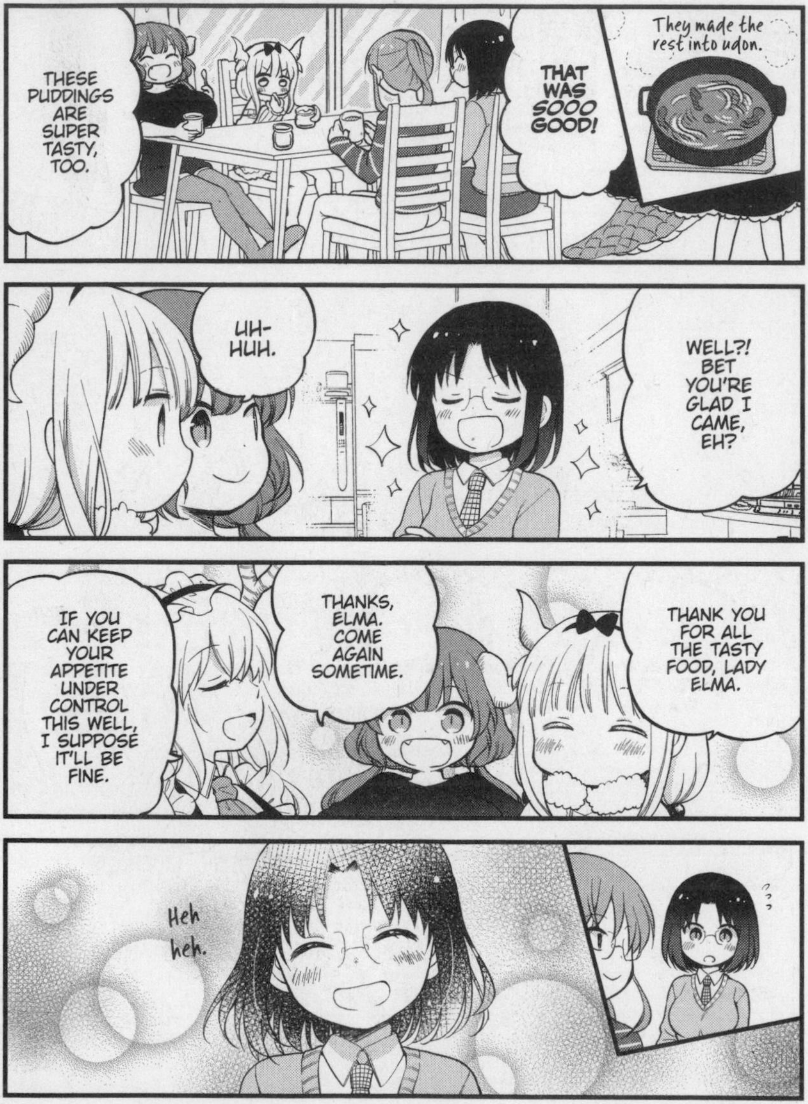
They made the rest into udon.
THAT WAS SOOO GOOD!
THESE PUDDINGS ARE SUPER TASTY, TOO.
WELL?! BET YOU'RE GLAD I CAME, EH?
UH-HUH.
THANK YOU FOR ALL THE TASTY FOOD, LADY ELMA.
THANKS, ELMA. COME AGAIN SOMETIME.
IF YOU CAN KEEP YOUR APPETITE UNDER CONTROL THIS WELL, I SUPPOSE IT'LL BE FINE.
Heh heh.

EXCITED

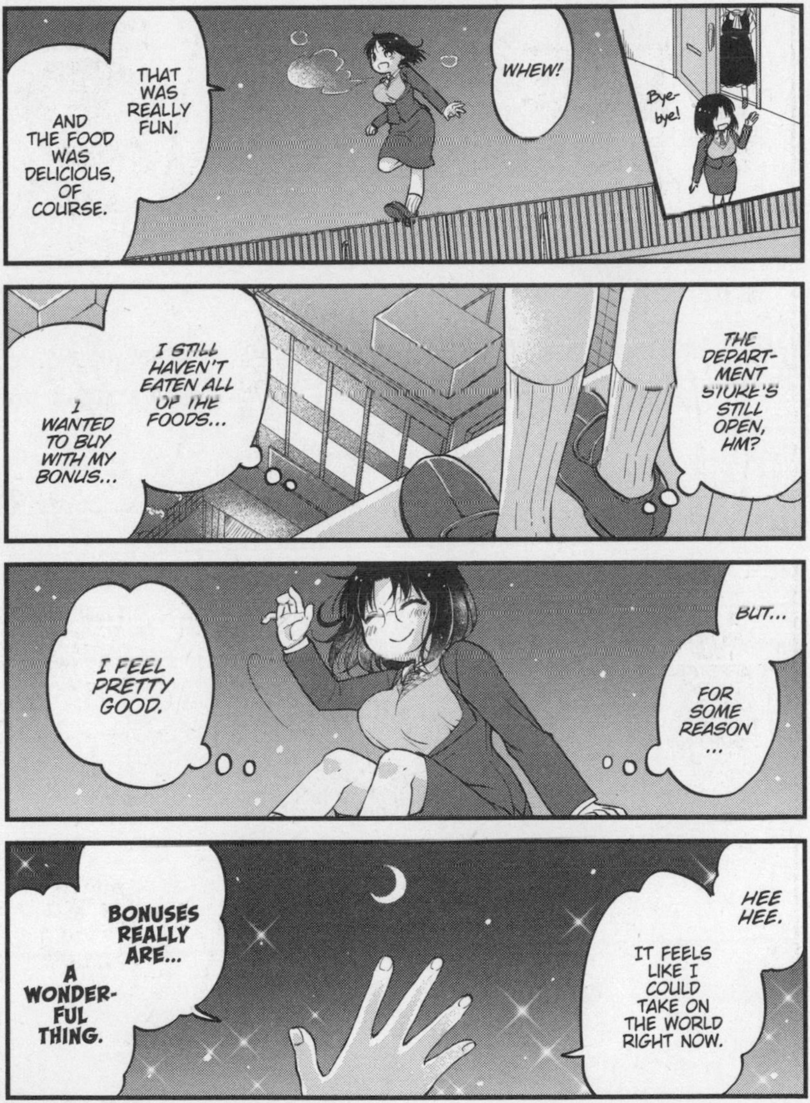
Bye-bye!
WHEW!
THAT WAS REALLY FUN.
AND THE FOOD WAS DELICIOUS, OF COURSE.
THE DEPART-MENT STORE'S STILL OPEN, HM?
I STILL HAVEN'T EATEN ALL OF THE FOODS...
I WANTED TO BUY WITH MY BONUS...
BUT...
FOR SOME REASON...
I FEEL PRETTY GOOD.
HEE HEE.
IT FEELS LIKE I COULD TAKE ON THE WORLD RIGHT NOW.
BONUSES REALLY ARE...
A WONDER-FUL THING.

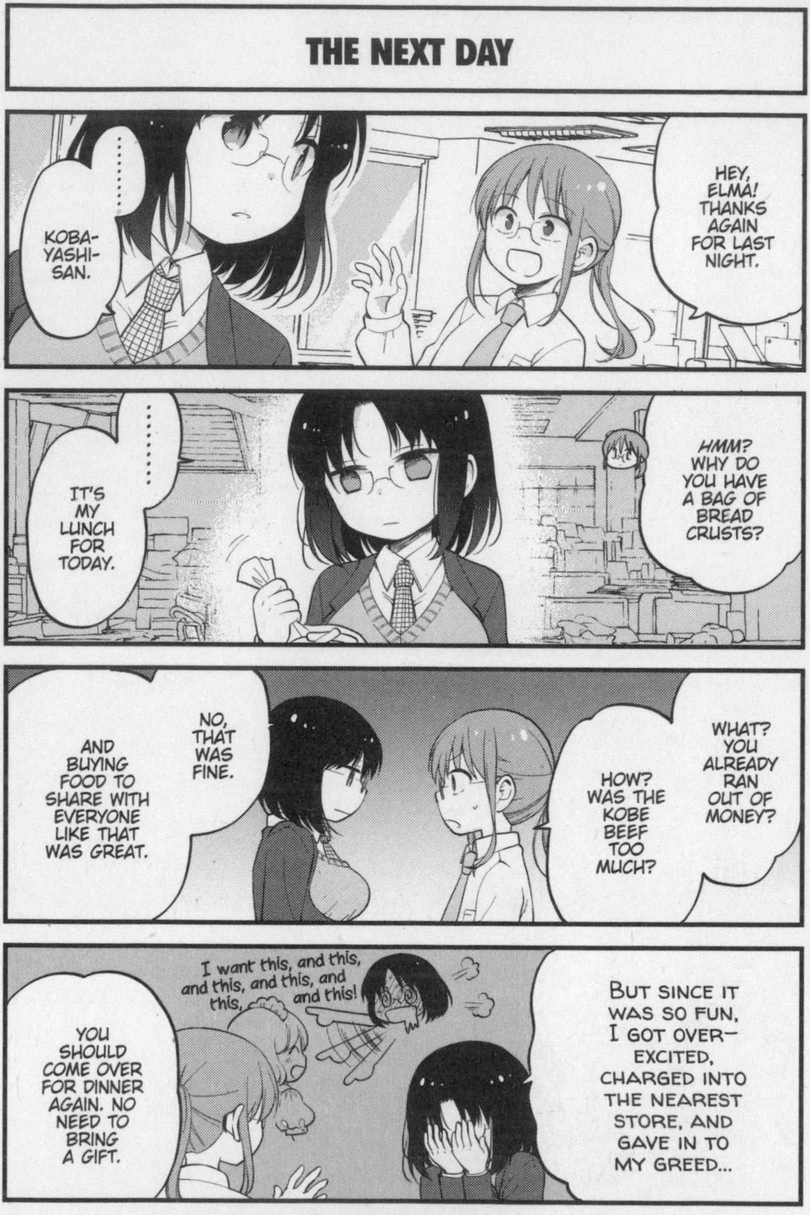
THE NEXT DAY
HEY, ELMA! THANKS AGAIN FOR LAST NIGHT.
......
KOBAYASHI-SAN.
HMM? WHY DO YOU HAVE A BAG OF BREAD CRUSTS?
......
IT'S MY LUNCH FOR TODAY.
WHAT? YOU ALREADY RAN OUT OF MONEY?
HOW? WAS THE KOBE BEEF TOO MUCH?
NO, THAT WAS FINE.
AND BUYING FOOD TO SHARE WITH EVERYONE LIKE THAT WAS GREAT.
BUT SINCE IT WAS SO FUN, I GOT OVER-EXCITED, CHARGED INTO THE NEAREST STORE, AND GAVE IN TO MY GREED...
I want this, and this, and this, and this, and this, and this!
YOU SHOULD COME OVER FOR DINNER AGAIN. NO NEED TO BRING A GIFT.

CHAPTER 18/END

If you fry bread crusts in oil or butter and sprinkle them with sugar, they make a tasty treat.

Yum!!

sizz

sizz

Miss Kobayashi's Dragon Maid

Elma's Office Lady Diary

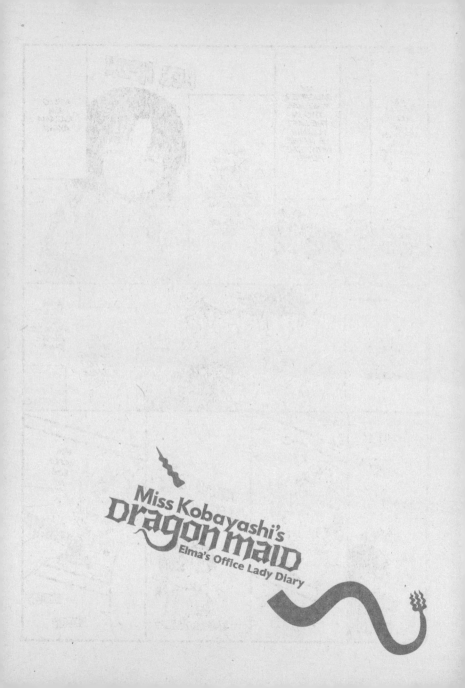

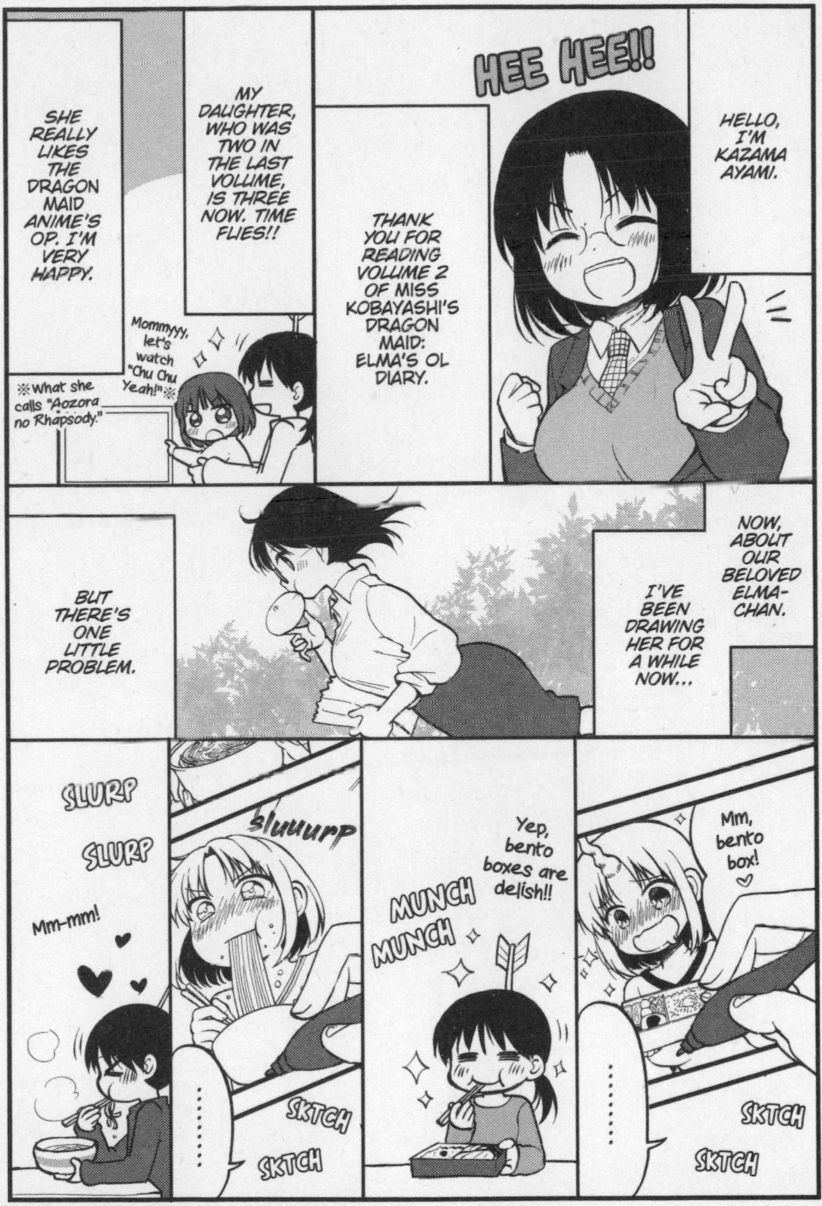
HELLO, I'M KAZAMA AYAMI.
HEE HEE!!
THANK YOU FOR READING VOLUME 2 OF MISS KOBAYASHI'S DRAGON MAID: ELMA'S OL DIARY.
MY DAUGHTER, WHO WAS TWO IN THE LAST VOLUME, IS THREE NOW. TIME FLIES!!
SHE REALLY LIKES THE DRAGON MAID ANIME'S OP. I'M VERY HAPPY.
Mommyyy, let's watch "Chu Chu Yeah!"※
※What she calls "Aozora no Rhapsody."
NOW, ABOUT OUR BELOVED ELMA-CHAN.
I'VE BEEN DRAWING HER FOR A WHILE NOW...
BUT THERE'S ONE LITTLE PROBLEM.
Mm, bento box! ♡
SKTCH
SKTCH
......
Yep, bento boxes are delish!!
MUNCH
MUNCH
sluuurp
SKTCH
SKTCH
......
SLURP
SLURP
Mm-mm!

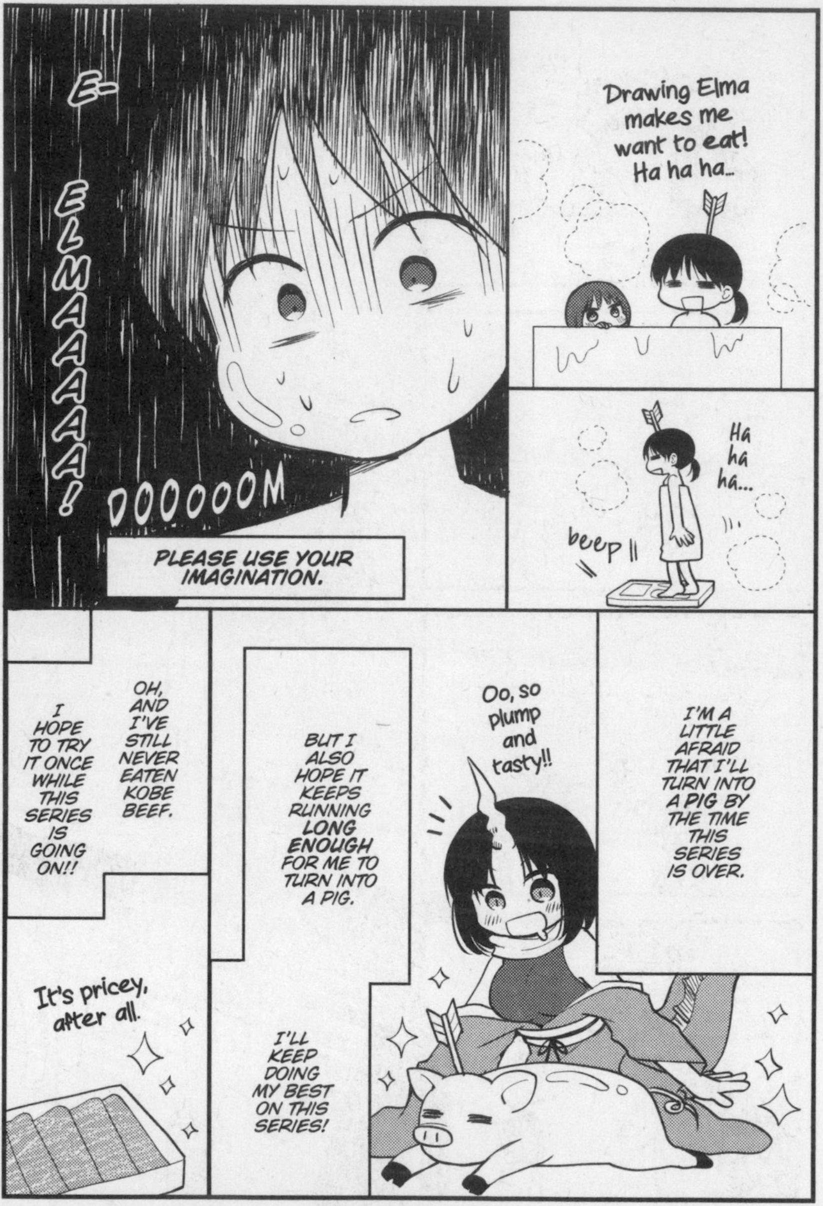
Drawing Elma makes me want to eat! Ha ha ha...
Ha ha ha...
beep
E-ELMAAAAAA!
DOOOOOM
PLEASE USE YOUR IMAGINATION.
I'M A LITTLE AFRAID THAT I'LL TURN INTO A PIG BY THE TIME THIS SERIES IS OVER.
Oo, so plump and tasty!!
BUT I ALSO HOPE IT KEEPS RUNNING LONG ENOUGH FOR ME TO TURN INTO A PIG.
I'LL KEEP DOING MY BEST ON THIS SERIES!
OH, AND I'VE STILL NEVER EATEN KOBE BEEF.
I HOPE TO TRY IT ONCE WHILE THIS SERIES IS GOING ON!!
It's pricey, after all.

A Bonus Comic Called an Afterword

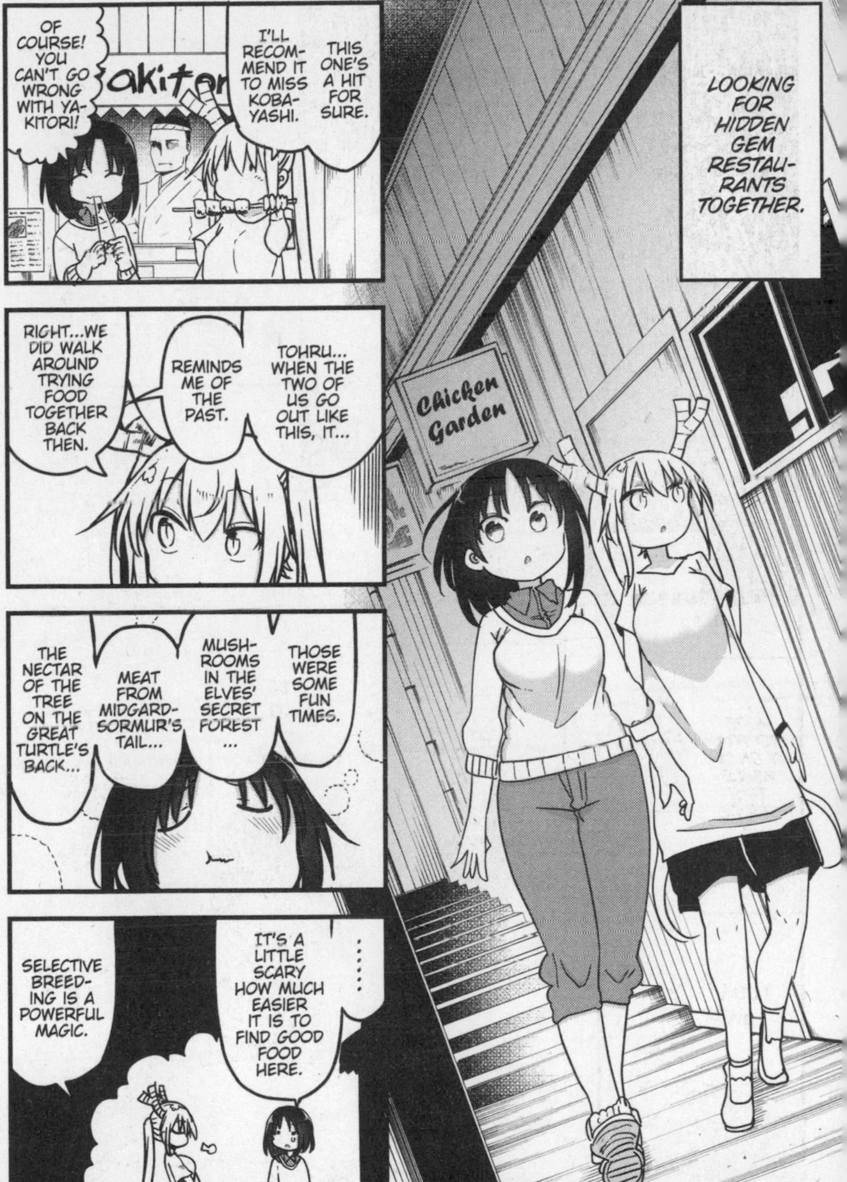
LOOKING FOR HIDDEN GEM RESTAURANTS TOGETHER.
Chicken Garden
THIS ONE'S A HIT FOR SURE.
I'LL RECOMMEND IT TO MISS KOBAYASHI.
OF COURSE! YOU CAN'T GO WRONG WITH YAKITORI!
TOHRU... WHEN THE TWO OF US GO OUT LIKE THIS, IT...
REMINDS ME OF THE PAST.
RIGHT...WE DID WALK AROUND TRYING FOOD TOGETHER BACK THEN.
THOSE WERE SOME FUN TIMES.
MUSHROOMS IN THE ELVES' SECRET FOREST...
MEAT FROM MIDGARDSORMUR'S TAIL...
THE NECTAR OF THE TREE ON THE GREAT TURTLE'S BACK...
......
IT'S A LITTLE SCARY HOW MUCH EASIER IT IS TO FIND GOOD FOOD HERE.
SELECTIVE BREEDING IS A POWERFUL MAGIC.

coolkyousinnjya

Miss Kobayashi's Dragon Maid

Elma's Office Lady Diary

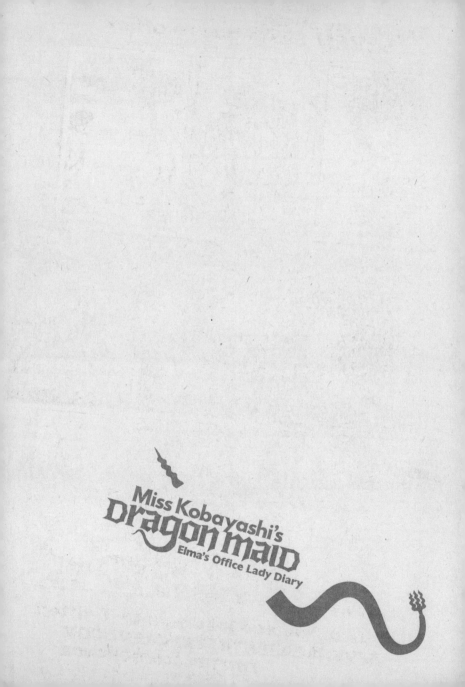

SEVEN SEAS ENTERTAINMENT PRESENTS

Miss Kobayashi's Dragon Maid
Elma's Office Lady Diary VOL. 2

original story by **coolkyousinnjya** story and art by **Ayami Kazama**

TRANSLATION
Jenny McKeon

ADAPTATION
Shanti Whitesides

LETTERING
Carolina Hernández Mendoza

LOGO DESIGN
KC Fabellon

COVER DESIGN
Nicky Lim

PROOFREADING
Danielle King
Stephanie Cohen

PRODUCTION MANAGER
Lissa Pattillo

MANAGING EDITOR
Julie Davis

EDITOR-IN-CHIEF
Adam Arnold

PUBLISHER
Jason DeAngelis

MISS KOBAYASHI'S DRAGON MAID: ELMA'S OFFICE LADY DIARY VOL. 2

First published in Japan in 2019 by Futabasha Publishers Ltd., Tokyo.
English version published by Seven Seas Entertainment.
Under license from Futabasha Publishers Ltd.

Seven Seas press and purchase enquiries can be sent to Marketing Manager Lianne Sentar at press@gomanga.com. Information regarding the distribution and purchase of digital editions is available from Digital Manager CK Russell at digital@gomanga.com.

ISBN: 978-1-64275-143-7

Printed in Canada

First Printing: August 2019

10 9 8 7 6 5 4 3 2 1

READING DIRECTIONS

This book reads from ***right to left***, Japanese style. If this is your first time reading manga, you start reading from the top right panel on each page and take it from there. If you get lost, just follow the numbered diagram here. It may seem backwards at first, but you'll get the hang of it! Have fun!!

1
2
3
4
5
6
7
8
9

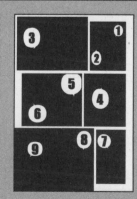